Licence to be Bad

JONATHAN ALDRED

Licence to be Bad

How Economics Corrupted Us

ALLEN LANE
an imprint of
PENGUIN BOOKS

ALLEN LANE

UK | USA | Canada | Ireland | Australia
India | New Zealand | South Africa

Allen Lane is part of the Penguin Random House group of companies
whose addresses can be found at global.penguinrandomhouse.com

First published 2019
001

Copyright © Jonathan Aldred, 2019

The moral right of the author has been asserted

Set in 10.5/14 pt Sabon LT Std
Typeset by Jouve (UK), Milton Keynes
Printed and bound in Great Britain by Clays Ltd, Elcograf S.p.A.

A CIP catalogue record for this book is available from the British Library

ISBN: 978-0-241-32543-8

Contents

I

The Shape of Things to Come

Over the past fifty years or so new ideas about how we should behave have corrupted our thinking. We have come to see black as white, bad as good: it's moral to be immoral. The change has been huge yet it has been achieved through many subtle, barely discernible steps.

Of course, we're not intrinsically less virtuous than past generations. And this is not a straightforward story about people knowingly behaving badly. Instead, it is about how we have been encouraged to believe that various actions and activities are acceptable, natural, rational, woven into the very logic of things – when just a few generations ago they would have seemed stupid, perplexing, harmful or simply wicked. There has been a transformation in the way we understand many of the ideas and values we live by: ideas about trust, justice, fairness, freedom of choice and social responsibility – ideas which profoundly shape our economy and society. Although these developments are relatively recent, they are now so ubiquitous and deep-rooted in everyday life that we are barely aware of them.

Take the global financial crisis that began back in 2007. It is widely agreed that much of the blame for the crisis lies with the regulators, the people employed by government to police the activities of banks and other financial institutions. 'Blame the regulators' is now a familiar argument – but it ought to shock us. We do not blame the police if our home is burgled. So why blame the regulators for the bankers' reckless (and sometimes criminal) behaviour? 'Bankers will be bankers' is the essence of the reply: there is no point in blaming them for it. And if one banker shows self-restraint, another will step in to exploit the opportunity. And markets rely on greed to function properly. Through the spread of these dangerous ideas, we have granted bankers an excuse to be greedy, permission to play the system: a Licence to be Bad.

It is not just bankers. Our troubles go much wider and much deeper. Look at Volkswagen. How did the biggest car-maker in the world morph from the modest, cautious manufacturer of a single model into a corporation which carefully plotted a cynical, large-scale deception of its customers?

At least part of the answer must surely reflect the change in corporate culture encouraged by a Chicago economist named Milton Friedman. In 1970 Friedman – who would later advise US President Ronald Reagan and Prime Minister Margaret Thatcher in the UK – wrote a landmark article in *The New York Times* entitled 'The Social Responsibility of Business is to Increase Its Profits'. In case of doubt, Friedman explained that profit was the *only* responsibility of business.

The influence of recent economic ideas has not been limited to the corporate and financial worlds. At around the same time that Friedman reframed the responsibilities of business, new ideas were reframing the responsibilities of individuals too.

Take an idea known as 'free-riding'. This theory implies that it is often irrational to cooperate because, even if you do, no one else will – and in any case your contribution is too small to make any difference. Although the theory's influence on society remains largely unacknowledged, its essential ideas have filtered out into our ordinary thinking, overthrowing the common sense of 'doing your bit'. We have all been corrupted, down to the small choices of daily life. We have come to believe that it is pointless to vote, harmless to access music, news and other online content without paying, and inevitable that people will exaggerate their insurance claims or avoid paying tax whenever possible. And we walk along busy city streets absorbed in our smartphones, paying little attention to avoiding collisions with other people. In all these cases we rely on the efforts or contributions of others, without which the collective activity in question would be impossible. On other occasions, there is no serious collective activity, because free-rider thinking leads us to abandon hope before we even begin. Many people despair about climate change in these terms.

How did we get to this? And how did we become a world in which, while the rich countries have become even richer, many more of their citizens rely on soup kitchens and food banks? Is it partly because we've been told that making the rich richer is good for the economy but making the poor richer is bad? How did so many of us come to believe all these things when, not so long ago, we had very different beliefs and values?

Whatever your views about bankers, corporate profits, voting, free online content, climate change or inequality, we often seem locked into our present way of thinking (some commentators have called it 'neoliberalism', but you won't see that word again in this book*). Economics appears to constrain the choices available to us. More than that, it shapes the questions we ask and the problems we see. The acceptable answers are influenced by our economics-derived morality. So if we hope for change, an essential first step is to understand how we came to this – where these powerful new economic ideas came from and how they came to have such a hold over us.

The answer is far from obvious. After all, by turns, we seem to ridicule economics and then defer to it. We did not adopt our present way of thinking through deliberate choice. But it didn't happen by chance. It wasn't a conspiracy, but from some angles it looks like one.

To see where it all began, travel to Geneva, Switzerland. Take a train going east, running along the edge of Lake Geneva (Lac Léman). At Vevey, alight and take the funicular railway which ascends Mont Pèlerin. Your hotel is just two minutes' walk from the top station of the funicular railway. In 1947 about fifty people made this journey to what was then called the Hôtel du Parc. Most of them were university academics, along with a few journalists and businesspeople. They were united by fear and loathing of the direction that many countries seemed to be taking.

At that time, in almost every country the state was assuming a bigger role than before. The Depression and mass unemployment of the 1930s was still a vivid memory; economic crisis had played a part in the rise of fascism and the subsequent catastrophes of the Second World War. As peace returned to Europe, no one wanted a return to

* I avoid the word because most people never use it, and those who do cannot agree on its meaning.

mass unemployment, and the new economics of John Maynard Keynes showed that governments had the power to prevent it. Keynes, who laid the foundations for modern macroeconomics, is probably the most influential economist of the last hundred years. It was Keynes who was responsible for the now-familiar idea that, in an economic downturn, governments should increase public expenditure or cut taxes to stimulate the economy. Keynesian economics complemented New Deal-style policies in the United States and the emergence of the welfare state in Britain following the Beveridge Report of 1942. Economist William Beveridge had been asked by the government to study unemployment insurance and related services and make recommendations. His landmark report argued for 'cradle-to-grave' state-provided social insurance.

Ironically, it was Beveridge who, back in 1931, had given a job to a man who would dedicate his life to undermining almost everything Beveridge believed in. When Beveridge, as Director of the London School of Economics, offered a lectureship to a little-known Austrian economist named Friedrich Hayek, he could not have foreseen the consequences. It was Hayek who organized the Mont Pèlerin meeting in 1947.

Hayek had been catapulted from obscurity to celebrity after the publication of his book *The Road to Serfdom* in 1944. His core argument was that the prevailing trend towards central planning and a larger role for government in the economy would set Britain on a road that ultimately led to the totalitarianism of Nazi Germany. *The Road to Serfdom* sold out within a few days of publication, and wartime paper shortages meant that reprints over the next year or so never kept up with demand. The book's controversial message led it to be turned down by three US publishers, until a Chicago economist – the aptly named Aaron Director – persuaded the University of Chicago Press to take it on.

Director published relatively little under his own name but, as well as his role in *The Road to Serfdom*, he was a guiding hand behind the work of several key thinkers, including Milton Friedman, his brother-in-law. As an undergraduate at Yale, Director had been an anti-establishment iconoclast who, with his close friend the painter Mark Rothko, produced an underground newspaper called the *Yale*

Saturday Evening Pest. In later life, though, Director was sufficiently conservative that he described Friedman, adviser to conservatives Reagan and Thatcher, as 'my radical brother-in-law'.[1]

The Road to Serfdom was a great success in the United States. Just as in Britain, the publishers had to battle the paper-rationing authorities to print enough copies to meet demand. But in April 1945 the *Reader's Digest* published a condensed twenty-page version with a print run of several million copies. At that moment, Hayek was on a ship bound for New York. When it docked, he was told the modest academic plans for his US visit had been cancelled in favour of a nationwide lecture tour. It began in New York Town Hall, packed to its capacity of 3,000, with many more listening in adjoining rooms.

In light of his burgeoning influence and celebrity, it was unsurprising that Hayek came to be seen as the intellectual leader of the group assembled at Mont Pèlerin (soon to be known as the Mont Pèlerin Society). Both Friedman and Director were in attendance. On 1st April, the first day of their meeting, Hayek set out the task they faced – saving Britain and the United States, among other countries, from what he and his fellow travellers saw as a descent into totalitarianism. The growing interference of government in the economy, Hayek believed, constituted a direct threat to individual freedoms, freedoms which could be restored only through the long, slow, patient rolling back of government intervention and the eventual return to a true free-market economy. Hayek was clear about the scale of the challenge.

Hayek saw that Keynesian economics was much more than just a set of policy recommendations for controlling unemployment. There was a rapidly emerging consensus in which a primary duty of government is to maintain full employment. (Even the bankers seemed to agree: in a government memo, Keynes noted that international financiers would disapprove of significant unemployment in Britain.)[2] More than that, Keynes insisted that governments have a duty to regulate and supplement market forces for the sake of wider social benefits. And it was taken for granted that governments were mostly competent, knowledgeable and could be trusted to pursue the greater good. This was the lens through which people now viewed the economy. Hayek realized that overturning Keynesian orthodoxy would require a different perspective – changing how people thought about the economy and government at a fundamental level. He concluded that the Mont Pèlerin Society should be 'concerned not so much with what would be immediately practical, but with the beliefs which must regain ascendance'.[3] It was a long-term project to change people's underlying 'common sense' beliefs. In other words, to lead us to a different way of seeing the world.

In this, Hayek and his Mont Pèlerin colleagues would eventually succeed far beyond their expectations. They knew they faced an enormous challenge to shift the prevailing worldview. In 1947, though, the Mont Pèlerin crowd were far outside the political and economic mainstream – not quite seen as cranks, perhaps, but not far off. It would take another three decades for their ideas to break through. With the benefit of hindsight, the turning point is easy to identify.

Today no one doubts that the 1979 election of Margaret Thatcher in the UK, and Ronald Reagan soon afterwards in the US, marked a fundamental shift in politics and economics. With the arrival of Thatcher and Reagan, the post-war Keynesian consensus was swept away. Thatcher had been elected leader of the British Conservative Party in February 1975. The Conservatives were hungry for power and, at a strategy meeting that summer, it was proposed that future party policy should explicitly follow a 'middle way', avoiding extremes of Left and Right. Thatcher interrupted, pulling one of Hayek's books from her bag and holding it up for all to see. 'This is what we believe,' she announced, and then slammed it down on the table.[4]

BATTERY CHICKENS FOR FREEDOM

When a British dairy farmer named Antony Fisher read the Reader's Digest version of *The Road to Serfdom*, it made a great impression on him. Hayek seemed to share Fisher's own gut instincts about individual freedom being under threat. Fisher wrote to Hayek to ask what he could do to help, and wondered whether he should go into politics. Hayek told Fisher that he could do something more valuable, explaining that a more powerful role in the ideological battle was played by 'second-hand dealers in ideas' – the journalists, political advisers, commentators and intellectuals who shaped and shifted public debate and political thinking. Hayek advised Fisher to work with the Mont Pèlerin Society to set up research institutes with the aim of influencing these second-hand dealers. In 1952 Fisher went to America to visit one of these fledgling institutes, the Foundation for Economic Education. Its co-founder was economist 'Baldy' Harper, who had been at the Mont Pèlerin meeting five years before. And, since Fisher was a farmer, Harper showed him a new farming method too. It was a new breed of fast-growing chicken, the broiler, which was being reared in tiny cages. With battery-chicken farming then unknown in the UK, Fisher saw there was a fortune to be made. So he brought broiler chickens to the UK.* He borrowed £5,000 to start a battery-farming business. By the time he sold it fifteen years later it was worth £21 million.

Fisher used his growing wealth to make Hayek's dreams come true. He began in 1955 by founding the Institute of Economic Affairs – a 'think tank', a research and lobbying organization set up to pursue the project laid out by Hayek at the first meeting of the Mont Pèlerin Society. It was this institute which, twenty years later, arranged for Thatcher and Hayek to meet for the first time – months before Thatcher waved Hayek's book in the air at the Conservative Party gathering. The one-to-one meeting between Thatcher and Hayek took place in the institute's boardroom. It lasted about thirty minutes, after which the staff of the institute gathered around Hayek for his verdict. After a long pause he said with obvious emotion, 'She's so beautiful.'[5]

The Institute of Economic Affairs is just one part of the Atlas

---

* Literally. According to Fisher's friend and biographer Gerald Frost (*Antony Fisher: Champion of Liberty*, Profile Books, 2002), Fisher brought twenty-four fertilized eggs back on the plane, hidden in his hand luggage: he wanted to dodge the slow process of getting a licence to import the eggs legally – a licence which might not have been granted. In public, Fisher was equally contemptuous of agricultural regulations. Unlike Hayek, he did not seem to recognize that even the free-est of free markets relies on a robust legal framework.

Economic Research Foundation established by Fisher in 1981 to nurture similar think tanks around the world. It has become a large international umbrella organization, a network which has grown over the years and now numbers more than 500 organizations in over 90 countries. As well as advocating free-market economics, the network includes specialist groups ranging from climate-change denialists to pro-tobacco-industry lobbyists. A common theme across the network is the reliance on funding from big corporations and plutocrats.

At this point, the conspiracy theories emerge. Beginning with the Mont Pèlerin Society, and culminating in the Atlas Foundation, the conspiracy theorists see the lofty philosophical ambitions of these organizations as mere cover for a secret, long-run plan to protect and then enhance the wealth and influence of rich and powerful business elites. And it is true that these organizations, while formally independent of the rich and powerful, have been bankrolled by them at every step. In a deeper sense, too, the Mont Pèlerin Society saw politics as subservient to economic interests. Hayek didn't just want laissez-faire, the old idea that politicians should leave the market and business well alone. Hayek didn't see markets and economics as something separate, existing in a different sphere from the rest of human life. For him, markets and economics were *all* of life. Hayek saw all human motivation as economic: 'there is no separate economic motive'.[6]

Hayek's ideas have come to shape contemporary culture as much as they have shaped our politics: over the last four decades the penetration of market economics deep into our daily lives has transformed what we value and how we think.

And yet the impact has not been quite what Hayek might have imagined at that inaugural meeting of the Mont Pèlerin Society, because economics has itself changed greatly since then. The rise of the society turns out to be just a small part of the story. And this is where the conspiracy theories break down.

Many of the most influential thinkers behind the triumph of market economics were Mont Pèlerin Society members, including Gary Becker, James Buchanan, Ronald Coase, Milton Friedman, Richard Posner and George Stigler. But they did not always share Hayek's views. And a few economists, such as Ken Arrow and Tom Schelling, were equally influential yet had a very different political outlook to the Mont Pèlerin gang.

In the following chapters I explore how the radical ideas of these thinkers did so much to make modern mainstream economics. It was these new ideas, more than a conspiracy by the rich and powerful, which produced the market-driven world we live in today. I focus on what's called *micro*economics (as opposed to the *macro*economics of how national economies function) because most of the major developments in economics since the Second World War have been in microeconomics. Microeconomics is economics at the individual, human level so, unsurprisingly, it has played a greater role in shaping how we, as individuals, see the world.

First, though, we need to peer through the fog of claim and counter-claim about modern economics. An important reason why we seem locked into current economic thinking is that the debate about it typically presents us with a choice between two equally unconvincing alternatives. On the one side, economics is a science uncovering truths about how we naturally, inevitably, think and behave. On the other, economics invokes a fantasy world populated not by plausible representations of people but by selfish, endlessly calculating decision-making robots – also known as *homo economicus*. The debate may be unsatisfactory, but the status of economics is of more than academic interest. The global financial crisis reminded us that bad economics can bite. If economic theories – used widely by financial institutions and their government regulators, among others – are fundamentally flawed, then no wonder we can have a global financial crisis and face the continuing risk of another one coming along at any moment.

From the 1950s onwards increasing numbers of economists began suffering from 'physics envy' – a yearning to re-make economics in the mould of a mathematical science like physics. And economics certainly started to *look* more scientific: mathematics became the privileged language in which economic arguments are expressed. Clearly, the use of mathematics can bring precision and rigour. A valid mathematical proof is indisputable; it seems to raise the tantalizing prospect of cutting through the tortuous on-the-one-hand-and-on-the-other arguments often characteristic of economics, to give a straight answer. As Chief Economist of the World Bank, Larry Summers (later US Treasury Secretary and President of Harvard) exuded this confidence: 'Spread the truth – the laws of economics are like the laws of engineering. One set of laws works everywhere.'[7]

But, of course, mathematics cannot give us laws of economics like the laws of nature or engineering. Mathematics can help make economic theories logical and consistent. It does nothing to ensure that these theories tell us something about the real world. Another problem with Summers's view is that it seems to banish political and ethical questions from economics because answering them involves unscientific value judgements which don't 'work everywhere'. Yet the questions still remain, because political and ethical considerations are inescapable in economics. So these value judgements are still made, but usually implicitly and obliquely. Much modern economics proceeds with a hidden political and ethical agenda but masquerades as an objective science. The result is an economics with an influence on our twenty-first-century lives which is all-embracing – and yet often far from simple or obvious.

A big part of that political and ethical agenda seems to build on a view of humans as essentially selfish. This brings us back to the complaint that economics is a set of highly unrealistic stories about selfish, hyper-rational *homo economicus*. In truth, many economic theories allow a wider range of human motivations than selfishness. And the problems of modern economics are not straightforwardly solved by making it more realistic.

Many economists proudly see themselves as unsentimental, straight-talking and brutally honest. For decades, the default starting point of mainstream economists has been to assume that selfishness is the natural, dominant determinant of human behaviour. This idea is there in the shadows behind slogans as varied as 'business is business' and 'rising inequality is inevitable in a market economy'. These economists and their supporters from outside economics (there are many) point to the founding father of economics, Adam Smith, who built his magnum opus *The Wealth of Nations* (1776) on the rock of humans as essentially selfish creatures. Modern economics has returned to this classical tradition, they conclude, after the aberration which began with Karl Marx and ended with the fall of the Berlin Wall, despite the best efforts of John Maynard Keynes to postpone the inevitable.

Unfortunately, this version of history goes wrong from the beginning. Adam Smith's ideas reflected the eighteenth-century intellectual society he lived in and don't easily translate to our world. The cornerstone of his Enlightenment thinking was the idea of enlightened self-interest, which is not at all the same as selfishness. Smith's enlightened self-interest required the development of cultivated behaviour, good manners and 'moral sentiments'. Smith worried, for example, that people's 'disposition to admire the rich and the great, and to despise or neglect persons of poor and mean condition' would lead to 'the corruption of our moral sentiments'.[8] This is far from the 'look after Number One' caricature of Smith used to justify selfishness today. Modern economics, then, has not returned us to some eternal truth laid down by Adam Smith. It has taken us somewhere different altogether.

The aforementioned straight-talking economists assume that we are always and everywhere narrowly selfish (but if that is true, why should we listen to these economists? Won't they simply be saying whatever they hope will get them a promotion/pay rise/Nobel Prize?). Other economists acknowledge that people may act altruistically, not just towards family and friends but in their kindness to strangers too: many people try to return a lost wallet found in the street.[9] However, seemingly altruistic behaviour is often interpreted as disguised selfishness. You give a gift to your girlfriend only because of what it might get you in return, according to Greg Mankiw (President George W. Bush's chief economic adviser and author of one of the bestselling economics textbooks of recent times). You act altruistically to signal your virtuousness to others, so that they will trust you enough to buy from you or employ you (and you can always cheat on them later). This approach mixes absurdity and tautology: every act can be interpreted as 'ultimately' selfish, but the broader the interpretation of selfishness, the less meaningful it becomes.

In an attempt to sidestep these difficulties, many economists today avoid talking about selfishness. Instead their theories and models assume that people are *rational*, a word given different meanings by different economists. More significant than the exact definition is the slippery power of the word, providing the opportunity to slide evasively between descriptive and prescriptive meanings. Labelling behaviour as rational might be descriptive – rational behaviour as normal or typical. Or it can be prescriptive – you *ought* to be rational. When faced with overwhelming evidence from psychology and behavioural economics that we often act irrationally, economists can respond that economic theories merely explore the 'what if?' implications of assuming everyone conforms to the economists' ideal of rational behaviour. These theories are not supposed to be accurate descriptions of reality. This seems innocuous enough, but the effect is that 'rational' provides scientific-sounding cover for the assumption that we ought to act like *homo economicus*, obsessively calculating in all our decisions – and that this calculating reasoning is somehow praiseworthy or superior, regardless of what we decide to do. Bad behaviour is licensed because it has been redefined as rational.

A general pattern begins to emerge here. Economic ideas – such as the idea of what it means to be rational – *change us* to become more like hyper-rational *homo economicus*. How can this happen?

We say that the most successful politicians 'make the weather': that is, they shape and bend our understanding of reality to fit their vision and values. The economists we meet in subsequent chapters have changed the weather too – and for the long term. Their ideas give us a way of seeing the world which, if we adopt it, becomes true. In other words, some economic ideas are at least partially self-fulfilling. Believing them goes a long way to making them true. If everyone assumes that everyone else is selfish, then everyone becomes more selfish. If all the buyers and sellers in a particular market assume that some economic theory of that market is true, then they behave more in accordance with the theory, and so market behaviour moves closer to that described in the theory. Some markets, notably in the financial world, couldn't even exist without an economic theory to explain them and give them rules: the financial products being traded are so complex that without a theory (or its manifestation as a computer model) to consult, traders cannot tell whether prices are cheap or expensive.

When economists see the chasm between economic theory and real-world behaviour their solution is often to change the world, not the theory.* Economist Richard Thaler recently won the Nobel Prize for his work leading to the *Nudge* idea. Nudge economists seek to change the environment in which we make choices, to steer us to choose as *homo economicus* would do – to make us behave in accordance with economic theory, even though we don't think like that. This approach, making our choice environment human-proof, assumes human decisions are generally inferior, and never superior, to those of machine-like *homo economicus*. We would want to choose what *homo economicus* does, the economists assume, if only our error-prone natures would let us.

This brings us to a more direct way in which economics can make the weather. It gives us a guide, a set of rules for living, which we are encouraged to follow. Sometimes these rules are peculiar.

DESIGNS FOR LIVING

In 1954 Dennis Robertson, a leading economist of his day, gave a lecture entitled 'What does the economist economize?' Robertson's answer was: Love. This answer would surely have met with approval from the Mont Pèlerin Society (Robertson himself was not a member, but his closest colleague and protégé Stanley Dennison was a friend of Hayek and a society member from the beginning).

Robertson used 'Love' as a shorthand for kindness, solidarity, generosity and other altruistic virtues. He argued that by promoting policies, laws and organizations which rely only on selfishness, economics and economists avoided wasting 'that scarce resource Love'. Robertson saw love and our altruistic virtues as akin to scarce resources depleted by each use – so they should be carefully hoarded for use in emergencies, rather than recklessly squandered in everyday

* As the joke goes, an economist is someone who asks, 'That's all very well in practice, but how does it work in theory?'

life. Many eminent economists share this same strange misunderstanding of humanity. In arguing that blood should be supplied through a market rather than a donation system, Nobel Prize-winner Ken Arrow worried about relying on donations: 'ethical behaviour', he stated, should 'be confined to those circumstances where the price system breaks down ... We do not wish to use up recklessly the scarce resources of altruistic motivation.'[10] Similarly, Larry Summers defended economists' reliance on selfishness: 'We all have only so much altruism in us. Economists like me think of altruism as a valuable and rare good that needs conserving.'[11]

It's true that a society in which people are endlessly exhorted to show solidarity with fellow citizens/comrades will soon discover the limits of altruism. But altruism is not depleted through use. That would be like the motorist who, after giving way to another driver in the morning rush hour, says, 'I have done my good deed for the day; for the remainder, I can act like a bastard.'[12] Our altruistic virtues are not like this. On the contrary, they are more like muscles which wither and atrophy if not regularly exercised. Aristotle emphasized that virtue is something we foster through practice: 'we become just by doing just acts ... brave by doing brave acts.'[13] Nowadays, we put it less poetically: Use it or lose it.

Again we see how economic behaviour can be self-fulfilling. By focusing on our selfishness, economics leads to the decline of our altruistic virtues, so we become more selfish – yet the irony is that all this is done in the name of preserving those altruistic virtues.

The neuroscientist Antonio Damasio made pioneering studies of patients suffering from damage to the part of the brain responsible for emotions. Damasio was trying to arrange the date of his next meeting with one such patient. While consulting his calendar for almost half an hour, 'the patient enumerated reasons for and against each of the two dates: previous engagements, proximity to other engagements, possible meteorological conditions ... [H]e was now walking us through a tiresome cost-benefit analysis, an endless outlining and fruitless comparison of options and possible consequences . . .'[14] This ended only when Damasio interrupted and simply told the patient when the next meeting would be.

We all know that no one can live as *homo economicus* does. And if being rational means engaging in endless calculations of costs and benefits, then we can't be rational either. So why have the economists' designs for living become so influential?

The interests of the rich and powerful of course have a major role to play but, as government insiders frequently report, no one gets to determine government policy by blatantly arguing 'because it will make me rich'.[15] They need a respected language in which to frame their demands. Economics has become that language.

Keynes concluded his most influential book with a declaration on the power of economic ideas:

> . . . Practical men, who believe themselves to be quite exempt from any intellectual influences, are usually the slaves of some defunct economist. Madmen in authority, who hear voices in the air, are usually distilling their frenzy from some academic scribbler of a few years back. I am sure that the power of vested interests is vastly exaggerated compared with the gradual encroachment of ideas . . . But, soon or late, it is ideas, not vested interests, which are dangerous for good and evil.[16]

Hayek, Keynes's intellectual enemy in many respects, agreed: he included this quotation from Keynes in his opening address to the Mont Pèlerin Society in 1947. It later became the motto of the Institute of Economic Affairs.

It is no exaggeration to see modern economics as partly filling the gap left by the decline of religion in modern societies. In the twenty-first century our way of seeing the world is unconsciously conditioned by its concepts and values. The language of economics profoundly limits the political and moral questions which can be asked. With modern economics as our guide, we just don't see the other questions. To change our society, or simply to decide whether change is necessary, we need to understand how constrained our thinking has become – how, without even realizing it, we veto or ignore alternatives to current orthodoxy.

And so we must look back to how these economic ideas emerged and spread. In subsequent chapters we follow a diverse range of economists on their intellectual journeys to become the high priests of our time. Like the real journeys we make, these economists often fail to take the shortest route. There are detours, accidental and otherwise. And, en route, some stops: ideas which get parked and left, motionless for years or decades, before their sudden reappearance in contemporary life. Some ideas begin well but are grossly distorted or misapplied by later thinkers. Some ideas are flawed from the start. In all this messy diversity we see the interplay of politics, culture and chance in shaping the spread of ideas. And the paradoxical quality of appealing, seductive ideas which turn out to do great damage. The stories of these high priests are varied, but together they show how economics has come to dominate our lives.

2

Trust No One

Oh, the RAND Corporation is the boon of the world;
They think all day for a fee.
They sit and play games about going up in flames,
For counters they use you and me, Honey Bee,
For counters they use you and me.[1]

In the fall of 1948 most of the newly arrived postgraduate maths students at Princeton University in New Jersey were cocky, but one was even cockier. Still only nineteen, he was always boasting about his mathematical prowess. No one recalls him attending any of the regular classes; nobody saw him with a book. Partly it was because he was dyslexic, but it was also because he thought too much reading would stifle his creativity. He took regular detours down Mercer Street in the hope of catching sight of its most famous resident, Albert Einstein. One day he succeeded. But a few weeks into his first term he decided a remote glimpse was not enough. He made an appointment to see Einstein.

He told Einstein's assistant that he had an idea about gravity, friction and radiation which he wished to discuss with the great man. Einstein listened politely, sucking on his tobacco-less pipe, while the twenty-year-old student wrote equations at the blackboard. The meeting lasted nearly an hour, at the end of which Einstein grunted: 'you had better study some more physics, young man.'[2] The student did not immediately follow Einstein's advice but, years later, did go on to win the Nobel Prize – although for economics rather than physics. The student was John Nash, and his Nobel Prize-winning idea would become central to how we think today about interactions between people with conflicting interests.

To understand Nash's brilliant idea – and the way it changed the direction of economics, as well as much of social science, biology, philosophy and law – we need to begin with the time, the place and the theory out of which it emerged.

The time and place was early 1950s Santa Monica, at the end of the Malibu Beach Crescent, just west of Los Angeles. The seaside promenade was lined with hotels and retirement homes, shades of cream and pink punctuated by bursts of vivid bougainvillea. The scent of oleander hung in the air. Santa Monica was an improbable setting for the offices of the RAND Corporation, a secretive think tank employing mathematicians and scientists to develop military strategy for potential nuclear war with the USSR. The Korean War had just begun and the Cold War was getting hot. The atmosphere at RAND combined paranoia, megalomania and a worship of abstract logic. Nuclear military technology was still in its infancy, and during the Second World War US generals had realized that they needed advice on the best way to deploy the latest weapons, from radar to long-range missiles, as well as the atom bomb. Such was the motivation for setting up RAND (an acronym for Research ANd Development) in 1948, initially as an offshoot of the Douglas Aircraft Corporation. RAND was described as 'the Air Force's big-brain-buying venture'.[3] Its mission, in the words of influential RAND nuclear physicist Herman Kahn, was to 'think the unthinkable'.

The intellectual framework for all this nuclear strategizing was game theory. It was the perfect tool for the RAND style of military thinking. Game theory assumes that humans are purely selfish and hyper-rational, in possession not only of all the information relevant to making decisions but of perfect and exhaustive powers of computation and logical reasoning.

John von Neumann is usually seen as the father of game theory. Nash may have been a genius, but he was almost a mathematical minnow in comparison to von Neumann.

DR STRANGELOVE AND THE
KAISER'S GRANDSON

The 1964 film *Dr Strangelove* satirized the Cold War with its tale of impending Armageddon triggered by a crazy US air force general launching a nuclear first strike on the USSR. If you have seen the film, it is hard to forget Dr Strangelove himself, gesticulating wildly from his wheelchair in a strange Mitteleuropa accent. Bizarre though it may seem, the film drew heavily on real events. In 1956 President Eisenhower held regular secret meetings with a Hungarian mathematician confined to a wheelchair who would be taken back and forth by limousine to the White House from his bed at Walter Reed Hospital in Washington. The patient was under armed guard day and night because he would frequently descend into deranged babbling, so it was feared he might spill military secrets if an enemy agent could get to his bedside. The patient, in what was to be the last year of his life, was John von Neumann, undoubtedly one of the inspirations for Dr Strangelove. (At one point in the film, Strangelove refers to research by the 'Bland Corporation'.)

Before his tragic decline 'Johnny' von Neumann's genius was so overwhelming that it is hard to summarize. He was a mathematical prodigy: at the age of eight, when given any two eight-digit numbers, he could divide one by the other in his head. Although he was credited with the invention of game theory, mathematicians regard von Neumann's work in pure mathematics as a greater achievement. He was undoubtedly one of the top few mathematicians of the twentieth century, often talked about as the greatest of all. Easier to describe is his memory: after just once reading any lengthy book, he could quote it verbatim in its entirety (he first performed this trick at the age of six, with pages from the Budapest telephone directory). One of the key people behind the invention of the atomic bomb and the modern computer, he could create and revise computer programs (involving forty lines of complex code) in his head alone. In the popular press he was seriously described as 'the best brain in the world'. At Princeton, he acquired legendary status among colleagues, the joke being that he was not human but a demigod who had studied humans and learned how to imitate them perfectly. Notably, this joke was told about von Neumann rather than his Princeton contemporary Einstein.

Von Neumann's opinion of Soviet Russia was as congenial to the RAND worldview as his game theory. Referring to the possibility of nuclear conflict with the USSR, he stated simply, 'it is not a question of whether but of when'. Given this premise, there was a kind of game-theoretic logic to von Neumann's advocacy of preventive nuclear war. Or, as he remarked in 1950: 'If you say why not bomb them tomorrow, I say why not today? If you say today at five o'clock I say why not one o'clock?'[4] For von Neumann, once the US had developed a hydrogen bomb (partly based on von Neumann's ideas), the only way for them to maintain their advantage in the nuclear game was to bomb the Soviets before they had built a hydrogen bomb too. Secretary of State John Foster Dulles was convinced by von Neumann's game-theoretic logic. Fortunately, President Eisenhower wasn't so sure.

Von Neumann's reasoning was straight out of the pages of *Theory of Games and Economic Behavior*, published in 1944, which von Neumann had written with Princeton economist Oskar Morgenstern. Like von Neumann, Morgenstern was an Austro-Hungarian émigré with a low opinion of the intellect of most people. Morgenstern cultivated an eccentric image: boasting that he was an (illegitimate) grandson of Kaiser Friedrich III, he rode around Princeton on horseback in bespoke three-piece suits. Morgenstern played an essential, but subordinate, role in developing the new theory, a kind of Dr Watson to von Neumann's Sherlock Holmes.

At that time, the late 1940s, the orthodox view in economics still looked back to Keynes's vision of the ideal economist as someone who was simultaneously a 'mathematician, historian, statesman, and philosopher'.[5] (Admittedly, this interdisciplinary economics often generated equivocal on-the-one-hand-but-on-the-other-hand advice, which led President Harry Truman to plead, 'Give me a one-handed economist!') Von Neumann and Morgenstern had no interest whatsoever in this Keynesian vision of economics; they bonded over their agreement that economics was in a mess. Von Neumann: 'economics is simply still a million miles away from . . . an advanced science such as physics'.[6] Morgenstern: 'Economists simply don't know what science means. I am quite disgusted with all this rubbish. I am more and more of the opinion that Keynes is a scientific charlatan, and his followers not even that.'[7] But if economics was a mess, theirs would be the double act to fix it. Their plan was to use game theory to turn economics into a proper science.

Theory of Games and Economic Behavior opened with a suggestion that the effect of game theory on economics would be akin to that of Newton's discovery of gravity on physics. Indeed, this claim underplayed the extent of von Neumann and Morgenstern's ambition. They had originally planned to call their book *General Theory of Rational Behavior*, because their ultimate hope for game theory was that it would become the single underpinning framework for analysing human relations.

The initial reviews were ecstatic. In an instant, game theory was transformed from an obscure corner of pure mathematics into a new science of social interaction which caught the public's attention: *Theory of Games and Economic Behavior* was a front-page story in the *New York Times* in March 1946.

This new science, however, contained a gaping hole. Von Neumann and Morgenstern's book distinguished cooperative from non-cooperative game theory. In cooperative games, players can make agreements or contracts before the game itself begins. Non-cooperative game theory assumes such agreements are impossible, because they are unenforceable (players will make promises then break them). But the book did not discuss most non-cooperative games. It only covered one type: *zero-sum* games between two players.

Zero-sum games are those in which whatever is good for one player is bad for the other. This framing of the analysis can make a big difference. The nuclear stand-off between America and the USSR was a perilous, indisputably 'non-cooperative' game – but was it zero-sum? Should the strategists at RAND and the Pentagon rule out altogether, in the very set-up of their analysis, the possibility of an outcome in which *neither* side wins? And also rule out an outcome where *both* do (the origin of the term 'win–win solution')? By adopting von Neumann and Morgenstern's zero-sum non-cooperative game theory, they could not consider such possibilities.

The lesson of this kind of game theory is simple. The best strategy is to calculate the worst-case outcome arising from each alternative you might choose, then choose the alternative that leads to the least bad of these worst-case outcomes. This *minimax* strategy is so called because you minimize your maximum possible loss. Effectively, you assume your non-cooperative opponent is trying to make you lose as much as possible (bad for you means good for them), so you minimize this risk. Von Neumann was widely regarded at the time as having 'invented' the minimax strategy,* and it was exactly this reasoning which led to his conviction that America should drop a hydrogen bomb on Russia before the Soviets developed one too.

But the real and intellectual worlds moved on fast. In 1953 the Soviet Union conducted its first hydrogen-bomb test, making von Neumann's advice redundant. And by this time minimax thinking had largely been superseded – by Nash himself, who had in the interim published a much more general approach to playing non-cooperative games which encompassed games involving more than two players and which were not zero-sum.

In 1950 Nash published the simple, elegant idea that made his name, nowadays known as the *Nash equilibrium*. Barely 300 words long, it had been accepted by the prestigious journal *Proceedings of the National Academy of Sciences*, a great achievement for a doctoral student. Von Neumann knew of this development in game theory but did not appreciate its significance. We know he knew, because Nash had arranged to meet von Neumann to tell him about it. Nash's meeting with von Neumann was even less successful than his meeting with Einstein a year earlier.

Again, twenty-one-year-old Nash felt he had an idea worthy of the attention of a world-famous genius. But this time the rejection was more dismissive. Nash had barely uttered more than a few sentences outlining the mathematical proof he had in mind when von

---

* In fact, it was discovered much earlier. A French mathematician who wrote one of the many stellar reviews of *Theory of Games and Economic Behavior* was also a book collector. In the 1960s he purchased a mathematical treatise from one of the stalls along the banks of the Seine in Paris. It included a letter describing the minimax solution to two-person zero-sum games. The letter was dated 1713.

Neumann cut in: 'That's trivial, you know. That's just a fixed point theorem.'[8]

In a sense, von Neumann was right. Nash's equilibrium theorem was *just* a (mathematically straightforward) extension of a well-known theorem. Nash's contribution was not as mathematically deep as any of von Neumann's major mathematical achievements. But by providing a more general approach to playing non-cooperative games, Nash's equilibrium idea effectively superseded von Neumann's game theory. And it casts light on a central aspect of what it means to be human – interdependence.

Since our choices are interdependent, an individual's best strategy depends on the strategies adopted by others. But in many situations – whether playing poker or competing against an arch-rival in business – you have to pick a strategy without knowing the strategies adopted by others. And, likewise, they will be choosing without knowing your strategy. Before Nash, reasoning in these situations seemed to fall ever deeper into a never-ending regress: 'If you think I will choose X, then I will do better choosing Y. But if you think that I will choose Y because I think that you think I will choose X, then you will change your strategy, and I may be better off choosing X after all. But if you think that I have realized *that*, then . . .' Put another way, chains of reasoning for a particular course of action often collapse once you realize that your opponent will probably be aware of that reasoning too.

Nash cut through this circular reasoning with the simple but brilliant insight that a particular pattern of social interaction will disappear as soon as anyone realizes they can do better by behaving differently. Hence, for a particular pattern of social interaction to persist, no one must have any reason to change their behaviour. And that must mean everyone has already adopted the best possible strategy *given* the strategies adopted by others. This is a Nash equilibrium. Even though, when making their decisions, no one knew what anyone else would do, it is *as if* everyone correctly guessed the strategy adopted by everyone else and picked their best response accordingly. The situation merits the 'equilibrium' label because it is stable: no one can do better by changing their behaviour.

Game theory has two obvious uses. First, as an aid to players in real-world games – a prescription telling you the best strategy to adopt in the situation you face. Second, as a tool for others to use in predicting what will happen – how the game will actually be played. The importance of this second use was obvious in the Cold War, as the entire world waited and wondered how the nuclear game between the US and the USSR would be played out. But it matters when the stakes are lower too: when Samsung and Apple play games with each other in the pricing and design of new smartphones, many outsiders try to predict what will happen – consumers, regulators and chip manufacturers all have an interest. In short, we look to game theory for an answer, a solution, comprising a prescription of how to play, or a prediction of what will be played, or both. Ever since Nash's 1950 paper, Nash equilibrium has been the basis of that answer: simultaneously a prediction of what a stable outcome must look like and a prescription of how to play.

Nash equilibrium bears the mark of a real intellectual breakthrough – an idea that had not occurred to anyone before Nash yet one that with hindsight seems entirely obvious. Together, von Neumann, Morgenstern and Nash had triggered a revolution in our thinking about human interaction. What happened next?

NON-COOPERATION ABOUT NON-COOPERATION

At first, nothing. Economists did not adopt game theory; a few mathematicians elaborated the mathematics of game theory as a project in pure mathematics; and RAND doggedly pursued a game-theoretic approach to military strategy, with few results of practical significance.* Despite the extravagant early praise lavished on their ideas by economists, there was virtually no progress in von Neumann and Morgenstern's grand project of doing for social science what Newton did for mechanics. Some spoilsports had even pointed out a crucial flaw in the analogy: balls, planets and all the other subjects of Newtonian

---

* RAND's failure to produce useful research was becoming a joke. By the late 1950s outsiders said that RAND stood for 'Research And No Development'.

mechanics are not aware of being studied. Humans *are* aware – and may change their behaviour accordingly.

Meanwhile, the project was plagued with people problems: indeed, it almost didn't get off the ground at all. Von Neumann's dismissal of Nash's equilibrium idea, combined with some relatively minor criticisms from his PhD supervisor, led Nash, who struggled to cope with intellectual criticism, seriously to consider abandoning research in game theory altogether. By the end of the 1950s the root of his problems would become clear: diagnosed with paranoid schizophrenia, he would spend ever-longer periods of time in hospital. Already, his condition dominated his behaviour: aggressively competitive, even by the standards of the elite young mathematicians he mingled with, he had almost no awareness of the brash abrasiveness which so alienated him from others.

While many of von Neumann's greatest intellectual accomplishments emerged in collaboration with others, and most of the (collaboratively written) *Theory of Games and Economic Behavior* was devoted to cooperative game theory, Nash was a loner. Indeed, he argued (in another path-breaking paper published just a year after his paper setting out the Nash equilibrium idea) that von Neumann's cooperative game theory was redundant. All cooperative games, Nash argued, should be understood as in fact non-cooperative: the seemingly cooperative phase, involving players making agreements before the game begins, should be seen as itself a separate, non-cooperative game. For Nash, in other words, what superficially looks like cooperation turns out to be nothing of the sort. This approach, which came to be known as the Nash program, was the first of many such programs across the social sciences from the 1960s onwards which 'explain' seemingly cooperative or altruistic behaviour as really non-cooperative and selfish underneath. Neither Nash nor his game theory did cooperation. From a comfortable post-Nobel Prize vantage point four decades later, Nash was phlegmatic about the initial rejection of his equilibrium concept by von Neumann and others, but his game-theoretic view of the world remains striking: 'I was playing a non-cooperative game in relation to von Neumann rather than simply seeking to join his coalition. And of course it was psychologically natural for him not to be entirely pleased by a rival theoretical approach.'[9]

Nash's descent into schizophrenia was surely one reason why game theory was not rapidly adopted by economists: the leading advocate of non-cooperative game theory went silent. Equally important was the attitude of von Neumann. In the mid-1950s he was busy with the development of the bomb and the computer. When he did have time for game theory, he reiterated his complaint that mainstream economic theory was mathematically primitive. In so doing he deeply antagonized many of the self-confessed 'mathematical' economists in academic economics at that time. Yet whatever von Neumann might have thought of their mathematics, these were the obvious people with sufficient mathematical skills to begin to incorporate game theory into social science. Von Neumann had alienated the academic audience likely to be most receptive to his game theory.

Given von Neumann's mathematical ambitions for social science, it was ironic that what finally propelled game theory beyond RAND and university maths departments was not maths but a story.

Albert Tucker was John Nash's PhD supervisor. In May 1950, just after persuading his wayward student not to abandon his PhD on game theory, Tucker was asked to talk about the new theory to a group of psychologists. Since his audience did not know the theory or the maths, Tucker decided to present a game he had learned about from some RAND researchers in the form of a little story. He called it the Prisoner's Dilemma.

Two members of a criminal gang have been imprisoned separately. The police have enough evidence to convict them both of a minor crime, but not the major one that they suspect them of committing. So they offer each prisoner the following deal: confess and implicate your partner and you receive immunity from prosecution while your former partner will be hit with a ten-year sentence. If you both stay silent, you will each be given a two-year sentence for the minor crime. The snag, however, is that if you both confess, the immunity deal is off and you will both be sentenced to eight years.

Assuming each prisoner cares only about their own sentence, what should they do? Although they have no means of communicating with each other, the prisoners believe they have both been offered the same deal. However, they can reason their way out of the dilemma.

'If my former partner in crime does not confess but I do, I get the lowest possible sentence. If he does confess, I will get a lower sentence if I confess than if I don't. So, either way, I should confess.' The trouble is, since both prisoners may reason alike, they may both confess and be given eight years in jail, significantly longer than if neither had confessed. Even if the prisoners could communicate and agree to stay silent, the outcome would surely be the same, because each prisoner would be tempted to break the agreement in the hope of a lower sentence.

In 1950 no one had any inkling that the Prisoner's Dilemma would later become the most influential game in game theory. Unsurprisingly, RAND was interested in the game for military reasons: the nuclear arms race between the US and the USSR was a classic Prisoner's Dilemma, both sides building more and better weapons in a futile attempt to gain an advantage. But the game's structure (rather than its story) captures more than just Cold War rivalries. It elegantly expresses the conflict between private and collective interest in thousands of real-world contexts. Firms producing similar products – OPEC oil producers or Coke versus Pepsi – cut prices to gain market share, but because their rivals do the same all firms suffer a fall in profit. The Prisoner's Dilemma describes this and many other 'races to the bottom'. Likewise, the so-called Tragedy of the Commons describes a Prisoner's Dilemma: given free access to a common resource, everyone will consume it regardless of what others do, leading to damage or destruction of the resource and making everyone worse off. The challenge posed by climate change is, too, widely agreed to be a Prisoner's Dilemma: everyone is better off if global carbon emissions are reduced, but every country is reluctant to reduce emissions, regardless of what other countries do. You and the other spectators face a Prisoner's Dilemma when deciding whether to stand up for a better view at a sports event: everyone stands, so everyone is worse off than if they had remained seated.

In the original Prisoner's Dilemma story, the reasoning described earlier implies that both players should confess. And this outcome is a Nash equilibrium: if your partner confesses, you do best by confessing too. So the blame for the damaging non-cooperation nurtured by this reasoning may seem to lie with John Nash's equilibrium idea.

But – although millions of students in social science, philosophy, law and biology are today introduced to game theory via the Prisoner's Dilemma and its Nash equilibrium 'solution' – the Nash equilibrium idea is not driving the outcome here. There is a more basic logic at work: regardless of what the other player does, your best action is to confess. Any predictions about, or agreements with, your opponent are irrelevant: you will always do better in Prisoner's Dilemma situations if you respond with a 'non-cooperative' action.

TRUST WITHOUT TRUE TRUST

Given the set-up of the Prisoner's Dilemma, this logic is unassailable. Rational players *must* play the Prisoner's Dilemma this way – and suffer the consequences, from longer jail terms to nuclear arms races. This follows directly from game theory's assumption that rational human behaviour is non-cooperative and distrustful. Von Neumann could not imagine it otherwise: 'It is just as foolish to complain that people are selfish and treacherous,' he asserted, 'as it is to complain that the magnetic field does not increase unless the electrical field has a curl. Both are laws of nature.'[10]

It is easy to shudder or scoff at this simplistic view of humanity – and that is precisely what critics did in 1944, when von Neumann and Morgenstern published their magnum opus. The influential British anthropologist Gregory Bateson remarked that 'premises of distrust are built into the von Neumann model', as was 'the more abstract premise that human nature is unchangeable'. There was, he concluded, nothing human about 'von Neumann's players', who 'differ profoundly from people and mammals in that those robots totally lack humour and are totally unable to "play" (in the sense which the word is applied to kittens and puppies)'.[11]

Players in game theory are unlike real humans. At best, they are partial and incomplete representations of humanity. What's more, game theory misses a crucial part of what it means to play games, because its vision of rational behaviour rules out all the play, all the fun. But so what? Even if game theory leaves a lot out, it might still give us valuable insights into social interaction – for instance, in contexts where the selfish, ruthless, calculating side of humanity is to the fore.

But what contexts are those? From the 1960s onwards, as game theory began to creep out of its academic niche into wider discussion in social-science departments and beyond, it became clear that the biggest challenge to the Prisoner's Dilemma was reality – the undeniable fact of cooperation in so many real-world contexts which look just like Prisoner's Dilemmas. Returning to the alleged Prisoner's Dilemmas mentioned earlier, firms often resist the temptation to cut prices, knowing a price war would harm them. Common resources are often sustainably managed, while countries have cooperated to limit carbon emissions. We don't all stand up at sporting events, and nuclear-arms-control measures were eventually agreed upon. If the Prisoner's Dilemma captures the essence of these interactions, why do we observe cooperation in the real world?

Real people in Prisoner's Dilemma situations can cooperate by agreeing to do so before they play the game. They trust each other to keep their promises. For most people, keeping promises and trusting others is normal, default behaviour, because they have been raised and educated to behave that way and experience confirms it generally makes life more liveable. Put another way, we escape the destructive consequences of following game theory's prescription of 'rational' behaviour in the Prisoner's Dilemma by rejecting this definition of 'rational'. As Nobel Prize-winning economist Amartya Sen put it in 1977, game theory's advice on how to behave in Prisoner's Dilemma situations shows us not how to be rational but how to be a 'rational fool'. The overwhelming evidence of cooperation in real-world Prisoner's Dilemmas suggested that not only was game theory bad at predicting how we *do* behave, its advice on how we *ought* to behave was suspect too. No one wants to be a rational fool.

But by the late 1970s game theorists had developed a response to this challenge with the theory of repeated games. In repeated games, people cooperate because they look to the future. People cooperate, even in Prisoner's Dilemma situations, for the sake of maintaining beneficial relationships in the future. Cheats, promise-breakers and the selfish generally find themselves shunned; they miss out on the benefits of future cooperation. This is the same cold and calculating view of human interaction as that underpinning the Prisoner's Dilemma – it *is* the Prisoner's Dilemma, but played repeatedly over time. If you know that you will meet the same opponent in another Prisoner's Dilemma situation in the future, you may cooperate now, for the sake of long-term benefits from cooperation – because if you break your promise or act selfishly now, you may find yourself punished by non-cooperative behaviour from your opponent in the future. The idea extends beyond two people: a group can hang on to some form of cooperation among its members by constant threats to punish selfish behaviour by those who fail to act in the group interest. The punishment is usually short and sharp – *tit-for-tat*, as the game theorists aptly describe it – but not too severe, as that would be too costly for those doing the punishing. One implication is that groups need not rely on external pressures such as law, coercion or social convention to sustain cooperation. Tit-for-tat will suffice, although to an observer it can look more like anarchy than stable society. The Mafia is a perfect example of tit-for-tat in action. Over a hundred years ago Pasquale Villari, a Neapolitan politician, observed, 'The Mafia has no written statutes, it is not a secret society, hardly an association. It is formed by spontaneous generation.'[12] In recent times, fans of Friedrich Hayek have invoked this aspect of game theory in an attempt to give mathematical credibility to Hayek's idea that seemingly anarchic societies with little or no government can sustain themselves through 'spontaneous order'.

Although the obvious political home for game theory seems on the Right – relentless competition between selfish individuals, self-organizing societies with no need for government – thinkers on the Left have pressed it into service too. They have argued that, contrary to appearances and von Neumann's views, game theory is compatible with a nicer, more trusting picture of human relations. Indeed, game theory can explain *why* we trust each other: I trust someone when I know they have an incentive to keep their promises. We are playing a repeated game in which we both know that any immediate gain either of us can make from breaking promises now is outweighed by losses from future punishment. The punishment may be inflicted not just by the victim of broken promises, but by the wider community: it is in everyone's interest that trust is possible and deals can be done. This way of thinking about trust may help us understand why some human relations and institutions work as they do. But it raises more questions than it answers.

To begin with, it implies that you can only trust those who have no incentive to break their promises to you. This game-theoretic perspective turns our normal understanding of trust upside down: it implies we can trust someone *only when we don't need to* – because it is in their interest to keep their promises anyway. Real trust means having faith in someone to keep promises, to do the right thing, because we believe in their good character, even in circumstances where we know they could profit by breaking promises, stabbing us in the back. Even in the competitive world of business, people need real trust more than the ersatz game-theoretic variety. There are too many situations where businesspeople are trying to do deals without any expectation of future interaction: they cannot assume they are playing a repeated game. Instead, they unconsciously rely on facts about human psychology which game theory ignores. It is, for instance, much easier to decide whether someone can be trusted if you meet them face to face. This is why, even in the era of Skype, business leaders are still willing to fly across the world for a crucial meeting.

Clearly, some game-theoretic explanations of trust and long-term cooperation seem to miss the point. But there is a more basic problem with this kind of response to the Prisoner's Dilemma. Even if strategies like tit-for-tat can help sustain cooperative behaviour when people interact repeatedly over a fairly long period, what about one-off interactions? Here the gap between theory and reality remains: game theory predicts that people will not cooperate in one-off Prisoner's Dilemma situations, yet they often do. Game theorists did not face up to this problem for many years. Most of them didn't accept that there *was* a problem. Instead they used a dodge which has often been used by economists when confronted with evidence of altruistic, cooperative or moral behaviour – reinterpret the evidence to make it go away. Thus, players who are apparently cooperating in a one-off Prisoner's Dilemma are not really doing so, because they are not actually playing a Prisoner's Dilemma. By definition, a pure Prisoner's Dilemma is a game in which each player cares only about their own prison sentence. Players who also care about their opponent's welfare, or believe in group solidarity, or know they will suffer the pangs of bad conscience if they break a promise to their opponent, and so on, are playing some other game. In the mathematical representation of the situation – which is, in the end, all that concerns game theorists – these other considerations would be captured in the single number representing the value or worth of a particular outcome for a player. These additional considerations would lead to a different number for most outcomes, compared to the pure Prisoner's Dilemma. Hence the new game is not the same.

The drawback with this dodge is that, taken to extremes, it can be used to define away *any* evidence that conflicts with the theory. It certainly makes it exceptionally difficult to find real-world evidence that is not vulnerable to this kind of dodge. It took until the 1990s for enough evidence of cooperation to emerge in a form which game theorists could not bypass or ignore: carefully designed experimental games played under lab conditions in which the information provided to participants – and, by extension, their possible motives – was strictly controlled. But by then game-theoretic thinking was securely embedded in economics and wider society. Its influence has become so strong that we fall back on it in times of crisis, to help define our civilization and identity. Three days after the 11th September 2001 attacks on New York and Washington, a *New Yorker* commentator tried to capture its significance:

> The calamity, of course, goes well beyond the damage to our city . . . it is civilizational. In the decade since the end of the Cold War, the human race has become, with increasing rapidity, a single organism . . . The organism relies increasingly on a kind of trust – the unsentimental expectation that people, individually and collectively, will behave more or less in their rational self-interest.[13]

Although, from the 1960s onwards, game theory began to influence everyday thinking, game theorists themselves were focusing on its limitations. In particular, they were becoming aware that in all too many contexts game theory seemed to have little to say.

CHICKEN

In 1955 the philosopher Bertrand Russell released an influential manifesto, co-authored by Albert Einstein, calling for nuclear disarmament. But Russell had an unintentionally greater impact on the disarmament debate just a few years later, by publicizing a game called Chicken. Painting a picture which could have come from the James Dean hit movie of the era, *Rebel without a Cause*, Russell imagined the US and the USSR as rival young drivers, speeding towards each other down the middle of a long, straight road. If neither swerved, both would die. But the first to swerve, the 'Chicken', would earn the everlasting contempt of his rival.

Chicken soon became a benchmark game in discussions among Cold War thinkers, game theorists and their students. In 1960 RAND strategist Herman Kahn adopted Chicken as a game to describe the nuclear stand-off in his influential and bestselling 652-page tome, *On Thermonuclear War*. Russell questioned why playing Chicken for nuclear high stakes seemed morally acceptable in RAND circles, while teenagers playing Chicken for much lower stakes were criticized:

> As played by youthful plutocrats, the [Chicken] game is considered decadent and immoral, though only the lives of the players are risked. But when the game is played by eminent statesmen ... it is thought that the statesmen on one side are displaying a high degree of wisdom and courage, and only the statesmen on the other side are reprehensible.[14]

In any case, Chicken was not a helpful bit of game-theoretic analysis, because it has *two* Nash equilibria, the first being 'your opponent does not swerve, you do' and the second being 'you do not swerve, your opponent does'. Game theory here makes no prediction about what will happen, or what should. The importance of this limitation was clear in the context of the Cuban Missile Crisis two years later when, in October 1962, both the US and the USSR refused to back down in their confrontation over the placing of Russian nuclear missiles on Cuba. It was obvious to both sides that Chicken was the game being played. However, what they both wanted to know was: which Nash equilibrium? In other words, who would swerve first? A mistake could mean annihilation. Most historians agree that the world has never come closer to full-scale nuclear war than during the Cuban crisis.

To recap, game theory's two obvious uses are to provide a prediction about how the players will behave, and/or a prescription about how they should. In games with more than one Nash equilibrium, like Chicken, game theory seemed to fail on both counts. Even game theorists began to ask: what's the point?

Worse still, over the coming years it became clear that games with multiple Nash equilibria were not rare exceptions. They were ubiquitous. Game theory provided no guidance in these situations. And by the time the importance and ubiquity of this so-called *multiplicity problem* became clear, Nash was in no position to help.

EMPEROR OF ANTARCTICA
WINS NOBEL PRIZE

Already, by early 1959, Nash's descent into madness had begun to accelerate. He was offered a top professorship at the University of Chicago, but wrote back explaining he could not take up the post because he was about to become Emperor of Antarctica. This was not an isolated incident. Around that time, Nash gave his expired driving licence to one of his students, writing the student's nickname over his own and telling the student furtively that it was an 'intergalactic driver's licence'.[15] Von Neumann had died two years earlier, so the two founding fathers of game theory were now silent. After the excitement of the early years, game theory had slipped, in the eyes of most economists, from the best hope for a comprehensive science of society to an intellectual dead end, bogged down with the multiplicity problem, which would preoccupy game theorists for years to come. As for Nash himself, by the 1980s many younger game theorists assumed he was dead. Other rumours circulated that he had had a lobotomy or lived in a secure psychiatric hospital. Yet in 1994 Nash, along with two other game theorists, John Harsanyi and Reinhard

Selten, won the Nobel Prize for economics. How did game theory make such a brilliant comeback?

There are two versions of the history of game theory in the forty-odd years that elapsed between von Neumann's death and Nash winning the prize. Let's begin with the official history. It is straightforward: Harsanyi, Selten and others made good progress on solving the multiplicity problem. Alongside other innovations like repeated game theory, the overall result was that game theory became useful again.

In the 1960s John Harsanyi explicitly set out the challenge game theory faced: solve the multiplicity problem and provide a determinate solution for every game, derived solely from general principles of rational behaviour. If this could be achieved, it would bring about the pure science of social interaction dreamed of by von Neumann, Morgenstern and Nash. The first major ascent in this Everest project was achieved by Reinhard Selten in 1965. To address the problem of multiple Nash equilibria, the obvious line of attack is to find grounds for ruling out some of these equilibria as inferior. Selten argued that some equilibria are inferior because they can only emerge when players make threats which are not credible. For example, the MAD (Mutually Assured Destruction) doctrine of nuclear deterrence relies on nuclear powers threatening catastrophic retaliation in response to a nuclear attack. But the threat is not credible if the recipient of the threat does not believe it would be carried out. In *Dr Strangelove* the Russians designed their Doomsday machine to trigger catastrophic retaliation automatically and irrevocably once an attack had been detected, removing any possibility of non-retaliation and hence making their threat completely credible.* In business, a monopoly firm in a particular market will often loudly threaten a price war to any firm considering entering the market as a competitor. If the new firm believes the threat, it may stay out of the market, allowing the monopolist to continue reaping big profits.

A threat is credible only if the player making the threat won't

---

* However, in the film the US did not know in advance that the Doomsday machine existed, rendering it useless as a threat. Director Stanley Kubrick ignored complaints about this plot flaw from economist and game theorist Thomas Schelling (see Chapter 6).

become worse off by carrying it out. Selten cleverly generalized and extended this idea, arguing that, at every stage in a game, players won't make choices that make them worse off, regardless of what they have said beforehand. Since 'what makes you worse off' depends on what you and the other players do later in the game, you find your best strategy by deciding what will happen at the end of the game and reasoning backwards from that, until you have decided your first move. This *backward induction* procedure can yield a determinate solution, a prediction of how to play, just as the game theorists hoped. But it yields some big surprises too.

Imagine a TV game show with the following format. The two players (let's call them Johnny and Oskar) know that the host has a maximum of $1,000 in prize money to hand out. The host starts by making an offer to the first player, Johnny – both players get to keep $100. If Johnny accepts the offer, both players leave with $100. If Johnny refuses, the host makes a new offer to the second player, Oskar: $50 for Johnny, $250 for Oskar – the total prize-money pot has increased by $100 but now it is to be split unequally. The game ends if Oskar accepts the offer, but if he refuses it is Johnny's turn again. Again, the total prize money pot increases by $100, but now it is to be split equally: $200 for each player. Again, the game ends if Johnny accepts the offer, while if he refuses the pot is increased by another $100 but split unequally: $150 for Johnny, $350 for Oskar. And so on, if both players keep refusing, until the host offers $350 for Johnny, $550 for Oskar. If Oskar refuses that, they both get $500 and the game ends.

It seems that, with just a bit of patience, Johnny and Oskar can share the maximum prize pot of $1,000 between them. But Selten's backward induction procedure implies otherwise. Both players know that Oskar will be better off accepting the host's last offer (he receives $550) than by refusing (he receives $500). So both players know that Oskar would accept that offer. So, reasoning backwards, Johnny knows he is better off accepting the host's previous offer ($400 each) than refusing it (he would receive $350 when Oskar accepts on the following round). The same reasoning applies to all previous rounds of the game too. Both players realize that they will *always* be better off accepting the host's offer than letting the game continue and getting a smaller prize when their opponent accepts in the next round. So Johnny should accept the very first offer of $100 and end the game immediately. Backward induction reasoning prevents either player from getting a bigger prize, because neither can trust the other to let the game continue past the next round. It is another variation on the familiar story of game theory: in the pursuit of hyper-rationality, cooperation is subverted and everyone is worse off.

Of course, people rarely think like this: in a large number of experiments with people playing games like the one just described, very few of them behave as prescribed by backward induction reasoning. In an attempt to suggest that people do use backward induction reasoning, if only they are smart enough, economists have recently repeated these experiments using chess Grandmasters as players. The results were ambiguous: some Grandmasters play as prescribed by backward induction reasoning; some don't. This brings us to a deep flaw in the logic of backward induction. In the game show just described, to conclude that you should accept the first $100 offer, you need to believe that your opponent is following backward induction reasoning and so will accept the first offer they receive. In other words, even if you are smart enough to understand backward induction reasoning, should you assume your opponent does too? The chess Grandmasters knew they were playing other Grandmasters, so for them it may have been a sensible assumption. But for most people, it isn't. If you are on the game show and your opponent refuses the first offer they receive, then you know, from observing this refusal alone, that they are not following the rulebook of game theory, because backward induction implies they should accept the first offer. More generally, in real-life interactions beyond the game show, we frequently deal with people who break the rules of game theory. It would be unwise to assume they will follow the rules in future. Game theorists call the rule-breakers 'irrational' and insist we should assume everyone is rational. No: given good evidence of someone's 'irrationality' in the past, it would be truly irrational to assume they will be 'rational' in the future.

The official history of game theory has largely ignored these problems. Some game theorists have always accepted that people often do not behave as game theory predicts. More modestly, they hold that game theory should not be understood as providing predictions, only prescriptions for how best to play. But games like the game show described above undermine even this modest view, because they show that following the prescriptions of game theory is not always the smart way to play a game after all. Which is where we must turn to the unofficial history.

A ZOMBIE SCIENCE OF HUMAN LIFE

Despite rumours to the contrary, Nash had been quietly working back at Princeton for some years before the Nobel announcement. On the afternoon of the announcement he gave a short speech. Nash's odd, uneasy sense of humour was still there. He noted that Nobel laureates are supposed to say how pleased they are to be sharing the honour. But Nash said he would have preferred to win the prize alone, because he really needed the money. He finished his speech by comparing game theory to string theory in physics, both subjects that researchers find intrinsically fascinating – so they like to pretend that both subjects are actually useful.[16] It was perhaps characteristic of Nash, especially after the Nobel announcement, to be playfully dismissive of game theory: around that time he described his own contribution to game theory as his 'most trivial work'.* But another of the laureates alongside Nash also raised concerns about the triviality of game theory. Reinhard Selten, who had used the paradoxical backward induction procedure in an attempt to solve the multiplicity problem, had turned away from such theoretical indulgences. From the late 1970s onwards Selten repeatedly stressed that game theory was too formal and mathematical to be a reliable guide to how people actually think in social interactions: 'game theory is for proving theorems, not for playing games'.[17]

However, there seems to be a clear exception to this negative verdict. Game theory can tell us the smart way to behave in some economic and social contexts – that is, contexts in which every player

---

* Perhaps Nash had finally accepted von Neumann's appraisal of his work, almost fifty years earlier.

knows that every player is well versed in game theory, as if they have a state-of-the-art textbook in hand. So if a chess Grandmaster is playing another chess Grandmaster, then both of them might reasonably assume their opponent has a sophisticated knowledge of game theory. Such a defence of game theory is (a bit) less useless than it seems. On 5th December 1994, the day John Nash left America for Stockholm to collect his Nobel Prize, Vice-President Gore was announcing the 'greatest auction ever' – an auction of airwave frequency spectrum licences to be used by mobile phones. Auctions are a type of game, and this auction was carefully designed using the latest game theory. When the auction closed in March 1995, the US government was delighted: it had received more than $7 billion in bids. The spectrum auctions, great revenue-raising successes for government, were hailed as a triumph of applied game theory. Here, at last, was a setting in which truly 'rational' players would interact – big corporations competing in an auction, each advised by a team of game theorists – leading to outcomes which could be predicted and tweaked by the game theorists designing the auction, on behalf of the government. Or so it seemed.

In reality, game theory did not provide the recipe for an ideal auction design to meet the government's objectives, because the theory could not adjudicate between conflicting auction designs. Different game theorists made different recommendations. This was not surprising, given that these theorists were employed as consultants for competing corporations. Moreover, game theorists didn't just provide advice on how to bid in a predetermined auction: they were employed from the very beginning of the process to help corporations lobby for particular auction designs, rules which would help skew the game in their favour. And the final outcome does not suggest hyperrational corporate players after all. Many successful bidders defaulted on their payments, and the later rise in failures and mergers in the telecoms industry was widely attributed to the burden of excessive auction bids.[18] The experience with a British spectrum-licence auction in 2000, also heavily influenced by game theorists, was similar: game theory did not tell the government how best to design the auction, nor did it adequately explain or predict the behaviour of bidders.

If game theory has limited use even in situations like these auctions, designed by game theorists as a potentially ideal playground for the theory, then why does it enjoy exalted status in economics today? There is no consensus answer, but there are common themes.

To begin with, the rise of game theory was not due to its successes or strengths but because economists turned to it to fix problems elsewhere in economics, or at least to find new techniques to break a stalemate in long-running debates. By the 1970s, for example, the regulation of big corporations was increasingly shaped by the ideas of lawyers and economists at the University of Chicago. This Chicago approach to 'law and economics' essentially argued that the less regulation there was, the better. Dominant corporations were dominant, they argued, because they offered better products at lower prices, not because of anti-competitive practices. Game theory gave opponents of the Chicago view a new framework which took anti-competitive behaviour seriously, a framework which impressed regulators and courts because of its high-status mathematical sophistication. Less politely, it was a new gimmick which might give you the upper hand in policy debate or legal argument. Elsewhere, ambitious economists were making imperialistic forays into aspects of life beyond the scope of markets and prices, and hence beyond the scope of the traditional tools of economic analysis. Game theory provided a new toolkit for these economists, who saw themselves as social engineers designing institutions and mechanisms to produce desired social outcomes. In their own terms, these academic users of game theory were remarkably successful: after Nash, Harsanyi and Selten in 1994, research essentially based on game theory led to Nobel prizes for eight more economists over the following twenty years.

In contrast, economists who questioned game theory faced ostracism. Rather than following the standard game-theoretic practice of making assumptions about human behaviour, Selten himself had become a firm believer in using lab experiments to study how people actually behave. As far as some game theorists were concerned, this reduced him to 'a turncoat, who has lost (or even worse) has left the path to the "pure and true" cause of game theory'.[19]

But Selten was an exception among economists. Game theory was not short of pure and true believers. Its seductive power should not be underestimated. Despite the problems with the theory, the temptation of a pure science of society, a grand unification theory for social science to rival that hoped for in physics, has proved irresistible. This seduction was reinforced by what Robert Axelrod, a US political scientist turned game theorist, called the 'law of the instrument': give an academic (or a child) a hammer, and they will find things to hammer. So game theory was used to 'explain' trust, although it is far from obvious that before game theorists came along there was any mystery about trust that needed explaining. Game theory is a kind of zombie science, a vision of human interaction which, no matter how broken it seems, never dies. Many thinkers abandon the project, but new recruits revive the grand dreams. As one recent convert solemnly intoned, 'game theory is a general lexicon that applies to all life forms. Strategic interaction neatly separates living from non-living entities and defines life itself.'[20]

These fantasies matter to the rest of us, in ordinary life. Game-theoretic ideas have spread out of academia to become part of common-sense thinking. But along the way, some subtleties have been lost. It is widely believed that cooperation is mostly for suckers and only the naïve rely on trust. In particular, game theory has been understood to prove, as a matter of irrefutable logic, that it is irrational to be altruistic, trustworthy or cooperative, even when the people you are dealing with are altruistic, trustworthy or cooperative. But this is a fundamental misunderstanding of the theory.

Yes, game theorists – especially in the early days of von Neumann, Nash and RAND – often *assumed* people are always selfish. But the circumstances under which game theory justifies or recommends selfishness are remarkably narrow. Nash's equilibrium idea essentially implies that *if* everyone else is behaving selfishly, you should do so too: selfishness is your best response. And their selfishness is then their best response to yours: we can get locked into non-cooperative situations. But crucially, in many contexts, we cannot assume that everyone else is behaving selfishly in the first place. And without this assumption, the explanation for why we get locked into non-cooperative situations disappears.

Put another way, game theory says we will end up in a Nash

equilibrium, but it does not explain which equilibrium – cooperative, non-cooperative or otherwise. It is a Nash equilibrium that everyone drives on the same side of the road, and there are two equilibria: everyone drives on the left, and everyone drives on the right. Game theory has little to say about which equilibrium will emerge, and why it differs across countries. Likewise, the QWERTY layout for keyboards is a Nash equilibrium: if everyone is using QWERTY to type, and almost all keyboards are manufactured with QWERTY, then you should learn to type using QWERTY too, and new keyboards will be made with that design. Therefore, the equilibrium will be maintained even though it is much slower to type in QWERTY than in rival layouts such as DVORAK: the equilibrium persists even though all keyboard users are worse off. But again, game theory does not explain why we got stuck in this slow equilibrium, with the slow QWERTY layout.

The key question, then, is often less about why a Nash equilibrium persists once the players are playing their equilibrium strategies, and more about whether we will reach that equilibrium in the first place: a question of history rather than game theory. (In the case of QWERTY, its convoluted form was precisely the point: it was invented to slow down typists in an era of mechanical typewriters with keys that were liable to jam when used at speed.) Most troubling of all for game-theoretic orthodoxy, even if a game has only one Nash equilibrium, it does not follow that we will reach it – that it will be the outcome when the game is actually played. Playing the Nash equilibrium strategy is only the best way for you to play the game *if* everyone else is playing the Nash equilibrium strategy too. But as we have seen, there are several good reasons why you might think others won't be playing their Nash strategy – because they are not selfish, or because they don't think like game theorists. This is a very basic hole in the theory, yet none of the textbooks mentions it.

At the climax of George Orwell's *Nineteen Eighty-Four*, Winston and Julia are literally in a Prisoner's Dilemma: each is held separately and tortured to try to force them to betray each other. But here, the prediction of game theory goes wrong. They don't betray each other. Orwell's understanding of what it means to be human makes love, friendship and loyalty paramount. These are concepts which have no place in traditional game theory. But why, exactly? Why can't traditional game theory encompass a full understanding of what it means to be human?

As we saw earlier, when people in a seeming Prisoner's Dilemma situation don't behave as predicted by game theory, game theorists respond by arguing that these players cannot really be in a Prisoner's Dilemma. The rules of that game specify that players must be narrowly self-interested, so by definition people such as Winston and Julia do not face a Prisoner's Dilemma. Once we incorporate Winston and Julia's concern for each other in the mathematical representation of the game, then it recommends that they should not betray each other. Their love, friendship and loyalty tilts the 'best strategy' calculation in favour of cooperation. More generally, the argument runs, *anything* a player cares about can be included in game theory, by adjusting the numbers representing the consequences which follow from each choice.

Yet game theory imposes one subtle but critical restriction: it is concerned not with the historical contexts of different choices, but solely with their consequences or outcomes.[21] Consequences are inherently forward-looking, while our moral concerns about fairness and responsibility typically look backwards: to the history of who did what, and why. This focus on consequences alone means that game theory must inevitably operate with a restricted, partial understanding of what it means to be human, an understanding which insists our future is always more important than our past. In later chapters we will find a similar pattern arising repeatedly elsewhere: the attempt to incorporate moral concerns within standard economic theories, in the process restricting, distorting or subverting them.

In the last months of his life von Neumann did something which shocked all who knew him. Perhaps even he had begun to look beyond game theory's limited view of humanity. Or perhaps it was just a side-effect of the mental and physical breakdown wrought by the cancer which now overwhelmed him. A firm agnostic throughout his life, he had himself baptized a Catholic. Confined to his hospital bed, he was regularly visited by Father Strittmatter, a Benedictine monk who received his confessions. It didn't seem to help: as Strittmatter recalled, von Neumann remained terrified of death until the end. As he drove away in a cab after von Neumann's burial, done with full Catholic rites, the Director of the Los Alamos Laboratory remarked to a physicist colleague: 'If Johnny is where he thought he was going, there must be some very interesting conversations going on about now.'[22]

3

Wealth Beats Justice: The Curious Coase Theorem

Here is a new idea for reducing unemployment: offer employers a bribe. For maximum impact it should not be done in a roundabout, secretive way but through an explicit cash offer made by the applicant during the job interview. Admittedly, it might be a tricky conversation. Picture the scene:

Human resources manager: [*rising from chair*] Well, thank you for coming in today. We should be able to let you know by tomorrow.

Ron [job applicant]: Erm . . . er . . . just one thing. There's this deal. You get $500 if you give me a job.

Manager: What? What do you mean?

Ron: It's a special incentive for taking me on. A sweetener!

Manager: [*embarrassed laughter*] Ah, I see. I'm sorry, but it doesn't work like that here. Thanks for your interest, but I need to bring the next person in now. I have a lot of people to see this afternoon [*moves towards the door*].

Ron: It's all above board. It's a government scheme.

Manager: [*sounding incredulous*] You mean there's a special scheme to pay me $500 for employing you?

Ron: Well, the company. Your company gets $500. As far as I can tell. It's all explained in the letter [*removes letter from pocket*].

Manager: Now I see [*reading letter*]. I've never seen one of these before. Hmmm . . . do you mind me asking if you have some kind of special status? This can't be for everyone who is looking for work, because I've not seen one before.

Ron: Oh, I don't know, I thought everyone qualified.

Manager: Hmmm . . . there seem to be two forms to fill, and we have to wait four months. I would have to get permission. It's a bit weird! And, of course, Accounts will need to be in the loop. Maybe we should forget about it. Anyway, I won't let it get in the way of considering your application, alongside everyone else's.

In truth, bribing employers is not a new idea. In 1983, with US unemployment above 10 per cent, there was an increasingly desperate search for policies which could bring the figure down. The state of Illinois decided to try something different. It randomly selected almost 4,000 people to take part in a year-long 'Hiring Incentive Experiment'.[1] They were told that, providing they found a new job within eleven weeks of becoming unemployed and stayed in the job for at least four months, their new employer could claim a $500 bonus from the state authorities. And the $500 offer was to be made by the unemployed person during the job-application process.

Probably because they anticipated the kind of uneasy, even hostile response that our imaginary Ron received, over a third of those invited to participate in the experiment refused to do so. Of those that did participate, only 4 per cent ended up with employers who received payment for hiring them. Some participants in the scheme did not get a job or lost it before four months had passed. Over a third of employers who qualified for the $500 payment did not get it simply because they failed to submit the final claim form to the Illinois authorities.

The economists who designed the experiment failed to anticipate the reluctance of many unemployed people to participate, or that their new employers would fail to claim free money ($500 in 1984 is equivalent to about $1,200 today). Moreover, the economists seemed unaware that offering your prospective employer a bribe to take you on might be embarrassing or awkward: the information given to participants included specific instructions on how to introduce the $500 offer, as if it were just another piece of advice on what to say in interviews.

The economists' odd view of the world was inspired by the Coase Theorem, a piece of economic theory attributed to the British economist Ronald Coase, who, coincidentally or not, was an Illinois resident. The theorem presumes that everyone, in all aspects of life, is always willing to do a deal: offering cash to get what you want or accepting cash in return for giving someone else what they want. The law, moral rules or social conventions – the social convention against bribing your way into a job, for example – will, ultimately, not get in the way of mutually beneficial deal-making. The economists essentially assumed the Coase Theorem would hold in reality.

Despite the poor performance of policies such as the Hiring Incentive Experiment – and its naïve view of deal-making – the Coase Theorem-based view of the world has in many ways triumphed. It began with a genuine revolution in legal thinking: Coase's 1960 paper 'The Problem of Social Cost', which inspired the Coase Theorem, became the most-cited law journal article.[2] Coasean ideas led to the belief that the ultimate purpose of law is to maximize the wealth of all citizens. To achieve this, the legal system should establish clear rules and rights, and then get out of the way of market forces and deal-making between individuals. This perspective led directly to policies which are now mainstream but were seen as shockingly radical when first proposed, such as the auctioning of mobile-phone and TV-broadcast spectra by governments, and government-created carbon markets in which different firms trade the 'right to emit' carbon dioxide into the atmosphere. More recently, the Coase Theorem has been invoked in proposals for other 'created' markets, including an inter-governmental trade in obligations to admit refugees, or population control via a market in procreation permits. Other than introducing markets into areas where they did not previously exist, the Coase Theorem is a do-nothing manifesto: the government should do nothing, it should not intervene, because private deals between affected parties can solve all problems.

And all this by accident.

THE ACCIDENTAL ECONOMIST AND HIS ACCIDENTAL THEOREM

Ronald Coase was born in December 1910, in the north-west London suburb of Willesden. Later, Coase would recollect having a 'weakness in his legs' as a child, a condition treated by putting him in leg irons, and his first school was a 'school for physical defectives'.[3] This seems to have led to him entering his next school, Kilburn Grammar, at the age of twelve rather than eleven. Five years later, this delayed entrance affected his choice of university subject. Wanting to study history, he was unable to do so: at that time a history degree was open only to those who had studied Latin, a subject not available to Coase because he arrived at Kilburn a year late. His second choice for university was chemistry, but he disliked mathematics, a requirement for a science degree. So, as he put it, 'I switched to the only other degree for which it was possible to study at the Kilburn Grammar School, one in commerce.'[4] By this accidental route, Coase ended up studying economics at the London School of Economics in 1929. He learned fast. The ideas for his first academic paper were already written up in a lecture he gave in Dundee three years later, aged twenty-one, and this first paper, 'The Nature of the Firm', was special: it was one of the two great contributions to economics that would lead to his Nobel Prize for economics over half a century later. (In a nutshell, 'The Nature of the Firm' tries to explain why firms exist at all: why, in particular, entrepreneurs choose to hire workers on an ongoing basis rather than 'contracting out' each and every task.) But it's his other contribution, 'The Problem of Social Cost', that we're concerned with here.

Many of the big ideas in economics have begun life as abstract exercises in pure theory, with the real-world applications – if any – added on as an afterthought. Coase's work was different. Throughout his long career (he published his last book, *How China became Capitalist*, at the age of 101), Coase criticized abstract theory, dismissing it as 'blackboard economics'. One of Coase's particular interests was public-sector monopolies, especially those involved with broadcasting, such as the BBC. After moving to the US in 1951, he studied the Federal Communications Commission, which allocated broadcast licences to radio and TV stations according to their judgement about what would best serve the public interest. Coase could barely conceal his contempt for what he saw as this state-diktat approach, pointing out that it was akin to 'a commission appointed by the federal government [having] the task of selecting those who were to be allowed to publish newspapers and periodicals in each city, town, and village'.[5] Coase proposed that slots on the broadcast spectrum should instead be auctioned off to the highest bidder, something then unthinkable to those working in broadcasting. Today, it is standard practice in many countries.

Coase's central argument was that the Federal Communications Commission (FCC) need not procrastinate over the allocation of broadcast spectrum rights. As long as the rights were clearly defined by law, and transferable, then they would inevitably end up in the hands of the broadcaster who valued them most. Whoever received the rights initially would make more money by selling them on than by keeping them – unless, of course, the initial recipient valued the broadcast rights more highly than anyone else. And because the broadcaster who valued them most was likely to make the best use of them, this was the best outcome for society at large. As it turned out, Coase's views didn't just meet with astonishment from the broadcasters and the FCC – remarkably, to modern eyes, the guardians of free-market economics were astonished and hostile too.

Coase sent his FCC paper to the *Journal of Law and Economics*, a new outlet based at the University of Chicago, which is where the academic shock-troops of free-market economics were mostly based. They thought that Coase's underlying idea – that who gets the legal rights to something has no effect on who gets it in the end – was straightforwardly false. Unlike to Coase, it seemed intuitively obvious to them that a firm is less likely to undertake some activity if it does not have the legal right to do so, because of the possible costs involved in violating the law: a firm, for instance, is less likely to produce something if it does not have the relevant patents, or if it might be sued for air or water pollution resulting from the production process. Accordingly, the editor of the *Journal of Law and Economics*, Aaron Director, asked Coase to remove his key conclusion from his paper: Coase had concluded that the legal position may ultimately have little effect on what is produced. When Coase refused, Director invited him to meet some Chicago economists to explain his arguments, over dinner at Director's home. The dinner-party setting seemed congenial enough; in fact, it was more like trial by ordeal.

Chicago economists in the early 1960s saw themselves as outsiders who had to battle aggressively against the political and academic establishments far away in Washington and Cambridge, Massachusetts. Gary Becker, a young Chicago economist who would also go on to win the Nobel Prize, later admitted that they all had 'chips on their shoulders'. This insecurity would manifest itself in aggression in workshops at which visiting academics would defend their ideas. One visiting speaker asked the workshop organizer George Stigler where he should sit to present his paper. Stigler replied, 'In your case – under the desk.' This was the atmosphere into which Coase descended at Director's home one evening in early 1960. The evening began with a vote. The twenty Chicago economists present disagreed with Coase; the only vote in support of Coase's argument was from Coase himself. Then Milton Friedman, leading the Chicago team, attempted to destroy Coase's argument. Stigler, looking on, later described what unfolded as 'one of the most exciting intellectual events of my life': '. . . Milton would hit him from one side, then from another, then from another. Then to our horror, Milton missed him and hit us: at the end of that evening the vote had changed. There were twenty-one votes for Ronald . . .'[6]

Coase found the evening at Director's house a gruelling experience. But the Chicago economists were now converts to Coase's ideas. Arguably, this was the precise moment when the modern idea of *privatization* was invented. For the Chicago economists immediately extended Coase's arguments about broadcast-spectrum rights to public assets more generally. They concluded that society overall would always be better off if public assets were simply auctioned off to the highest bidder. If auctioning is impossible (or politically unacceptable), then rights over public assets should be given to somebody, anybody – it does not matter whom, because Coase had argued that in a free market they would inevitably end up in the hands of those who valued them the most.

Director encouraged Coase to write up his argument in detail, which was soon published as 'The Problem of Social Cost'. Coase introduced the argument through a story about two farmers. Suppose, he said, a rancher's cows stray on to a neighbouring arable farmer's crops and damage them. If the two farmers are free to negotiate a deal to address this problem, then there are two possible outcomes. If the cost of restraining the cattle (say, by erecting a fence) is less than the cost of the damage to the crops, then the cattle will be restrained; conversely, if the cost of restraining the cattle is greater than the value of the damaged crops, then the crops will get damaged. The facts about relative costs will determine the outcome of the negotiations, regardless of whether the law gives rights to the rancher or to the arable farmer. However, the legal rights will determine who pays to fix the problem – for instance, if the cost of building a fence is less than the value of the damaged crops but the rancher's cattle have a legal right to roam, then the arable farmer will have to pay the rancher to build a fence. The message of Coase's story can be simply summarized: if there are no costs or other obstacles to their deal-making, then the outcome of the farmers' negotiations will be the same, regardless of the legal position.

Yet, almost immediately after Coase's triumph at Director's house, a crucial gap started to open up between Coase's views and those of his new Chicago supporters. Assuming that Coase's story was intended to be realistic, the Chicago economists concluded that in many disputes in life the involvement of the courts is a costly waste of time. More generally, they held that the role and purpose of the legal system should be entirely rethought and the need for government intervention via the legal system dramatically reduced. These conclusions remain hugely influential in the twenty-first century. But they rest on a misunderstanding.

Coase regarded his story as obviously fiction, a kind of thought experiment to show the fantastic conclusions that follow from the story's *fictitious* assumption: that there are no costs or other obstacles to private deal-making or, in Coase's words, the assumption of 'zero transaction costs'. While this style of reasoning is familiar to philosophers as a *reductio ad absurdum*, the Chicago economists missed the point: they treated the zero-transaction-costs assumption as essentially realistic, and as a result duly embraced the absurd conclusion.

Their mistaken interpretation of Coase's argument rapidly became hard to dislodge because it was elevated to the status of a 'theorem'. In 1966, Stigler made the first mention of 'The Coase Theorem' in print, introducing it into the third edition of his successful textbook.

Soon, a version of the theorem was appearing in most textbooks, along the lines of 'It does not matter how the law distributes rights, because bargaining among affected parties will lead to the same outcome.' That this conclusion relies entirely on the highly unrealistic assumption of zero transaction costs was often downplayed, if it was mentioned at all.

It's important to stress that the Coase Theorem is not what it seems. First, it is not something that Coase ever stated or proposed; second, it is not a theorem, because it does not take the form of a set of assumptions leading, through logical deductions, to a conclusion. (But as we seem stuck with the name now, I will continue to use it here.) And this so-called 'Coase Theorem' in fact suggests the *opposite* of what Coase argued. Indeed, although the Coase Theorem has been enormously influential, it has been subject to strong and persistent criticism from a notable source: Ronald Coase himself. Almost thirty years after the publication of his ground-breaking paper Coase commented wistfully: 'My point of view has not in general commanded assent, nor has my argument, for the most part, been understood.'[7] Yet his complaints were ignored. For Coase, receiving the 1991 Nobel Prize for economics was rather ironic, because it was awarded on the basis of widespread and fundamental misunderstanding of his work. It is time to let the real Coase speak.

COASE VERSUS CHICAGO?

Coase used his story about the farmers to argue not that the law is irrelevant but precisely the opposite: that the law does matter, because who has the legal rights to something will influence the outcome of private bargaining over it, unless there are literally *no* costs or obstacles to the bargaining process. And Coase rightly emphasized that, in the real world, there are *always* some obstacles, which lead to what Coase named transaction costs. These costs are ubiquitous because they are so varied and include any type of impediment – not necessarily financial – which discourages the affected parties from doing a deal to resolve a dispute. Before a bargain is struck, there are the costs of discovering who to bargain with and the costs of communicating with them. You may be willing to pay your neighbour(s) to agree to let you play loud music at your party until late at night, but first you need to determine which neighbours will be disturbed by the noise. Like-wise, while a laundry wanting to draw clean water from a river (cleaner than the minimum legal standards ensured by prevailing regulations) may be willing to pay to get cleaner water, it may be hard to identify which upstream factory is causing the water pollution. Then there are costs directly involved in negotiating a deal, most obviously the time and effort involved, as well as the cost of gathering all relevant information. The laundry will need to decide how much it is willing to pay the factory, so it will have to estimate the cost of alternative solutions, such as alternative water supplies or treating the water to clean it inhouse. Finally, once a deal has been done, there are costs involved in monitoring the outcome to be sure that the other party has stuck to the agreement. And if they haven't, there are further costs in trying to enforce the deal, perhaps through the courts.

Transaction costs imply that the thing being argued over may not go to the individual, firm or organization which values it the most. This is because transaction costs often prevent deals being done, even when the deal is beneficial to all parties. If, for any of the parties involved, the overall transaction costs involved in arranging and enforcing a deal exceed the expected benefits from doing so, then the deal will not happen. But if a deal beneficial to all parties does not happen, then the outcome is in a sense wasteful: it wastes an opportunity to make *all* parties better off. Economists call this kind of outcome 'inefficient' because of the waste of available benefit. Here, government can play an obvious role in intervening to bring about an increase in overall benefit. For example, rather than assuming that the laundry and factory will make a deal, which may not happen because of transaction costs, the government could tax the water pollution caused by the factory, the underlying idea being that the amount of the tax should reflect the cost of the pollution (such as the extra cost faced by the laundry drawing dirty water). Coase's general conclusion was that the presence of transaction costs can indeed justify government intervention, because private bargaining alone will lead to inefficient outcomes.

At this point you might hazard a guess as to how the story of Coase versus Chicago economics unfolds. The Chicago economists invoke the Coase Theorem to justify privatization, auctioning off public assets, market-based policies such as carbon markets, and so on. Against this, Coase emerges as a champion of government intervention.

That guess would be wrong. Consistent with his suspicion of the sweeping generalizations of 'blackboard economics', Coase argued that neither the free market nor government intervention is always superior. It depends on the circumstances. There is no alternative to a careful, case-by-case analysis to decide the best policy. So Coase, rather than being a cheerleader for government intervention, was a sensible pragmatist about it. Beyond that, he had an insight which not only reconciled him to the Chicago economists, it made him an intellectual hero among them. It was an insight which seemed to destroy many ideas about morality and fairness – ideas often invoked to justify restrictions on free markets.

Until 'The Problem of Social Cost', economics had followed common sense in analysing situations in which one party harmed another. If a factory pollutes the water used downstream by a laundry, then the solution to this problem involves getting the factory to stop polluting, or to compensate the laundry. If a design flaw in a car means that it is dangerous to drive under certain circumstances, then the solution is to require a recall of the faulty cars and compensate the drivers who have already suffered harm. Coase summarized the general perspective here as 'one in which A inflicts harm on B and what has to be decided is: how should we restrain A?' Coase demolished this way of thinking at a stroke: 'The real question that has to be decided is: should A be allowed to harm B or should B be allowed to harm A? The problem is to avoid the more serious harm.'[8] It is obvious that this is a crucial question to ask. But no economist had ever asked it before. As a leading US judge, Richard Posner, later commented, 'Coase is living proof . . . that it requires a very unusual mind to undertake the analysis of the obvious.'[9]

Coase's simple insight was that when two parties come into conflict *both* are harmed by the presence of the other. When the cattle farmer's cows stray on to the neighbouring arable farmer's crops, which farmer is responsible? There would be no problem, no crop damage, without both farms being present and adjacent. It is the conjunction of the two farms which 'causes' the crop damage, not one farmer alone. When a factory pollutes the water used by a laundry, it imposes costs on the laundry – but banning the pollution imposes costs on the factory. This perspective implies that common-sense ideas about blame are meaningless. There is no way of establishing the victim and the villain by examining who imposes costs on whom, because costs flow in both directions. Coase concluded that the decision about whether or not to allow a firm to emit pollution was 'no different from deciding whether a field should be used for growing wheat or barley'.[10] That is, all that matters is maximizing total product, output or value.

Coase's analysis stopped there. However, by the early 1970s his Chicago followers, now just as likely to be in the university law school as in the economics department, went much further. They extended the analysis from the world of economics to that of law and morality. Applying Coase's ideas to accidents, for example, they argued that both the injurer and the injured may be said to cause an accident, because both parties must be present for an accident to occur. From this, it is a short step to conclude that both parties are equally to blame for the accident. Traditional ethical and legal ideas about motivation, responsibility and rights are cast aside in this new approach, which soon became known as the 'law-and-economics' school of legal thinking.

The growth of the law-and-economics movement – a powerful network of academics and judges – is a good example of big ideas having unintended consequences. Coase overturned centuries of legal thinking about accidents – by accident. He did not intend to trigger a revolution in law: as he put it, 'I have no interest in lawyers or legal education.'[11] Instead, he saw his ideas as showing the ways in which markets and other economic arrangements are dependent on the wider legal system. But his followers put it the other way round: legal rights should be determined by economics (and hence *not* by ideas about justice, fairness, responsibility, motivation, and so on). The law-and-economics people wanted to use economics to explain and reshape the law. Their inspiration was Coase, and the consequences were momentous.

THE REVOLUTION OF 1968

For historians, 1968 is a momentous year of revolutionary upheaval, centred on the student protests in Paris. That's only half right. 1968 did bring about a revolution, but it began in Chicago, not Paris.

For a long time the legal establishment ignored the law-and-economics people. They were seen as a band of libertarian eccentrics with off-the-wall ideas. The establishment debate was not about whether these ideas were right or wrong, but whether they were worth taking seriously at all. Their dismissiveness was overturned by one man, who almost single-handedly turned law-and-economics into a respectable, albeit controversial, school of thought, and who in the process became the most cited legal academic of the twentieth century.

After graduating top of his class from Harvard Law School, Richard Posner assisted Supreme Court Justice William Brennan in 1962–3, then took a series of important legal posts in Washington, culminating in work for the Solicitor General, with responsibility for 'antitrust' – regulating monopolies and other anti-competitive practices by firms. These impeccable mainstream credentials would soon prove invaluable in getting his intellectual adversaries to take him seriously. But first he needed a cause. It didn't take long. When Nixon became president in the autumn of 1968, the new administration asked Chicago economist George Stigler to set up a task force on antitrust. Stigler asked Posner to join. Posner saw himself as a liberal – he voted for the Democrats, not Nixon – but, increasingly turned off by the Vietnam protests and student riots, he agreed. His transformation from liberal to Nietzsche-reading libertarian accelerated when he joined Chicago law school in 1969 and spent more time with Chicago economists Milton Friedman, George Stigler and Gary Becker.

From a legal perspective, the Chicago boys' ideas about antitrust were revolutionary and posed a series of complex challenges to legal orthodoxy. From the Chicago perspective, their ideas were a simple application of the Coase Theorem. Coase had argued that before intervening to prevent A harming B governments should bear in mind the cost to B. Posner applied this to antitrust. Take the phenomenon of predatory pricing, which occurs when a dominant firm in a sector cuts prices aggressively – even making losses in the short term – in order to take customers away from rival firms and force them to leave the market. These bullying tactics are common practice among large retailers when they first open in a small town; after the small shops have closed, the big retailer raises prices because it now has a monopoly. The conventional wisdom among lawyers and free-market economists was that regulations or other measures are required to prohibit these kinds of bullying practices by dominant firms in order to protect smaller firms and so preserve competition, which will benefit consumers and wider society. Posner and the Chicago economists pointed out that this reasoning ignored the interests of the bully. An objective assessment of the interests of society overall should include the interests of the dominant firm too.

Posner had a particular approach to objective assessment in mind. He called it 'wealth maximization'. If the introduction of antitrust regulations result in financial losses to the dominant firm which outweigh the financial gains to the smaller firms, then, according to Posner's approach, antitrust regulation is a bad idea. More generally, the Chicago law-and-economics movement has developed arguments which favour protecting dominant firms – or, as critics of the movement see it, protecting corporate bullies. So, for example, Posner and his followers have had a huge impact on intellectual property law in arguing, paradoxically, that the virtues of free markets are best achieved through extensive legal intervention to give the owners of patents and copyrights powerful monopoly rights over their creations. The biggest contemporary beneficiaries of this legal largesse are corporations which hold monopoly rights over products that are hard to avoid – Apple, Microsoft, Pfizer, Glaxo, and so on. And the Posnerian belief that wealth maximization beats corporate justice lay behind the opposition to the suggestion that banks should be punished for their role in bringing about the global financial crisis which began in 2007. A Posnerian echo could be heard in the objection from Alan Greenspan (former Chairman of the US Federal Reserve) that while punishing the banks might be 'soul satisfying', it 'is rarely economically productive'.[12]

Posner's support for big corporations came not just through his scholarship. In 1977 he co-founded the consulting firm Lexecon. It has grown enormously (it is now Compass Lexecon, following a merger) and has provided many big corporations with law-and-economics ammunition to protect their interests. And it has also provided lucrative employment and consultancy for those trained in law-and-economics.

Posner's wealth-maximization principle doesn't just apply to corporations. That barely scratches the surface. To appreciate the breadth of its impact on legal thinking, a clarification is in order. For Posner, it's not so much a question of 'wealth maximization beats justice' as something much more ambitious: wealth maximization *is* justice.

In attempting to argue that 'justice' has no meaning other than as a kind of synonym for wealth maximization, Posner went into full-frontal collision with the liberal legal establishment. Even with his elite CV, Posner's views might have seen him ignored by this establishment. But he made himself impossible to ignore through a series of abrasive, high-profile confrontations with his opponents, provoking them to respond. Posner liked Chicago economics not just for its right-wing leanings but for its methods, and he copied them, arguing that wealth maximization was a much more objective, scientific approach than traditional legal analysis. As far as Posner was concerned, traditional legal doctrines were 'just baloney'.

The liberal establishment was provoked into responding to Posner's interventions, with the result that law-and-economics, rather than being shut out, was let into the room. The debate shifted from whether or not Posner's ideas were worth taking seriously to discussion about the details of his economic arguments. With this shift in focus on to the economic nitty-gritty, legal thinking was sidelined. Lawyers began to retool with economics. And this is how the revolution of 1968 came to endure, because the new terms of debate made it possible for legions of academic lawyers to build lucrative careers rewriting entire fields of law based on Posner's opening salvos. As one protégé, Douglas Baird, later Dean of Chicago law school, put it:

> In the early seventies people like Posner would come in and spend six
> weeks studying family law, and they'd write a couple of articles

explaining why everything everyone was saying in family law was 100% wrong. And then the replies would be 'No, we were only 80% wrong' . . . Doing great work was easy . . . I used to say that this was just like knocking over Coke bottles with a baseball bat . . . I was interested in bankruptcy law which was inhabited by intellectual midgets . . . It was a complete intellectual wasteland. I got tenure by saying 'Jeez, a dollar today is worth more than a dollar tomorrow.'[13]

Admittedly, the tone of the new law-and-economics was brutal – Posner called his caustic approach an 'acid bath' – and some of Posner's friends were bullies, but that does not mean the ideas are wrong.[14] But how exactly can wealth maximization *be* justice?

POSNER IN WONDERLAND

'When I use a word,' Humpty Dumpty said in rather a scornful tone, 'it means just what I choose it to mean – neither more nor less.'

'The question is,' said Alice, 'whether you can make words mean so many different things.'

At first glance, in redefining justice as wealth maximization Posner seems to be doing neither more nor less than Humpty Dumpty. In fact, there were two parts to Posner's argument.

In 'The Problem of Social Cost' Coase had implied that, while judges talk of 'justice' and refer to elaborate legal doctrines, the effect of their decisions is, in most cases and on average, to favour the maximization of what Coase called 'total social product'. Posner interpreted this product as wealth and developed a comprehensive historical analysis based on Coase's suggestion, concluding that 'the logic of the common law is an economic logic':[15] consciously or not, judges promote wealth maximization through their court decisions. Posner's findings remain controversial to this day, but there is general agreement that they contain at least a kernel of truth, partly because court decisions which altogether ignore the resulting balance of gains and losses seem more likely to be overturned on appeal. If a decision imposes big losses on one party, then they are more likely to appeal; if the other party has gained relatively little from the decision, they are less likely to devote time and money to defend their position. Conversely, decisions which ensure that gains outweigh losses are less likely to be appealed. This argument is fine as far as it goes – but that is not very far. Even if court decisions on average ensure that gains outweigh losses, it does not follow that they maximize wealth regardless of more traditional considerations of justice. And even if wealth maximization did turn out to be the (unconscious) effect of judicial decisions, it does not follow that wealth maximization is a desirable goal on ethical grounds – indeed, it may conflict with the demands of justice.

This brings us to the second part of Posner's argument, in which he attempted to construct an explicit justification for wealth maximization. However, the inspiration for Posner's approach came not from ethics but from economics: in particular, the strand of thinking in economics which holds that judgements about fairness and justice are no more than expressions of feeling, and that differences of opinion on these matters are 'differences about which men can ultimately only fight', as Posner's colleague Milton Friedman put it.[16] Posner saw wealth maximization as 'scientific' because it avoids judgements about fairness and justice. Wealth maximization identifies objective improvements in the total size of the economic pie without the need to fight over how the pie should be divided up.

But this perspective is mistaken even on its own terms. Wealth maximization is not scientific in the sense of avoiding ethical judgements, because the decision to maximize wealth is itself an ethical judgement – a decision to prioritize wealth over other moral considerations, ranging from the distribution of the pie to the responsibility for accidents. For instance, we saw earlier that the Chicago boys applied Coase's ideas about harm to accidents: the party injured in an accident is equally to blame for their injury, because without them the accident would not have occurred. Posner went even further, arguing that the law should say a defendant negligently caused an accident only if that legal judgement would maximize wealth. That is, a defendant is said to be negligent only if the cost of preventing the accident is less than the expected cost of the accident itself (calculated as the money value of the injury multiplied by the probability of injury occurring). If finding a defendant negligent would *not* maximize wealth, then, according to Posner, the law should conclude that the cause of the accident lay elsewhere. Posner noted that a convenient excuse in such cases would be to attribute the accident to 'an act of God'. Posner's version of justice has no place for what most people regard as justice – determining negligence on the basis of the chain of cause and effect and the motives, competence and care of the parties involved.

In a similar vein was Posner's 1978 'The Economics of the Baby Shortage', which argued that the highly regulated process for adopting babies should be scrapped. Posner recommended replacing it with a 'fully-fledged' free market in babies in order to maximize wealth by realizing the 'gains from trade from transferring the custody of the child to a new set of parents'.[17] For Posner and his Chicago colleagues, this proposal was an obvious application of the wealth-maximization principle, rolling back legal restraints in order to 'solve' a practical problem. For everyone else, it was further confirmation of how far Posner and reality had parted ways, morality left trailing behind in his wake.

Posner's reference to the 'gains from trade' from buying and selling babies invokes the Coasean world of deal-making. By the 1970s most Chicago lawyers and economists had begun to accept that the Coase Theorem does not hold in the real world because of the ubiquity of transaction costs. Instead, they saw the theorem in utopian terms. In an ideal world, a Posnerian Wonderland, everyone would have unlimited opportunities to do deals for mutual benefit. Accordingly, the project of Chicago law-and-economics was to reshape the real world into this Wonderland as far as possible. First, legal impediments to deal-making should be stripped away. Even if the deal involves selling a baby, the law should not in general intervene because that would prevent valuable gains from trade. Second, if the courts become involved as a result of transaction costs preventing parties from making deals, the courts should simply bring about, by judicial decree, the wealth-enhancing deals that the parties *would* have made in an ideal world without transaction costs. This was dubbed the 'mimic the market' approach to judicial decision-making. Again, wealth maximization is substituted for justice as the explicit purpose of the legal system.

It is easy to ridicule this approach when baby-selling or moral issues more generally are involved – which is much of the time. But in narrowly economic contexts it seems right to allow parties to engage in mutually beneficial deal-making as much as possible. So should unrestricted deal-making be allowed in everyday or economic matters when there are no obvious moral questions at stake? There is another way of posing this question. Coase had imagined a world in which people with conflicting interests would make mutually beneficial deals without recourse to law or government intervention. Coase was absolutely clear that this is an entirely hypothetical world, because in the real world transaction costs always exist. But is this hypothetical Coasean world something we should strive towards?

Coase himself had almost nothing to say on the matter, probably because he did not see its practical relevance. But then, he did not anticipate the transformation of his thought experiment in unfettered deal-making into the utopian vision of Chicago law-and-economics.

If we set morality aside and assume, with Posner, that wealth maximization is our only goal, there are still problems with this utopian vision. To begin with, deals may be wealth maximizing for the parties concerned but not for society at large. Two big firms in an industry may form a cartel or other price-fixing agreement which maximizes their joint profits but at the expense of consumers.

Another problem is that unfettered deal-making does not imply that mutually beneficial deals will be made. Imagine I'm in one of the labyrinthine souks of Marrakesh and I want to buy a teapot. But we need to agree a price. Suppose the maximum I'm prepared to pay is more than the minimum the stall-holder is prepared to accept. Then a mutually beneficial deal is possible: settling on some price in between would leave us both better off than not reaching a deal. Of course, neither of us knows this. We may fail to agree a price, because I wrongly believe that the stall-holder will drop his price no further or simply because his best offer is still too high and I can't face haggling any more. Even when people are prepared to negotiate at length because there is a lot at stake, neither side knows how far the other is prepared to go, and each party's determination to get the best possible terms may prevent any deal being agreed, even though there are terms which would leave both sides content – if only they knew.

Practical problems such as these are important. But perhaps there is a more basic worry. For most of us, a life of constant, endless deal-making hardly sounds utopian. What would it look like?

THE COASE THEOREM TRIUMPHANT

On 1st September 2014 a woman on a flight from New York to Palm Beach, Florida, put down her knitting and reclined her seat. The woman seated immediately behind began screaming and swearing in complaint, and the resulting fracas had the pilot so concerned that he diverted the flight to land sooner, at Jacksonville. This was not a freak incident.[18] Four days earlier, a flight from Miami to Paris was diverted to Boston because a Parisian on the flight objected to someone trying to recline the seat in front of him. The flight crew became involved, the Parisian became angry, and he was later charged with the offence of 'interfering with an airline flight crew'. Just three days before, on 24th August, another flight from New York was diverted after two passengers argued over one of them using a 'Knee Defender', a $21.95 device that blocks reclining.

Commenting in *The New York Times*, the journalist Josh Barro pointed out that he had already identified the solution to this problem. In a 2011 article he had invoked the Coase Theorem to argue that passengers should be encouraged to strike deals with those sitting in front of and behind them.[19] Most airlines give passengers the 'right to recline', but if passengers could do deals, then travellers wishing to preserve their knee space from recliners in front could pay them not to recline. Barro explained that the 'right to recline' is irrelevant. Giving everyone the right to knee space will work just as well: as long as airlines give passengers *some* set of clear and consistent rights and officially encourage them to bargain with each other, then, according to the Coase Theorem, the outcome will be the same. Passengers will do deals so that seats will end up reclined, or not, according to who values their extra space most – recliners or those behind them. The outcome will be efficient in the economic sense of the resource (space) going to who values it most. And no fights.

Proposals such as this have become mainstream; they no longer come just from Chicago-school loyalists. Yet Coase, who died in 2013, may be turning in his grave. This kind of proposal works fine in the world of 'blackboard economics' ridiculed by Coase. All the conditions for low transaction costs are met: just two people are involved in each deal; the right being haggled over is clearly defined and simple; no information need be gathered before passengers can decide how much the right is worth to them; cheats can be easily spotted. And yet something is obviously wrong. People do not see every social conflict as ripe for a deal. Many passengers are likely to want a peaceful flight uninterrupted by haggling over their seat position. Barro makes no mention whatsoever of this drawback. Perhaps it had not occurred to him – like the economists who designed the Hiring Incentive Experiment, who were surprised that some unemployed people did not want to participate and that some employers who were offered cash did not take up the offer.

Some passengers may go further and argue that Coasean bargaining is simply not the right way to decide whether airline seats should recline. Here are some possible reasons: the alleged efficiency of this approach ignores the costs in time and effort negotiating; rich people will get everything they want, again; airlines should decide whether seats can recline on the basis of the best available medical advice concerning back problems, sleep needs, and so on. If medical experts judge that airline seat configurations may trigger or exacerbate health problems in a significant number of passengers, then the law should be changed to increase space (perhaps reflecting the increase in average leg length since regulations were first introduced in the 1950s).

The ideas behind these objections go beyond the debate over the 'right to recline'. The wider point is that other values may be more important than efficiency. Coasean bargaining is often defended by its supporters on the grounds that it is democratic and anti-elitist; that, unlike regulations and government interventions, it does not impose the values and priorities of regulators, judges and politicians on ordinary people. But this argument is duplicitous. Coasean bargaining – and the Chicago law-and-economics project more generally – *does* impose a value on society. The value of efficiency is given priority throughout, even when not articulated in terms of explicit wealth maximization. The Chicago approach will be anti-democratic if it does not give people what they want – if what they want is to use a range of moral principles, rather than bargaining, to resolve conflicts and organize society.

These tensions emerge strongly when there is more at stake than the right to recline. When Posner first argued that judges in their decision-making should aim to 'mimic the market', the legal establishment was outraged. But nowadays we barely notice an approach which goes further, *creating* markets to solve conflicts over rights, rather than simply mimicking them. This is not just market creation in the sense of decriminalizing existing black markets, such as Posner's support for a free market in kidneys and other organs. Markets are created out of nothing, designed by economists and legislated into existence by governments. This brings us to perhaps the biggest impact of the Coase Theorem.

Today, the biggest created market is the carbon market, with the greatest potential to affect humanity by saving the planet from catastrophic warming – or not. The 'carbon market' is shorthand for a $150 billion global trade in carbon dioxide and other greenhouse gas emission permits – a little-known network of national and international trading systems which grew out of nothing from 2005 and which now, with the 2016 launch of China's carbon market, covers countries which are collectively responsible for almost half of global GDP. Carbon markets are repeatedly hailed as the most important component of any strategy to tackle climate change: the mainstream political consensus in many countries is to rely on them to make meaningful carbon emissions reductions possible. So it matters whether or not they work.

The economic thinking behind the development of carbon markets drew explicitly on the Coase Theorem. The theorem is supposed to show that it does not matter which countries (or firms) are given permits to emit X units of carbon because, in a free market for emissions permits, they will end up in the hands of those who value them the most. All the political authority with overall responsibility for cutting emissions needs to do is to decide the total emissions target for the economy or economies as a whole. The market does the rest. The Coase Theorem seems to save governments from the politically painful job of deciding how the emissions rights should be divided up between, say, airlines, electricity generators and car manufacturers (and car drivers). And the best news of all is that, according to the Coase Theorem, the overall emissions target will be achieved *at the lowest possible cost*. Across all emission-producing activities covered by the emissions target, emitters must choose between buying permits to emit or reducing their emissions (by cutting production or adopting cleaner technology). So emitters who do *not* buy permits, those who value them least, will be those for whom reducing emissions is cheaper than buying permits. Across the economy, the emissions cuts needed to meet the overall target will be concentrated where they are cheapest to achieve, leading to the lowest overall cost. Clever.

Unfortunately, there is a chasm between the blackboard economics of this argument and the reality. It is a short-term argument, focusing on the cheapest way of achieving emissions reductions now, ignoring the further reductions which will be necessary in the future and the way in which current choices may increase the costs of these future reductions. Carbon markets encourage emitters to exploit the cheap short-term ways of cutting emissions, the low-hanging fruit, the easy wins, and buy permits rather than attempt anything more. Emitters lack the incentives to innovate and invest in new technologies, so economies get locked into old, dirty technologies, which in the long term are likely to be more costly. For example, carbon markets encourage an electricity generator using a coal-fired power station to fit filtering equipment to obtain some cheap emissions reductions. But further reductions in future in the emissions from coal-based electricity generation will be very expensive or impossible. To achieve larger reductions in the long term, a less costly strategy overall would involve legislation to require the phasing out of coal-based electricity as soon as possible and strong incentives to innovate to bring down the cost of cleaner technologies.

Another legacy of the Coasean worldview is the idea that pollution is not harmful in any absolute or objective sense: it is only harmful from the subjective perspective of the person, organization or country suffering as a result. This 'pollutee' is just as much to blame as the 'polluter': it was their fault for getting in the way. From this perspective, it is absurd to think of carbon-emitting economic activity 'harming' the environment. Or at least one-sided: the limited carbon-absorbing capacity of the planet harms economic growth too. It follows that big carbon emitters have no special responsibility to reduce their emissions. The moral dimension of carbon-emitting activity is lost. Insofar as climate change is recognized as a problem, big emitters can say, 'Not my problem,' and attribute responsibility to the carbon market, in particular those who decide the total emissions target the market is supposed to meet. When the Chair of the Chicago Climate Exchange was asked whether some sellers on the Chicago exchange would actually be emitting less as a result of selling permits, he replied: 'That's not my business. I'm running a for-profit company.'[20]

Once the responsibility for tackling climate change is understood as lying elsewhere, then carbon markets become just like any other market. In the right conditions, speculators pile in. In 2008, early on in this bonanza, they were invited to a conference in London with the promising title 'Cashing In on Carbon'. The marketing blurb promised that the conference 'does not really concern itself with climate change issues . . . It is aimed squarely at investment banks, investors and major compliance buyers and is focused on how they can profit today from an increasingly diverse range of carbon-related investment opportunities.'

'On or about December 1910, human character changed . . .' So wrote Virginia Woolf about the rise of modernism, from the music of Stravinsky, the art of Picasso, the architecture of Le Corbusier, to the writing of Woolf herself.[21] The poet Philip Larkin declared that his 'essential criticism of modernism' was its 'irresponsible exploitations of technique in contradiction to human life as we know it.'[22] Ironic, then, that Ronald Coase, born in December 1910, should have been a victim of the rise of modernism in economics. His subtle ideas, explored through careful case studies, were shorn of their nuance and solidified by his followers into A Theorem – one which contradicted economic life as Coase knew it. Indeed, throughout Coase's work runs the rejection of unrealistic 'blackboard economics', which focused on exploiting modern mathematical techniques. Coase remains the only Nobel Laureate in economics whose work includes no equations.

As we have seen already, and will see throughout this book, Coase's essential criticism remains valid: there is a worrying gulf between social and economic reality and its idealized portrayal in economic theory. Economists are in love with fancy mathematical tools and software. But we need to update Coase's metaphor: nowadays the arena where economists play is more video game than blackboard. The tools may now be digital, but the trouble they can cause when economists naïvely apply them to reality is just as great as in Coase's day. Imagine an economist reared on *Grand Theft Auto* let loose in real-world LA with a fast car and an Uzi. Carbon markets, the strengthening of intellectual property protection, redefining the meaning of 'negligence' and the campaign to replace the adoption system with a free trade in babies: all these projects have real-life consequences that go far beyond mere ivory-tower tinkering.

A nagging question remains. How could Coase have been so misunderstood for so long? Obviously, the misinterpretation of Coase persisted because it was ideologically appealing to many in Chicago, as well as providing a fertile basis for academic careers in the new law-and-economics, as well as lucrative careers in firms like Lexecon. Equally, Coase had not exactly helped himself be understood: he introduced his key ideas through a thought experiment, a *reductio ad absurdum*. Invoking a hypothetical world does not seem a good idea for someone keen to make economics more realistic. Why did Coase do this? No one seems sure, but an important part of the answer is that even great thinkers often focus on solving what with hindsight turn out to be yesterday's problems. Coase was preoccupied with how previous economists had analysed problems such as pollution. The standard analysis assumed there were no transaction costs but nevertheless called for government intervention. Coase wanted to show that in this strictly blackboard world of zero transaction costs, government intervention would be unnecessary because the polluter and pollutee would make a deal. So, given Coase's backward-looking gaze, his starting point of a zero transaction cost world made sense. But it helped entrench a disastrous misinterpretation of his ideas by future generations.

By the 1970s Coase had begun to refer tentatively to such a misinterpretation, but he did not shout loudly enough and was drowned out by influential Chicago voices including Becker, Friedman and Stigler. His slowness and quietness remain a puzzle. In 1995 Coase was invited by historians to comment on his reticence: he replied blandly that he just waited until he had something to say. Perhaps it was loyalty to his Chicago colleagues which prevented him from speaking out sooner. Not until the 1980s did Coase make clear that the misunderstanding of his work was on a grand scale, but by then it was too late. The misinterpretation had become the mainstream; careers had been built on it. Coase observed sadly, 'The world of zero transaction costs has often been described as a Coasian world. Nothing could be further from the truth. It is the world of modern economic theory, one which I was hoping to persuade economists to leave.'[23] The usual spelling is 'Coasean', *not* Coase's choice of 'Coasian'. Poor Ronald Coase – he didn't even get to control the spelling of 'Coasean world', let alone what it means.

4

The Government Enemy

In the early 1950s John von Neumann and John Nash were not the only geniuses associated with the RAND Corporation. RAND was the incubator for another intellectual revolution, as significant as game theory but completely independent of it. And this time the genius behind it was a lowly intern.

The earliest and most enthusiastic adopters of game theory had been the military analysts at RAND, who wanted to use its powerful mathematical tools to outwit the Soviets in Cold War nuclear strategizing. But logical rigour was everything to the RAND thinkers, and by 1948 a possible flaw had been spotted in the logic of analysing nuclear conflict in game-theoretic terms. Whether the game is Scrabble or Armageddon, game theory views the players in just the same way, as rational individuals. But was the dense black web of Stalin's sprawling Soviet state best seen as an *individual*? In other words, who exactly was playing the nuclear-war game against the US? Surely not Stalin himself. The opponent should be thought of not as an individual but as a group, a collective. However, this interpretation poses a problem for game theory, because its players are assumed to have clear preferences between the alternatives they face. This assumption seems plausible for a hyper-rational individual but mysterious for a group. It raises some difficult questions: what does it mean to speak of the preferences of a collective, a group of people? Where do these preferences come from? And does it make any sense to talk about a group being rational?

Some things never change in office life. If you have some really tricky, abstract questions which can't be avoided, ask someone who can't say no, who hopefully won't mind looking stupid. Ask the intern.

In the summer of 1948 a graduate student from New York named Ken Arrow was an intern at RAND. His answer to these questions was contained in a RAND report he completed the following year called 'Social Choice and Individual Values'. By 1951 it was developed into a short book of the same name, whose influence was such that, two decades later, it helped Arrow win the Nobel Prize for economics at the age of fifty-one – younger than any other winner before or since.

It is hard to convey Arrow's status among economists. After the Second World War, most academic economics changed – first in America and then worldwide – from a discipline that was recognizably like politics and history to something which looked more like a branch of applied mathematics. Ken Arrow was probably the single most influential figure in that radical repositioning of economics. Arrow just did economics differently from almost everyone who went before him, and more successfully than the few who had tried. Arrow established the benchmark for how the most prestigious research in economics – economic theory – should be done. He is frequently mentioned on lists of the 'greatest' Nobel laureates in economics, while his contributions arguably qualified him for three Nobel prizes, because of his work in effectively establishing three major fields of economic theory. Five of his students would also win the Nobel Prize.

Like many of his generation, Arrow's studies had been disrupted by the war. Serving as a weather officer in the US Air Corps from 1942 to 1946, his work in the Corps established a pattern which would be repeated over the following twenty years: using mathematics for military ends, with his first published research, 'On the Optimal Use of Winds for Flight Planning' being from this period. Arrow and his statistician colleagues were required to forecast the number of rainy days a month in advance. They sent a memo to the General of the Air Corps, noting that their forecasts were unsurprisingly very poor and arguing that their group should be disbanded. Six months later the general's secretary replied: 'The general is well aware that your forecasts are no good. However, they are required for planning purposes.' The forecasting continued.[1]

Arrow's life through the 1950s and '60s seems unremarkable, but then much about his life during this period remains classified: his central role in US military thinking gave him a 'top secret' level security clearance from 1949 to 1971.

The central mathematical result at the heart of *Social Choice and Individual Values* is what became known as the *Impossibility Theorem*. While the mathematical proof appeals only to specialists, the implications of the Impossibility Theorem have reached – and astonished – a wide audience. The easiest, shortest summary – the one which proved the most popular – can even fit nicely on a bumper sticker. It goes like this: DEMOCRACY IS IMPOSSIBLE. But this was a bumper sticker which could be worn with pride on the cars of an entire generation of academics studying politics who, after reading Arrow's work, were more likely to call themselves political *scientists*.

How could this nihilistic view of democracy be taken seriously and presented not as a politico-philosophical argument but as an unimpeachable fact of mathematical logic? Arrow did not need to get bogged down in millennia-old debates about the feasibility of democracy, nor could he. His ideas were too different, too new. Indeed, he was able to sidestep most of the intellectual history of democracy altogether.

Social Choice and Individual Values invented a field of economics called 'social choice theory'. Before Arrow came along, the field did not exist; it had no name, just a few dabblers. Arrow's intellectual ancestor was less Aristotle, more Alice in Wonderland. The Reverend Charles Lutwidge Dodgson – better known as Lewis Carroll, the author of *Alice's Adventures in Wonderland* – was a mathematician at Oxford in the second half of the nineteenth century. As well as maths and *Alice*, Dodgson did some pioneering thinking about voting systems. Before Arrow, Dodgson's was by far the most comprehensive analysis of voting systems, but it was hidden away in unpublished pamphlets, so Arrow did not know about it when he began work on the seemingly obscure questions posed by the RAND analysts in the summer of 1948.*

* Fifteen years later, with his stellar reputation already secure, Arrow could admit that he had shown 'a certain want of diligence' in tracking down the existing research on voting systems.

Arrow certainly did not know that his answers, far from being a footnote to RAND's military analysis, would change the way we understand democracy: in the light of Arrow's work, democracy would come to seem fundamentally flawed, at best embodying a series of unconvincing compromises.

THE IMPOSSIBILITY THEOREM

In order to use game theory to construct Cold War nuclear strategy, RAND needed to assume that the Soviet opponent was rational. Since rationality in game theory essentially just means being consistent, it is a relatively easy test for an individual, even a paranoid megalomaniac like Stalin, to pass. But if a 'player' in the nuclear game is really a group of individuals, it is far from clear that groups are consistent in their views or choices. Arrow's analysis of this problem began by assuming that if a group of people – whether Soviet military strategists or a bunch of friends – can be said to have a 'collective preference' about something, then that collective preference must be derived from the preferences of the individuals in the group. So Arrow's attention turned immediately to voting systems: the various ways of combining the preferences of individual voters to determine a collective choice or preference.

In particular, Arrow wanted to know if the collective preference emerging from any sensible voting system would be consistent. Defining what he meant by 'sensible', he spelt out a set of principles, desirable features which he thought any sensible voting system should have. With these in hand, there seems an obvious way to proceed: study a variety of voting systems which possess the desirable features, assessing for each system whether the collective decisions which emerge from them are consistent. This is the approach researchers before Arrow would have taken. But Arrow did something profoundly different.

First, he saw that a voting system can be understood in a general mathematical way. It is like a computer program in which each voter enters their preferences, preferences that the computer amalgamates using a set of rules, and then announces the collective preference.

Next, Arrow expressed in mathematical terms both the desirable features of voting systems and his idea about what it means for collective preferences to be consistent (we will return to this later). Putting all this together generated a completely unexpected incompatibility: there is, Arrow concluded, *no* voting system – including systems as yet unimagined – which both possesses the desirable features and produces a consistent collective preference. This was the Impossibility Theorem.

The essentials of the theorem were already there in the memo Arrow wrote as a RAND intern, which took him five days in September 1948.[2] Arrow was a modest man. He recalled that he thought of the Impossibility Theorem only when all his other attempts to answer RAND's questions had failed. Even genius interns have to sweat.

Arrow was lucky too. He could never have developed the Impossibility Theorem without knowledge of a then little-known mathematical language, the logic of relations, which he became aware of only through a series of unexpected events. First, because his father lost everything in the Great Depression, family poverty gave Arrow no choice but to attend City College in New York for his undergraduate education rather than a more prestigious university. Yet at that time City College had some impressive lecturers: the leading philosopher of logic Bertrand Russell was due to take up a Chair (professorship) there, and Arrow, already interested in mathematical logic, signed up to take Russell's course. But second, Russell was fired before he even arrived, for 'moral indecency'. The mother of a potential student (more potential than actual: she was only twelve) brought a lawsuit against City College on the grounds that Russell's well-publicised philosophy of 'free love' would endanger the morals of female students. The trial judge thundered that the college was creating a 'Chair of Indecency'.* Then came the third twist. The college was unexpectedly able to find a distinguished replacement for Russell. Alfred Tarski, one of the twentieth century's greatest philosophers of logic, left his native Poland in August 1939 to lecture at a

---

* A *New York Post* cartoon, titled 'The Chair of Indecency', showed Russell, pipe in hand, sitting on a pile of his books, including his classic of mathematical logic, *Principia Mathematica*, which inspired Arrow.

conference at Harvard. As it turned out, he was on the last ship to leave for the US before the German and Soviet invasions of Poland and the outbreak of war. As a Jew, Tarski could not return to Poland; lacking an income, he was glad to be offered a job at City College. In spring 1940 he lectured Arrow on the logic of relations. Tarski was not just an expert on this new kind of logic; he was its pioneer. Arrow's knowledge was cemented when Tarski, recognizing Arrow as a gifted student, asked this eighteen-year-old undergraduate to be the main proofreader for his definitive text on logic, published in 1941.[3]

Social Choice and Individual Values immediately garnered wide acclaim. But outside a narrow circle few could follow Arrow's mathematics, and even fewer were interested. And to begin with, it was a *very* narrow circle. There was, for instance, a missing step in the proof of the Impossibility Theorem, a gap not spotted by reviewers before publication, probably because the mathematical language used was so new and unfamiliar that it obscured the omission. (The problem was spotted and easily fixed a few years later.) This mathematical barrier has helped both supporters and critics of democracy in subsequent years to ignore the details of Arrow's work and to associate it instead with cruder, bumper-sticker messages. To go beyond that, we need to delve deeper, to get at least a flavour of what it means to speak of 'consistent' collective choices and how they can be mathematically impossible.

Since it is couched in purely mathematical terms, the Impossibility Theorem claims universal applicability. The mathematics does not place any restrictions on who is voting, how they are voting and what they are voting about (as long as there are at least three alternatives to choose between). It could be the Soviet military planners deciding which US city should be their primary nuclear target – or it could be some teenagers deciding whether to go out for pizzas, burgers or sushi. So when introducing a 'paradox of voting' on the second page of *Social Choice and Individual Values*, Arrow could have illustrated the paradox in a wide range of contexts. But of course, he used an example that reflected his RAND work, a choice between the three alternatives 'disarmament, cold war or hot war'. Suppose the decision-makers are three RAND analysts, Tom, Dick and Harry, with the following preferences: Tom prefers disarmament to cold war, and cold war to hot war; Dick prefers cold war to hot war, and hot war to disarmament; Harry prefers hot war to disarmament, and disarmament to cold war.* Bear with me. Now, if Tom proposes disarmament, then Dick and Harry could propose hot war, because they both prefer it (in a vote between hot war and disarmament, hot war wins). Similarly, if Harry proposes his first choice, hot war, Tom and Dick can form a coalition to outvote it, since they both prefer cold war to hot war. And again, if Dick proposes his first choice, cold war, Tom and Harry can form a coalition to outvote it, since they both prefer disarmament to cold war.

There is no overall winner because any proposal can be defeated by a counter-proposal from two out of the three voters. In other words, the group's preference is inconsistent: disarmament beats cold war, cold war beats hot war, but hot war beats disarmament. Arrow's Impossibility Theorem showed that problems akin to this paradox arise for any number of voters, with any voting method, in any context: the problems follow from the *pattern* of voter preferences, not what the preferences are about. In this sense, the Impossibility Theorem has universal applicability.

The Impossibility Theorem was misunderstood and misrepresented from the outset. Readers of the theorem more or less split into two groups: those who didn't understand the maths but found the impossibility result astonishing; and those who grasped the maths and were not astonished by the apparent impossibility. Many in the latter group, meanwhile, sniffed that the paradox discussed by Arrow was not new. It was known as the Condorcet Paradox, discovered by the French philosopher-mathematician Marquis de Condorcet back in 1785 (Arrow, though, did not know this – blame his 'wanting in diligence' research). More to the point, mathematical economists quickly saw ways to avoid the problem posed by the theorem, describing voting arrangements which ensure consistent collective choices after all. But it leaves a puzzle. If the problem posed by the Impossibility Theorem can readily be solved, why did *Social Choice and*

---

* The names don't matter, of course, but why assume white males? Just look at the RAND strategists in those days.

Individual Values have such a huge impact? Perhaps Arrow was just in the right place at the right time. Someone else might not have been so lucky.

AMERICA 1, SCOTLAND 0

Duncan Black was born poor but clever in Motherwell, Scotland, in 1908. After studying mathematics and economics at Glasgow University he became a lecturer at the new Dundee School of Economics, where he befriended another young new lecturer there, Ronald Coase. Black was already interested in voting systems, in particular how committees might vote to reach a collective decision. Like Arrow, his career was put on hold by war duties. Black was a night-time 'fire-watcher' at Warwick Castle – ready to sound the alarm if German bombers appeared – and it was on one lonely night in February 1942 that he 'saw in a flash' a key idea about voting. This turned into Black's *median voter theorem* – the idea that if voters have straightforward preferences in an electoral competition between two candidates, the winner will be the one who gains the support of the centrist (median) voters. In 1946 Black had another important insight, but his 'stomach revolted in something akin to physical sickness' as he realized the negative implications of his insight for finding reliable voting systems.[4] Black only later learned that his insight was not new – it was the Condorcet Paradox again (which had also been rediscovered by Dodgson in nineteenth-century Oxford, then forgotten again). Black's first major publication on the subject was in 1948, three years before Arrow's book. Then, in November 1949, Black submitted another important paper to the leading journal of mathematical economics, *Econometrica*. Being the first to publish new ideas is highly regarded in academia, so Black's status in the field seemed secure.

But Black was not so lucky. He always worked alone: Ronald Coase described him as 'unworldly, modest, diffident'; another academic colleague quipped 'he was an expert on committees but I never saw him sit on one'.[5] Unlike Arrow at RAND, Black was not surrounded by mathematicians and none of his colleagues knew anything about his research. Moreover, Black heard nothing from *Econometrica* about his paper until he chased the editor for news eighteen months later, in May 1951. The editor replied that Black's paper could be published – but only on condition that it was completely revised to acknowledge that Arrow was the originator of these ideas, because Arrow's book had been published a month or so earlier. Black was furious, because Arrow's prior publication was due to *Econometrica*'s slowness. And his fury increased when a possible explanation for that slowness emerged: the editor was biased, being a research director at the Cowles Commission in Chicago, where Arrow had just written most of his book.

Still, this could have been merely a temporary setback for Black. Instead, his defeat was long term: his work on social choice theory both before and after Arrow's book received only a fraction of the attention and praise lavished on Arrow. Arrow *had* been in the right place at the right time. It wasn't just that Arrow's links with RAND and Cowles brought him contacts and an influence unimaginable in isolated Dundee; his intellectual world was equally far removed from Black's. Black saw himself as a disinterested scholar developing a pure science of politics: when, in 1948, a RAND researcher wrote to Black asking for advice on suitable reading for RAND staff, Black, not wanting to assist a secretive, militaristic organization like RAND, chose not to reply. Arrow, in contrast, had a subtle but clear philosophical and political outlook which fitted well with the self-image of RAND as a defender of freedom. It was this broader philosophical and political vision, woven through *Social Choice and Individual Values*, which ultimately had an impact far beyond the Impossibility Theorem alone. Arrow inadvertently set out a framework which would be adopted by many cheerleaders for 'free markets' in future years.

In the aftermath of the Second World War scepticism about the wisdom of decisions made by more or less democratic processes was not hard to find. Hitler had come to power through a democratic vote. In *The Road to Serfdom*, Hayek emphasized how talk of the 'common good', 'public interest' and 'social purpose' could be used as convenient cover to take us down the road to totalitarianism. Yet he also argued that none of these concepts exist, because a society of free individuals can never reach agreement on common goals. No wonder Arrow's Impossibility Theorem was popular with Hayek's supporters: Arrow seemed to have provided a mathematical proof of Hayek's argument.

For the free marketeers, Arrow apparently had more to offer. If democracy was impossible, Arrow seemed to hint at a replacement. In the first few pages of *Social Choice and Individual Values*, he stated that there were two types of 'social choice': voting, to make political choices; and markets, to make economic ones. For Arrow, voting and markets were so 'analogous' that the distinction between them should be 'disregarded'. So as far as the Hayek–Chicago axis was concerned, the obvious response to the Impossibility Theorem was to replace politics and voting with economics and markets. This was a big new step beyond Adam Smith, nineteenth-century laissez-faire and other traditional forms of conservatism – a vision not just of freedom from state interference in the market but as far as possible replacing the state altogether. And this vision looms large over twenty-first-century life, in every presumption that markets are the default way of making decisions that were formerly handled by politics.

Yet there is a basic problem with this market euphoria. If markets are perfectly analogous to voting, *then the Impossibility Theorem applies to markets too*, and hence, as Arrow put it just after first stating his theorem, 'the market mechanism does not create a rational social choice.'[6]

But this part of Arrow's message was ignored.

MATHEMATICAL PHILOSOPHY

No serious student of Arrow's work could conclude that he obviously favours markets over democracy as a means of giving people what they want. It bears repeating: Arrow argued that the Impossibility Theorem poses a challenge to the legitimacy of both markets and voting. More importantly, as those who grasped Arrow's mathematics realized almost immediately, the logical 'impossibility' of democracy could be avoided in a number of ways, by weakening or tweaking one or more of Arrow's assumptions. Each of these tweaks opened the door to various possibilities for reliable voting systems.

Did Arrow feel embarrassed by the ease with which his Impossibility Theorem could be sidestepped? Not at all. Avoiding the impossibility was the whole point: although almost everyone called it 'Arrow's Impossibility Theorem', the name Arrow gave it was the *General Possibility Theorem*. Friends joked that Arrow was an incurable optimist, but it was more than that. Arrow knew from the outset that his theorem would not hold if any of the assumptions were weakened. His purpose had never been to prove that meaningful democracy is impossible. Instead, he aimed to map out the terrain of compromises: the theorem showed that voting arrangements involving more of one desirable feature are only possible if another desirable feature is to some extent sacrificed. It would be up to others to take Arrow's map and argue for a particular destination in terms of voting arrangements.

For instance, Arrow had asserted that collective preferences should be consistent, in the sense that if A is preferred to B and B is preferred to C, then A must be preferred to C. This consistency requirement was not met in the Cold War voting example described earlier: a majority preferred disarmament to cold war, a majority preferred cold war to hot war, *but* a majority preferred hot war to disarmament. Arrow's consistency requirement is appealing because it rules out voting arrangements which lead to situations like this: it rules out voting arrangements which fail to yield a clear winner in all circumstances. But there are other ways of ensuring that voting arrangements always yield a winner. In 1998 Amartya Sen won the Nobel Prize for economics partly for his work in this area. Sen argued that Arrow was asking too much of voting systems: often, Sen pointed out, all we need to know is the winner. But Arrow's approach looks for voting systems which give us more information – the 'collective preference', a complete ranking of all the alternatives from top to bottom, not just the selection of a winner. Sen proposed a mathematical framework for voting systems which just identify winners: this is much less demanding than Arrow's approach and many plausible voting systems are possible. In many circumstances, this seems worth the sacrifice of not knowing which alternatives come second, third, and so on.

To explore another important escape route from the Impossibility Theorem, we need to spell out two of the desirable features of voting systems which Arrow had specified. They came to be known as 'Universal Domain' and 'Independence of Irrelevant Alternatives'. Universal Domain asserts that a voting system must be able to handle any kind of opinion or preference expressed by individual voters. Independence of Irrelevant Alternatives requires that the voting system's ranking of any two alternatives should depend only on how individuals rank these two alternatives, and nothing else. At first glance, these principles seem to capture the spirit of democracy, ensuring that the opinions of individual voters take priority in determining the collective decision. However, when Universal Domain says 'any', it truly means any, in a mathematical sense: any logically possible preference over the alternatives is allowed. Again, Arrow may be needlessly setting the bar too high here: in a democracy, we need not accommodate any kind of preference, as though allowing for people to choose their rankings over the alternatives entirely randomly, perhaps by tossing a coin. There will be some logically possible preference patterns which just make no sense and can be ruled out. Moreover, probably every democratic country or society throughout history has set limits on the preferences which citizens can express and the choices available to them at the ballot box. The limits are often themselves the outcome of some formal or informal democratic procedures, ranging from the agenda agreed by citizens' elected representatives to the adoption of explicit constitutional prohibitions, such as the ban on 'anti-democratic' political parties in Germany. If such limits are legitimate, then Arrow's Universal Domain assumption can be dropped and so the Impossibility Theorem does not apply.

Arguments such as these, about the trade-offs involved in weakening one of Arrow's assumptions for the sake of saving the others, raged on for decades, generating a vast academic literature – but one largely ignored by outsiders, who were happy to stick with the 'democracy is impossible' bumper-sticker version.

Yet Arrow's influence went far beyond the Impossibility Theorem. He laid out a framework for thinking about politics and economics which he presented as scientific, universally true and capturing the essence of democracy, which he took to be twofold: individual freedom to express any kind of opinion or preference about any subject, and collective decisions based on these individual preferences alone. But this vision of democracy was largely hidden in the mathematical statement of 'Universal Domain' and 'Independence of Irrelevant Alternatives'. (Or, as mathematically inclined readers soon labelled them, 'Axiom U' and 'Axiom I'). In other words, Arrow set out his personal philosophical views – because that is what they were – as though they were universal laws of algebra, expressing them in mathematical language, and unfamiliar mathematical language at that.

Taken together, Arrow's two axioms define democracy in terms of a strong form of individualism and moral relativism, ruling out any kind of social philosophy that might legitimately override individual opinion on occasion. Arrow's principal target was totalitarian philosophies such as Soviet Communism (which pleased readers from Hayek to RAND to Chicago economists), but his axioms U and I also banished potentially more benign philosophies, from Rousseau to Kant. In practical terms, Arrow's seemingly inoffensive abstract axioms mean that individual preferences, no matter how mean, selfish, racist or nasty, can never be overruled, even if they conflict with law, the constitution or human rights.

Arrow's approach fundamentally misunderstands the meaning of democracy. Democracy is about more than voting systems which add up citizens' sacrosanct fixed preferences. In a democracy, preferences are *not* sacrosanct – not just because they might be nasty but because they may be the product of propaganda or deceptive marketing: in all these cases, we try to persuade citizens to change their minds. More generally, democracy involves public deliberation, debate and persuasion, hopefully bringing about some reconciliation of differing points of view. Even if these attempted reconciliations are only fractionally successful, these processes will lead to a narrower range of voter preferences than Universal Domain demands. Without any kind of reconciliation, the impossibility of establishing a consistent collective preference seems hardly surprising.

No one – apparently including Arrow himself – seemed immediately aware of the full implications of the political philosophy hidden in his maths. He seems to have got away with it because philosophically inclined critics struggled to follow the argument, woven as it was into layers of mathematical definitions and deductions. Arrow inspired a generation of academics to search for a science of politics, which they took to be expressible in purely mathematical terms, based on premises assumed to be universally true. When contemporary Western governments attempt to impose electoral democracy on countries which have never experienced it, their presumption that there are universal truths about democracy, valid in all times and places, reflects the extraordinary reach and influence of Arrow's kind of thinking.

But before we get to these contemporary effects, we need to follow the story of this new science of politics from the well-ordered world of Arrow in the 1950s through the political and economic turbulence of the 1970s: Watergate, the quadrupling of the oil price, rampant inflation, rising unemployment and ballooning government debt. In 1978, at the height of these crises, Arrow was asked to contribute to a debate on whether American democracy and capitalism had a future. The thrust of Arrow's essay is clear from its title – 'A Cautious Case for Socialism'.[7] If there was to be an intellectual revolution overthrowing politics in favour of markets, Arrow was not the man to lead it. It would take a very different kind of person, more prophet than mathematician.

POLITICS, HEAD LICE AND ROOT CANALS

James McGill Buchanan was born in 1919 in Murfreesboro, Tennessee, where he grew up on the family farm. Every morning before going to school he milked the cows. His poor Southern background strongly shaped his attitudes in later life. Remembering stories told by his grandparents about the occupation of the defeated Confederacy, Buchanan always retained a deep distrust of national government: he described himself as always 'anti-state, anti-government, anti-establishment . . . The robber barons were very real to me'.[8] And 'for me, government has always been something to be protected from rather than to be the provider of assistance'.[9] Buchanan was one of those people who grow up with firm beliefs and spend the rest of their life repeatedly discovering that they were right all along.

Within six weeks of arriving at the University of Chicago Buchanan had become a 'zealous advocate' of free markets, under the influence of teachers including a young Milton Friedman. He never wavered thereafter. But his ideology, rather than straightforward free-market orthodoxy, was of his own making. Buchanan was a moralist at heart, with the fire of a preacher from the Bible Belt – a secular, ascetic puritan. He did not believe parents should bequeath their wealth to their children (although Buchanan had none), and he never had any formal affiliation to a political party.

Buchanan found his distrust of what he called the 'East Coast establishment' confirmed first in the Navy, and then, when applying for academic jobs, when he felt repeatedly passed over in favour of less well-qualified applicants from Ivy League universities. He complained that he had been 'subjected to overt discrimination'[10] – although he could hardly worry about a glass ceiling after winning the Nobel Prize for economics in 1986. Buchanan's career was spent mostly at universities in Virginia rather than Ivy League establishments. This physical separation from US academic elites was reinforced by a political separation: Buchanan and his colleagues saw the mainstream faith in 'neutral' bureaucrats who serve the public interest as leading down the road to communism. They called their own approach *public choice theory*, a bizarre name, given their belief that the public cannot make coherent collective choices, and indeed that there are no such things as the public interest, the public good, public service or public servants.

Unlike Arrow's work, public choice theory is easy to summarize. As Buchanan put it in a letter to Hayek, public choice theory is 'politics without the romance': for Buchanan, everyone concerned with politics – including politicians, bureaucrats and voters – is motivated solely by the pursuit of narrow, selfish ends. Public choice theory is almost entirely devoted to tracing out the implications of this single, simple idea.

Nowadays there is a wide consensus that government is bloated, incompetent, inefficient, vulnerable to capture by special interests and that its interference in ordinary life knows no bounds. Put another way, as several surveys have found, many in the US compare Washington politics unfavourably to head lice and painful dental work on your root canals. Public choice theory has done more than help shape this consensus view: it has *become* the consensus about government and politics. Beginning in the shadow of Arrow's work in the mid-1950s, public choice theory was built up over the following twenty years into a comprehensive analysis of every aspect of politics. However, this intellectual revolution had little immediate impact on the real world of politics beyond academia: it was like a timebomb waiting to explode.

The detonator was the political and economic crises of the 1970s. Buchanan and his followers were ready with an explanation for how governments across the West had got into this mess. They called it 'political overload'. According to public choice theory, the selfishness of politicians makes them focus solely on getting elected and re-elected. So they will try to adopt the policies which will win them the most votes. Good for democracy, surely? No, because a policy which commands majority support among the voters may not best serve the interests of all citizens, since many citizens do not bother to vote. And there is a bigger problem: selfish voters are not wise voters.

On the contrary, public choice theory argues, selfish voters are 'rationally ignorant'. Each voter's single vote is highly unlikely to make any difference to the outcome, so, according to public choice theory, it is not worth the time and effort involved in obtaining information about candidates and/or policies. Instead voters will choose to remain ignorant to some degree and ignore altogether those policy impacts which have little effect on them in isolation. This wilful ignorance combines with selfishness in a dangerous way. If a politician promises a big new project for your community – perhaps a new school or hospital – but the costs of the project are borne by taxpayers generally, then public choice theory suggests the promise might win your vote, partly because the extra tax falling on you personally is likely to be small. The psychological power of the politician's promise is clear: the benefit is local, soon, tangible and explicit, whereas the tax cost is general, later, vague and unacknowledged. As an election approaches, all politicians and their parties make promises like these, each promise bidding to win the votes of a different group or constituency. The bidding war is unconstrained, ultimately leading to political overload – a situation of exploding government debt with tax revenue continually falling short of public expenditure.

This story was new in the 1970s. Today we take it for granted, one reason why 'politics' has become a dirty word. And yet as an explanation for political and economic crises – in the twenty-first century as well as in the 1970s – it is incomplete, self-contradictory and ignores the facts.

IT'S THE VOTERS, STUPID

Public choice theorists were among the first economists explicitly to equate rational behaviour with selfishness. An influential early statement of public choice theory is Anthony Downs's *An Economic Theory of Democracy*, published in 1957. Downs flatly asserted: 'whenever we speak of rational behavior, we always mean rational behavior directed primarily to selfish ends'.[11] In sharp contrast, Arrow never assumed people are selfish. He merely took people to be rational – meaning consistent – in pursuing their goals, whether those goals are selfish or selfless, noble or base. Remarkable, then, that Arrow was Downs's doctoral supervisor – and *An Economic Theory of Democracy* was Downs's doctoral thesis, published without any changes. Perhaps Downs's divided loyalties explain his complete volte-face just five years later, when he acknowledged the mixed motives behind political behaviour, not all of them selfish. But it is the original *Economic Theory of Democracy* which was handed down to generations of students, without Downs's later retractions, and became one of the most cited books on American politics.

If we dig into the details of the 'political overload' argument, it does not withstand scrutiny. There is something paradoxical at the heart of the argument and public choice theory more generally: although voters are 'rational', they are easily fooled. The overload argument portrayed voters as suckers, seduced by promises of public spending and oblivious to the cumulative effect of the overall spending package on government debt and future tax levels. Yet robust evidence rapidly emerged that electorates do not vote solely on the basis of the packages of public spending promises dangled before them. They judge politicians on their competence in managing the economy, too, even if this is poorly defined and hard to assess.[12] For Buchanan, the problem was more one of voters' moral degeneracy than their stupidity. He blamed the Keynesian fiscal permissiveness (government 'tax and spend') beginning in the 1960s for the growing moral permissiveness of the time, accusing Keynesianism of helping cause 'increasingly liberalized attitudes toward sexual activities' and 'a declining vitality of the Puritan work ethic', among other sins.[13] Whatever the exact limitations of voters in public choice theory, the theory is distinctive in stressing such limitations: it is unlike most other traditions in economics, including ones concerned with reducing the size of the state.

Emerging at roughly the same time as public choice theory was a new brand of macroeconomics associated with reducing the size of the state – monetarism. Monetarists, led by Milton Friedman, were as hostile to Keynesianism as Buchanan was, but for different reasons: monetarists believe that public spending to stimulate the economy is futile. Any increase in public spending must be paid for in the future through higher taxes. Everyone knows this, and their response is to reduce their own spending now – belt-tightening to help pay for future tax rises – and so the stimulus effect of public spending is immediately cancelled out by reduced private spending. In this story, the voters don't forget about future tax, they fixate on it. Both monetarists and public choice theorists argue for reduced public spending then, but their stories directly contradict each other.

Even *within* public choice theory, the foolish voter assumption is applied in a partial and self-contradictory way. If voters are consistently fooled by public spending promises, then there would be no point in asking voters to support a government committed to spending cuts and fiscal austerity. But that is what many public choice theorists did: Buchanan was involved directly or indirectly in all the American 'tax revolt' campaigns of the 1970s, and the administration of Ronald Reagan, elected in 1980, contained many of Buchanan's students, including one of Reagan's economic advisers. And again, if electoral competition forces selfish politicians to outbid each other in their public spending commitments, then there is little hope of electing governments committed to breaking the cycle. So the election of Reagan, and Thatcher in the UK the year before, both outwardly committed to reducing public expenditure, was itself powerful evidence that voters and politicians are not always foolish and selfish in the way public choice theory assumes. The contradictions here are hard to avoid. Among economists aiming to shrink the state, even close colleagues took different sides. Milton Friedman thought that voters could be persuaded to support policies and politicians committed to reducing the size of the state, while his Chicago friend and colleague George Stigler was very doubtful. Stigler dodged the nihilistic implications of his own view: 'Milton wants to change the world; I only want to understand it.'[14]

There are other ironies too. First, if we should assume that politicians, bureaucrats and voters are all selfish because everyone is, then academics are, too, including public choice theorists. The public choice perspective tells us not to trust public choice theorists as objective scientists or neutral observers. Instead we should expect them to write and say whatever it takes to advance their own careers. Although Arrow and Buchanan were clearly motivated solely by their academic values and interests, it is not hard to find evidence of economists with more selfish concerns (such as some financial economists in the years leading up to the global financial crisis, as shown in the 2010 documentary *Inside Job*).[15] More generally, evidence of self-serving behaviour in government goes beyond politicians and bureaucrats to include the external consultants and analysts who advise, for instance, moving public services to the private sector because public-sector workers cannot be trusted. The lesson here is that if we take public choice theory seriously, we should apply it comprehensively and even-handedly, to include all those involved in the policy-making process, including academics, consultants, lobbyists and advisers from the private sector.

Second, public choice theory predicts that many people will not bother to vote, because the costs of voting, albeit small, are outweighed by the expected benefits, which are even smaller, because the probability of a single vote swinging the result is almost zero. And yet of course people do vote in large numbers. Downs was sufficiently puzzled by the fact of significant voter turnout that he labelled it a 'paradox', and public choice theorists remain worried that this 'paradox of voter turnout' suggests voters are not rational calculators after all.

Wait a moment. It is *so* easy to turn public choice theory against itself – a public choice critique of public choice theory. It seems too easy, too much of a self-referential academic game, because there is clearly a basic truth in the public choice theorists' perspective on politics: some politicians, voters and bureaucrats do seem largely motivated by selfish concerns. And this is not a new idea. Over 500 years ago the Italian diplomat Niccoló Machiavelli described in detail the elaborate strategies adopted by selfish, cynical politicians and bureaucrats. Public choice theory began as a reaction against a naïve and simplistic view widespread after the Second World War: that once some desirable policy change has been identified by economists or other 'experts', benign politicians and bureaucrats will always do their best to bring it about. Buchanan and his colleagues saw themselves – rightly – as outsiders intent on subverting this fantasy. But by the 1980s they were definitely insiders.

Beginning with Thatcher in the UK and Reagan in the US, public choice theory conquered mainstream politics. At least on the surface, it seemed to mesh neatly with monetarist macroeconomics, pessimism about democracy based on Arrow's theorem and Hayek's ideas about freedom, to create a powerful case for more markets, less government. And some key facts seemed to be tilting in favour of the theory. Despite occasional upticks, the trend in voter turnout seemed inexorably downwards in most developed democracies. Public expenditure continued to rise, even under governments claiming to be determined to reduce it. Why? If not the public choice story of selfish and short-sighted politicians, bureaucrats and voters, then what?

In fact, a compelling alternative explanation for the growth of public expenditure has been familiar to economists since the 1960s, but it's an explanation that remains completely hidden from political debate.

SMARTPHONES AND STRING QUARTETS

Some things are getting cheaper, and others more expensive.

Well, of course. But this is true in a more fundamental sense too: over time, some things are getting cheaper, and others more expensive *in terms of average incomes*. Mass-produced manufactured goods are becoming ever cheaper. The proportion of an average worker's pay needed to buy a TV or a washing machine today is lower than it was ten years ago and much lower than thirty years ago (and the product being bought is much better). But the reverse is true for labour-intensive services: childcare costs, retirement-home bills, university fees, luxury meals and live theatre tickets are all relatively more expensive as a proportion of average income. When the first smartphones were released in the late 1990s, their price was roughly the same as thirty classical concert tickets. In the late 2010s the price of a smartphone is equivalent to about two tickets.[16] The reason for this divergence is that while productivity (output per hour worked) has been rising for decades in manufacturing – due to economies of scale, innovation and automation – it has risen only modestly in labour-intensive services. Productivity growth in manufacturing and the economy in general allows wages to rise without pushing up the prices paid by consumers. But wages in labour-intensive services will not simply stagnate because productivity growth in these sectors is weak. If pay in these service sectors falls behind the rest of the economy, employers will be unable to attract and retain workers. Instead, wages in labour-intensive services must rise roughly in line with average wages across the economy. Since there is little compensating increase in productivity – it's not as though those better-paid workers are producing more stuff – firms are forced to raise prices. Over time, then, the prices of labour-intensive services rise inexorably relative to the prices of all other goods and services. Put differently, the proportion of national income spent on labour-intensive services will continually increase over time.

William Baumol was the economist who first noticed this phenomenon, which soon became known as Baumol's *cost disease*.[17]

(Coincidentally, Baumol studied at City College, New York, at the same time as Ken Arrow, although Baumol majored in economics and art rather than Arrow's major in maths.) Baumol's cost disease is especially virulent in services for which the number of hours provided by workers is part of the definition of the service being offered. In these services, productivity cannot be increased by reducing hours worked, because that would mean a different service. As Baumol observed, musicians' productivity in 'producing' a live performance of a Mozart string quartet has remained unchanged since Mozart's day: it still requires four musicians and takes as long to play. Similarly, a one-hour consultation with a doctor is just that: the service provided would not be the same if it were thirty minutes with the doctor and thirty completing an online diagnostic questionnaire.

The implications of Baumol's cost disease are shocking. The proportion of US GDP spent on healthcare is growing by around 1.4 per cent per year. Baumol recently predicted that this trend will broadly continue, implying that US spending on healthcare will rise from its current level, around 18 per cent of GDP, to about 60 per cent by 2100.[18] Data from other countries shows the cost disease too, albeit usually less pronounced than in the US: in Britain the trend in healthcare spending takes it from about 10 per cent of GDP now to 50 per cent by 2100.

Unbelievable? Baumol's forecasts are worth taking more seriously than many economists' predictions, not least because Baumol first described the cost disease in the 1960s and made some empirical 'extrapolations' at that time which have largely been proven correct.* More generally, the data supports the cost disease phenomenon. From 1978 to 2012, average price and wage increases in the US were 110 per cent and 150 per cent respectively. Over the same period healthcare costs rose by around 250 per cent, while the price of a university education rose by about 440 per cent. In many countries, a substantial part of healthcare provision is from the public sector. But the US data show the cost disease can arise in healthcare dominated by private provision too. The cost disease – both the data and

* Fifty years later Baumol admitted that he had been 'too cowardly' to call them predictions back in the 1960s so he settled on 'extrapolations'. Even the originators of counter-intuitive ideas sometimes find them hard to take seriously.

Baumol's explanation – suggests that the growth in public expenditure due to increased healthcare spending is not due to lazy or inefficient public-sector workers: it is inherent in the service being provided.

No political genius is required to realize why mainstream politics of all shades remains silent about Baumol's cost disease. It seems to point to a frightening future in which key services such as healthcare and education become completely unaffordable. There is no cure. The unaffordability remains, irrespective of whether the services are publicly or privately provided.

Yet, thankfully, the cost disease is much less unpleasant than it sounds. While healthcare, education and other labour-intensive services are getting relatively more expensive, they are becoming more affordable.

Something can become *relatively* more expensive simply because other things have become cheaper – it can still be more affordable than in the past. So it is with labour-intensive services. The most important measure of affordability for society is the labour input, the number of hours worked to make something. This is the real cost incurred by humanity in producing things. Since productivity is rising almost everywhere in the economy, the labour required to produce the same output is falling in almost all sectors: things are becoming more affordable in terms of labour input. Put another way, productivity growth across the economy allows average wages to rise faster than prices so, overall, most goods and services are becoming more affordable as our purchasing power increases. If Baumol is right and US spending on health is 60 per cent of GDP by 2100, there will still be enough left to spend on everything else – because, as a proportion of GDP, many things will be cheaper.

This is a subtle story, which is one reason why it is rarely told. And, once we look more closely, it gets more subtle still. Clearly, there *is* room for productivity improvement in labour-intensive services over time. Even performing Mozart quartets requires less labour than it did back in the eighteenth century. When four Viennese musicians travel to Frankfurt to perform a Mozart quartet, it takes them several hours to get there. When Mozart made the same journey in 1790, he recorded that it took six days in great discomfort – and he was pleasantly surprised that it did not take longer.[19] Today, some software packages make more accurate diagnoses than doctors, while university lectures can be recorded and made available to millions online. Yet there are limits to productivity growth in services such as healthcare and education. When the service provided is bespoke, tailored to the requirements of the person receiving it – physiotherapy, assessing a dissertation – it is essentially unique. There is little scope for economies of scale. And good-quality bespoke services are often *defined in terms of* low productivity. If a school increases class sizes, this is usually seen as a decline in the quality of the education provided, not an increase in teacher productivity.

Another complication. It might seem that, as the relative price of labour-intensive services rises, we will respond as we often do when the price of something rises: we will buy less. But in richer societies we are demanding more, not less, of key services such as healthcare and education, with greater numbers entering higher education and receiving treatment for unpleasant but minor health problems.

Finally, while the rising cost of services such as healthcare and education may be due to Baumol's cost disease, that leaves open the possibility that costs are higher still when the services are publicly rather than privately provided. We have seen that the evidence for this possibility is not promising, because leading examples of private provision, such as US healthcare, show costs rising at least as fast as their public counterparts. Still, the idea of public bad, private good has become so deeply embedded that it is worth briefly assessing its greatest policy triumph – privatization.

The clearest test of this idea is the massive privatization programme launched in Britain immediately after Margaret Thatcher's election as prime minister in 1979. The most comprehensive long-term study of these British privatizations shows that the results did not live up to the rhetoric.[20] Since the privatized firms in question were mostly monopolies or oligopolies facing little competition, they made substantial profits. And management salaries rose significantly (with no evidence of firing poor managers in pursuit of better ones: there was minimal management turnover). Advocates of privatization had claimed that the profit motive would drive privatized firms to cut costs. But in reality, rising salary costs and shareholder dividends essentially cancelled out any cost savings: overall, privatization made little difference to long-term trends in productivity and service prices.

In sum, what does Baumol's cost disease tell us? It provides a more convincing explanation than public choice theory of much of the rise in public expenditure in many countries in recent years. The cost disease goes to the heart of what is distinctive about services like health and education. These services have inherently low productivity (because we value small class sizes and time with our doctor). And there is no theory or evidence to suggest that goods and services are usually provided at lower cost or more efficiently by the private sector. Yet there is no unaffordability crisis here. True, the price of services such as health and education will carry on rising relative to other goods and services, but not as fast as the growth in our purchasing power. Nevertheless, big political problems lie ahead. If these services are publicly provided, then taxes must inevitably rise over time, just to maintain current service standards; privatization, meanwhile, will achieve nothing except the probable exclusion of the poorest from access to these services.

THE POLITICS WE DESERVE?

The cost disease implies tax rises to maintain existing public services like health and education. It's easy to be pessimistic about the unwillingness of twenty-first-century democracies to accept such tax rises. And this pessimism is at least partly due to the influence of public choice theory, which suggests that politicians would never propose tax rises and voters would never agree to them. Of course, we have had pessimism about the possibilities of politics since we have had politics, but even Machiavelli believed that most politicians have honourable motives as well as base ones. In comparison, public choice theory offers just a crude, one-dimensional caricature of selfish politicians, bureaucrats and voters. Not unrelated, the fashionable dismissal of almost any role for the state is unprecedented in modern times.[21] Even Friedrich Hayek's *The Road to Serfdom* accepted a wider role for government, including some degree of social insurance or 'welfare state'.

As recently as the 1960s surveys regularly showed that ordinary people more or less accepted a view of politics in which politicians and bureaucrats mostly tried to pursue the public interest, and voters 'held power to account'. It is no coincidence that public choice theory emerged from academia at broadly the same time – the late 1970s – as modern cynicism about politics took root. This is not to suggest that we have consciously embraced public choice theory: Buchanan, Downs and co. have not become household names. The influence of public choice arguments has been more subtle: many of them are akin to self-fulfilling prophecies. Take the claim that bureaucrats and other employees of the state – in many countries this includes most doctors and teachers – have solely selfish motives. Against this, there is clear evidence that many of these employees embrace an ethos of public service and strive to meet standards of professionalism appropriate to their work, such as the Hippocratic oath taken by doctors. Policies inspired by public choice theory will corrode these ethical codes and standards: if you assume the worst of people, they will live down to your dismal expectations. The result will be a decline rather than an improvement in public-service quality and efficiency.

Another self-fulfilling prophecy concerns voter turnout. By suggesting that voting is pointless, Downs's *Economic Theory of Democracy* sowed the seeds for a decline in voter turnout. Inheriting from Arrow the concept of voters as no more than bundles of fixed preferences, Downs added the assumption that these preferences are purely selfish. Downs saw voters as just like selfish consumers, and the competition between parties for their votes as like that between rival businesses for market share. This kind of competition is not won through attempts to persuade voters in a process of public debate and argument but instead through modern marketing techniques. And assuming voters are narrowly selfish implies that their concerns are one-dimensional – economic well-being – so the terrain on which elections are won and lost will be equally one-dimensional. The winning strategy here is clear: adopt the policies favoured by centrist voters. This is Duncan Black's median voter theorem (but Black saw it as an exercise in pure theory rather than a realistic model of how voters behave).

From the 1960s onwards this analysis filtered through to influence mainstream political parties, which relied increasingly on marketing rather than argument. Their policy packages became more alike as they hugged the centre, seeking to appeal to the median voter. Predictably, the result was declining voter turnout: there is less point in voting if all parties with a chance of forming the government have similar policies. And when marketing replaces political argument, the language becomes less emotive, less impassioned and voters lose interest.

Voter engagement has been further undermined by criticism of the political process from an unexpected source – political insiders themselves. The anti-political attitude of public choice theory has been seemingly embraced by the politicians and bureaucrats it portrays as so cynical, selfish and short-termist. The bureaucrats at the United Nations, the World Bank and the European Commission have been arguing for decades that policy-making should be 'depoliticized'. As an influential minister in the UK's Blair government explained, 'what governs our approach is a clear desire to place power where it should be: increasingly not with politicians, but with those best fitted in different ways to employ it . . . This depoliticization of key decision-making is a vital element in bringing power closer to the people.'[22] The same insider cited the setting of interest rates by the Bank of England and the setting of a national minimum wage by an independent commission. If politicians themselves have come to believe that they should not be trusted to make decisions (for example because of their temptation to manipulate interest rates for electoral reasons), and that unelected technocrats should be handed much of the political power, no wonder voters come to believe these things too. Traditionally, politicians might regard handing over power to unelected officials as a failure to fulfil their democratic responsibilities, a repudiation of their own electoral mandate. That politicians and organizations such as the World Bank are *proud* of this activity shows that they have a rather more pessimistic view of democracy. Ironically, the fact that depoliticization seems driven by a sincere desire by political insiders to bring about better government suggests that they are not so selfish after all. They need to believe in themselves.

We get the politics we deserve. If each of us assumes politicians, bureaucrats and voters are all selfish, and each of us acts accordingly, then we cannot expect much from politics. Our assumptions about human nature are not, as public choice theory would have it, above and beyond politics: they *make* our politics. So does that mean, to get better politics, as the song goes, all you need is love?

We cannot pretend to trust politicians and politics more than we really do. But we should be aware that every decision not to do so comes with a cost. There is a cumulative drip-drip effect of seemingly innocuous assumptions slowly dissolving the democratic glue that holds us together. Who imagined that comparing competition between political parties to that between firms for market share would lead to most voters deciding that mainstream parties are 'all the same', and alarming levels of disaffection with democracy?

If we don't like the way contemporary politics works, then any attempt to change it must begin by assessing all these assumptions case by case, on the best evidence available. Trust is not easy to rebuild, but we do have a choice.

We can't trace the origins of our contemporary political malaise to a single event. But if we are looking for a decisive Big Bang in the history of ideas which set us on our current path, Arrow's *Social Choice and Individual Values* is a convincing candidate. The impossibility theorem is a remarkable intellectual achievement. Yet even if society's goals cannot be derived from individual voter preferences using Arrow's questionable ideal of a voting system, it does not follow that democracy is impossible or that ideas of the common good or public interest are mythical. Rather, Arrow's impossibility theorem reminds us that voting systems involve ethical compromises. And the solution of many public choice theorists – contracting out politics to the market – does not escape the need for these compromises. It just ignores them.

Arrow, by turns an apolitical mathematician and a cautious social-ist who left meagre materials for biographers, remains an inscrutable figure in the history of economics. He was an unwitting revolution-ary in the assault on politics. And he was only there by chance. How different would modern politics look if Arrow had not learned the maths he needed – if Bertrand Russell had not been accused of 'moral indecency'?

5

Free-riding, or Not Doing Your Bit

'From now on I'm thinking only of me.'

Major Danby replied indulgently with a superior smile: 'But, Yossarian, suppose everyone felt that way.'

'Then,' said Yossarian, 'I'd certainly be a damned fool to feel any other way, wouldn't I?'

– Joseph Heller, *Catch-22*

One of the biggest media events of 2013 was the birth of a child. Not any child, but George, Prince of Cambridge, third in line to the British throne. Interest in the birth was global: on the day of the birth, 22nd July, the BBC News website received more traffic than ever before, with 19.4 million unique browsers. An estimated ninety separate TV crews spent a long day camped outside a London hospital waiting for the birth to be announced. In the midst of the media frenzy, a BBC reporter standing outside the hospital expressed grave concern about the challenges that George's parents would face: 'A major problem is the intense media interest which will surround the boy.'

Wait a moment. Isn't there something a bit odd, even hypocritical, about a BBC reporter worrying aloud about this? Presumably the BBC realizes that it plays a major role in sustaining intense media interest in the British royal family. When challenged about the harm done to the family by saturation media coverage, the BBC has always pointed out that its involvement alone does not cause the problem. In the barely imaginable parallel universe involving BBC silence on royal matters, the argument goes, there would still be more than enough other media organizations to ensure saturation coverage. So, if there is a problem, the BBC is not responsible for it.

This is a variation on an argument that has become very familiar in recent decades: *it makes no difference whether or not I do my bit.* I might worry about climate change, but it makes no difference whether or not I cut my carbon emissions by consuming less, driving less, flying less. So why bother? And although I may be horrified by the latest African famine, my charitable donation makes no difference. So why bother? Again, it makes no difference whether or not I vote, so why bother? Since it makes no difference, doing my bit in all these cases would not be virtuous. It would be completely futile. The only sensible decision is to *free-ride* on the contributions of others.

Facebook UK seems to think so too. In 2014, despite UK sales of over £100 million, it paid only £4,327 in UK corporation tax. By 2018, its tax payment had risen to £15.8 million – but sales had grown to £1.3 billion, so it still paid barely more than 1 per cent in tax. Facebook free-rides on the contributions of other taxpayers, who pay for state-subsidized improvements in UK internet infrastructure – enabling almost two-thirds of the UK population to use Facebook. Facebook can free-ride because we let it. We might boycott Facebook over fake news, but not over their tax avoidance, because free-riding is normal behaviour nowadays. We just shrug our shoulders and mutter, 'Wouldn't you . . . ?'

And yet for most of human history, when people have confronted these kinds of situations, they have reached the opposite conclusion. The term 'free-riding' was first used in 1850s Wisconsin to refer to travelling on a train without paying. But the wider contemporary meaning of 'free-riding' – enjoying the benefits made possible by the contributions of others without contributing yourself – was unknown outside academia till the 1970s. The transformation of the phrase 'free-riding' from obscure academic jargon to everyday speech is a recent one.

Of course, people have been free-riding for as long as there have been communities large enough for free riders to sponge off. But they didn't call it that. The wider usage of the word 'free-riding' in the last fifty years or so reflects a fundamental shift in the status of this kind of behaviour. Over this period, free-riding behaviour began to shed some of the negative connotations with which it had always been associated: quite suddenly, it became the smart thing to do. 'Free-riding' wasn't just a new label for old behaviour but a new argument that such behaviour was acceptable: an argument mostly based on some economic theory not even invented until the 1930s and still confined to academia as late as the 1960s. As ideas go, free-riding is very new.

The emergence in the 1960s of a hippie countercultural mentality of fatalistic powerlessness provided fertile ground for the spread of this new idea. The activist Abbie Hoffman's *Steal This Book*, a defining statement of 60s hippiedom, exemplifies the contradictions in free-riding. Rejected by over thirty publishers, it sold over a quarter of a million copies in the first six months after publication, and countless copies were stolen – but without the buyers there would have been very few copies produced for the free-riders to steal. Hoffman thought it was immoral *not* to steal from the 'Pig Empire' (the US), and ruefully acknowledged his contradictory success: 'it's embarrassing when you try to overthrow the government and you wind up on the bestsellers list.'[1]

HOW DID FREE-RIDING BECOME SMART?

In Plato's *Republic*, Glaucon tells the story of a shepherd, Gyges, who witnesses an earthquake in which a chasm opens up in the earth. In a Hollywood disaster movie, Gyges would leave the earthquake zone as fast as his SUV would carry him. But it's not that kind of story. Gyges descends into the chasm. He finds a gold ring, which he puts on, and rapidly discovers that by twisting the ring, he can make himself invisible. It's that kind of story. Gyges does not spend much time contemplating how to do good with his new powers. On the contrary, with the help of the ring, Gyges quickly gets into the royal palace, whereupon he seduces the queen, murders the king and seizes the throne. Glaucon argues that all of us would steal, murder and seduce if we had such a ring: we obey the law only because we face penalties for disobedience.* The rational action is to pursue your own

---

* Although we don't have magic rings, another form of invisibility is now available to users of Twitter and other social media. Celebrities are often abused and harassed on Twitter by followers who rely on online invisibility to escape sanction.

self-interest, even if it harms wider society, if there is no penalty for doing so. Effectively, Glaucon recommends free-riding whenever you can do so without penalty. Socrates rejects Glaucon's reasoning, arguing instead that everyone should obey the law even in the absence of sanctions. Free-riding is implicitly but emphatically rejected.

In the eighteenth century Adam Smith reached a similar conclusion to Socrates. Smith noticed that it can be smart for people to co-operate for mutual benefit, even if, individually, they can do better in the short term by not cooperating. The particular case of cooperation for mutual benefit that most interested Smith was business people co-operating to arrange a cartel or some other form of price-fixing: 'People of the same trade seldom meet together, even for merriment and diversion, but the conversation ends in a conspiracy against the public, or in some contrivance to raise prices.'[2] Smith and his followers concluded that in a capitalist economy there is a strong tendency towards cartels, monopolies and other forms of anti-competitive activity.

Price-fixing might seem an abstruse technical issue, but in the following century Marx took Smith's argument further, substantially raising the stakes in the process. Marx argued that the competition on which capitalism relied was being subverted by various forms of anti-competitive activity. Indeed, for Marx, capitalism was headed for self-destruction partly through the tendency of competition to be eroded away. By the 1930s many people agreed, concluding that communism was the answer. Today, it is easy to forget how the world looked to many people then. In an open letter to the *Manchester Guardian* in March 1933, George Bernard Shaw and twenty other prominent British socialists robustly defended Stalin's regime and rejected the evidence then emerging of mass famines in the Soviet Union. (Shaw remained a fan of Stalin. In 1950, asked for his choice for 'Man of the Half-century', Shaw suggested three – Stalin, Einstein and 'one whom I cannot modestly name'.)[3]

Against this background, there was a large audience in the West hungry for ideas which could be used to defend capitalism. And, specifically, for ideas to answer the question left open by Adam Smith: how to preserve competition when firms have a natural inclination to subvert it, to cooperate for mutual benefit?

One answer provided by thinkers after Smith, such as John Stuart Mill and Jeremy Bentham, was that people are often too short-sightedly irrational to collaborate for mutual benefit. For example, a firm which stood to gain more in the long term by joining a cartel or other price-fixing agreement would be tempted instead by the short-term profits from cutting prices and gaining market share over rivals. This argument had merit but now seemed too flimsy a basis on which to build a defence of capitalism. It was not enough to respond to the challenge posed by Marx merely by noting that firms are often too short-sighted to realize that their long-term interests lie in subverting competition. A big idea was needed.

Free-riding was that idea. It provides the crux of a powerful argument suggesting that competition is rational and natural after all. In this way of thinking, collaboration by firms is not smart but foolish, because every firm can free-ride on the collaborative efforts of other firms in the industry. As a result, cartels and other attempts to undermine competition will collapse. To see why, we need to explore a specific example of collaboration in a bit more detail.

Suppose that a small firm has agreed to restrict its sales to help uphold a price-fixing agreement. The firm will soon realize that it can make more profit by quietly ignoring the agreement and selling more. The agreement will not collapse immediately, because the extra sales made by one small firm will have a negligible effect on the market price.[4] In other words, the business owner will be thinking along the lines of *it makes no difference whether or not I do my bit to maintain the price-fixing agreement.* The firm should sell as much as it can, while free-riding on the higher price made possible by the sales restraint of other companies in that market. The snag is that since all firms in that market think like this, the agreement will soon collapse – or never get started in the first place, because firms anticipate the collapse. The logic of the argument suggests that price-fixing agreements are unsustainable – even though if companies could somehow sustain them they would all be better off.

This obscure technical argument about price-fixing, developed in the 1930s, has turned out to have a giant impact on modern life, because it is the genesis of all those now familiar free-riding arguments which conclude that cooperation is futile. But first the free-riding idea needed someone to bring it out of its relative obscurity in economic theory and apply it to wider society.[5]

Enter a farm boy from North Dakota. Mancur Olson was born in January 1932 in North Dakota's Red River Valley, into a Norwegian-American farming family.[6] Even when, decades later, he had become famous throughout the world of academia, he retained his Norwegian accent and humble farm-boy manner. As the awards and honours rolled in, he continued to begin his curriculum vitae with his social-security number – as if he needed to prove who he was. One characteristic pronouncement, delivered in the flat voice of the prairies, was 'Look for a problem that is interesting and important – never mind how it is classified – and tackle it. That is my advice to Mancur Olson, and that is my advice to everyone else.'[7]

As the eldest of three sons, Mancur was allowed to sit in on adult conversations about the prospects for the farm. There were many discussions about the difficulty in getting small farmers to work together, despite their shared interest in getting a fair price for their crops. The Olsons observed that back in Norway, and in the other Scandinavian countries, there seemed to be a much stronger tradition of getting people to work together for common interests, achieving both economic growth and a measure of equality for society at large. Mancur Olson never forgot these conversations, and by the time he came to write his PhD dissertation he was preoccupied with why some groups seem able to work together for their common interest, while others cannot. Like Ken Arrow's, Olson's early career involved military service – as a lieutenant in the US Air Force in 1961–3 – and time at RAND. Olson's breakthrough came when he took the economic theory of perfect competition between firms and applied it to a vast range of social situations. In his aptly titled 1965 masterwork *The Logic of Collective Action*, Olson built on the earlier argument about price fixing: small firms realize that there is no point in restraining their sales for the sake of the agreement, because, since their sales are a negligible part of the total market, their restraint makes no difference. True to his roots, Olson chose the example of a small farmer to apply this thinking: 'A farmer who placed the interests of other farmers above his own would not necessarily restrict his production to raise farm prices, since he would know that his sacrifice would not bring a noticeable benefit to anyone. Such a rational farmer, however unselfish, would not make such a futile and point-less sacrifice . . .'[8]

To push home his point about there being no virtue in doing your bit – making a sacrifice – when it makes no difference to anyone, Olson continued: 'Selfless behavior that has no perceptible effect is sometimes not even considered praiseworthy. A man who tried to hold back a flood with a pail would probably be considered more of a crank than a saint, even by those he was trying to help.'[9]

This striking metaphor brings out Olson's key insight. If it makes no difference whether or not you do your bit, then there is no point in making a futile sacrifice. So there is nothing immoral about free-riding: it's just the rational thing to do. Free-riding might seem selfish, but in these situations self-sacrifice helps no one. In arguing that rational people free-ride rather than cooperate, so that collective action is hard to sustain, Olson had a bigger target in mind than small farmers. He went after Marxism. Explicitly rejecting what he called 'Marxian theories of class action', he argued instead that the opportunity to free-ride will prevent groups acting together in pur-suit of their common interests. Only if there is some form of coercion will groups act collectively. As an illustration, Olson concluded that labour or trade unions must be coercive, otherwise they would not survive. For Olson, the trade union movement had the same authori-tarian overtones as the Soviet economies.

Unsurprisingly, Olson's revolutionary analysis was well received on the Right. Their intellectual leader, Friedrich Hayek, arranged for *The Logic of Collective Action* to be translated into German. By the 1980s, Olson's analysis appeared to fit neatly into the intellectual underpinnings of free-market worldviews such as Reaganomics and Thatcherism: cooperation and collective action are generally hard to sustain, so competition must be the natural state of affairs.

And yet, there is a puzzle. Despite the seemingly unassailable logic of Olson's argument, free-riding still has a dodgy reputation. Nowa-days it feels like many of us rely on *it makes no difference whether or not I do my bit* thinking to let ourselves off the hook in a wide range of situations – even though we don't really believe the argument. One reason for our unease might be that heavy-duty free-riders, the kind of people that devote their lives to free-riding, tend not to be very admirable, impressive or nice.

FREE-RIDERS V. LITTLE PEOPLE

Tax evasion is a strong form of free-riding. At the end of the 1980s Leona Helmsley, one of the biggest US tax evaders of the decade, explained her views about tax to her maid: 'We don't pay taxes. Only the little people pay taxes.'[10] Helmsley's lack of sympathy for other people was legendary, so we should not take this kind of arrogant flaunting of tax avoidance as typical of tax avoiders in general.* But even among people who need to maintain a reputation for being law-abiding, aggressive minimization of your tax bill is no longer something to be coy about. Former US Treasury Secretary Tim Geithner repeatedly forgot to pay tax on his earnings from working at the IMF. After an IRS audit, Geithner paid back taxes on only two of the four years owing, relying on the Statute of Limitations to avoid paying the rest. This suggests that Geithner (or his accountant) felt no moral obligation to pay all tax originally due. Geithner did pay the remaining two years' worth of tax – but later, just before being nominated for Treasury Secretary.[11] There has been a similar shift in corporate culture. When CEO Eric Schmidt was asked in 2012 about Google's tax-avoidance strategies, he replied, 'We are proudly capitalistic. I'm not confused about this. We pay lots of taxes; we pay them in the legally prescribed ways. I am very proud of the structure that we set up. We did it based on the incentives that the governments offered us to operate.'[12]

The size of Google means that its tax avoidance makes a meaningful difference to government revenues.[13] But for the rest of us little people, Helmsley's notorious phrase has it the wrong way round. For us, tax avoidance seems to make sense: it makes no difference to what the government can afford to do whether or not I pay my little

---

* Helmsley showed no sympathy towards those close to her. She left two grand-children nothing in her will, but left $12 million to her dog, a Maltese named Trouble. When the dog bit her housekeeper, Helmsley reportedly said, 'Good for you, Trouble, she deserved it!' (*New York Daily News*, 30 August 2007).

bit of tax. Restraining myself, refusing to engage in tax avoidance, appears to be pointless self-sacrifice.

If you resist this conclusion – perhaps because you *do* pay all your taxes – it is worth pausing to think if you nevertheless free-ride in other contexts instead. It is easy enough to do so, almost without noticing. As well as travelling on trains without a ticket, I free-ride if I sneak into a sports match or a music festival without paying. Or take a coffee from the office machine without putting money in the honesty box. Or accept that my community needs to recycle most household waste but don't bother to sort my own household re-cycling. Or exaggerate the value of an item lost when making an insurance claim. These free-rides are probably still regarded as mor-ally wrong by most of us. Yet according to the compelling logic of the free-riding argument, free-riding is the only rational thing to do, assuming that the likelihood of punishment or some form of social sanction is minimal. Maybe our morality just needs to catch up with our understanding of economics?

Maybe in some cases it already has. Many people illegally down-load music or read newspaper content for free online, relying on others to pay. Maybe you browsed this book and others in a book-shop, but while standing there you learned via your smartphone that it is cheaper on Amazon, so you didn't buy anything in the shop. Organizations from Ryanair to the UK National Health Service repeatedly poach skilled workers who have been expensively trained elsewhere. All these free-rides are widely regarded as acceptable. And free-riding is so *normal*. Nowadays accessing free music or other con-tent online is too commonplace to mention; past generations would have needed no less than Glaucon's invisibility ring to get free music from the record shop.

It is easy to see how the free-riders might justify their actions. Maybe I entered the sports match without paying because I've been a loyal fan for ages, buying season tickets in previous years. Now the club is owned by a billionaire but ticket prices have risen sharply, and I'm unemployed and short of cash. I take a coffee from the office machine without paying because I know that the suggested price I am supposed to pay has been calculated to allow for 'forgetfulness'. The machine still covers its costs even if not everyone pays. I'm taking one of the spare coffees. I do some illegal downloading because I pay for some music, the cost of supplying downloads is virtually zero and the band members are all millionaires. I inflate my insurance claim and deflate my tax return because I know several of my friends have done so, and so I assume most people do. Or perhaps I exaggerate my insurance claim because previously I made a legitimate claim but the insurance company refused to pay out on a technicality.

Some of these justifications are worth taking seriously in themselves. They invoke powerful ideas about fairness. However, as reasons for free-riding, they miss the point. Free-riding may or may not be fair or virtuous. But free-riding is always the smart thing to do, because you gain; and always the rational thing to do, because your contribution makes a negligible difference to the collective endeavour, so no one loses if you withdraw it. Yet the fact we use these *other* reasons to justify free-riding suggests that, despite the force of the argument for free-riding, we don't like to admit to the little free-rides sprinkled across our daily lives. The mystery only deepens.

Perhaps the explanation is straightforward. Perhaps we reject the logic of the free-riding argument after all. What if the little people rebel? What if everyone tried to evade tax whenever possible? What if everyone decided to free-ride whenever possible? The consequences for society would be disastrous.

There are two problems with this easy reply. First, it doesn't provide a positive reason to do your bit. As Yossarian in *Catch-22* realized, if everyone else is free-riding or otherwise acting selfishly, and you don't, no one gains and you lose. A society cannot survive on the back of a single taxpayer. Collective endeavours need more than a single contribution, so if everyone else is free-riding you don't achieve anything by doing your bit. Second, the free-rider can simply respond, 'But not everyone *does* free-ride. So I can rely on the contributions of others.' It is true that not everyone can free-ride. As a free-rider, I need other people to contribute and should encourage them to do so. So maybe I am inconsistent, or at least hypocritical, in discouraging other people from free-riding while doing it myself. But being a bit of a hypocrite seems better than a needless contribution to a collective endeavour which will happen anyway. And if it won't happen, doing your bit is as senseless as trying to hold back a flood with a pail.

In the wake of Mancur Olson's work, free-rider thinking spread across society in the 1970s. If Olson and his followers were right, previous generations were all making a huge mistake in their thinking about when and why to cooperate. They understood cooperation and the meaning of an individual contribution to a group effort in an entirely different way. How, for instance, did previous generations persuade people to pay their taxes? Partly, of course, with the threat of punishment if you were caught cheating. But just as importantly there was a shared understanding that it is in each individual's interest to pay their taxes. A diverse range of economists and philosophers agreed that if cooperation secures benefits for all concerned, that alone is good enough reason for each individual to contribute voluntarily to the cooperative enterprise.[14] A 1930s Italian economist even described people who do not voluntarily pay their taxes as 'a pathological group against which society must defend itself'.[15] So, back then, free-riding was regarded as acting *against* your own best interests – irrational, or even pathological.

If we're looking for a flaw in the argument for free-riding, this older perspective on doing your bit seems long overdue for a revival.

MAKING THINGS HAPPEN BEATS BEING INDISPENSABLE

What are you going to do at work next week? In my typical week, there are plenty of things which *must* be done. There is also a long list of other things to do, over which I have some discretion. But there is never enough time to do all of them. (Sound familiar?) I could decide to make a list of all the things I want to happen, then rank them in order of priority. In deciding the ranking, various considerations would come into play, such as the relative desirability or importance of the different things; the pleasure or otherwise of doing them myself; whether or not a colleague would do them if I don't; and, sometimes, the desire to be the person who makes a particular thing happen. Once I have things ranked in order of priority, I would simply work down the list from the top, until I ran out of time.

Do you make decisions in that way? No, I don't either. But we might see it as a hyper-rational way of making decisions, in some sense an ideal. And yet it is fundamentally incompatible with the thinking behind free-riding, because of one of the considerations just mentioned – whether or not a colleague would do something if I don't. According to free-rider thinking, if something is going to happen any-way, regardless of whether or not I do it myself, then it would be irrational to waste any time on it. It should not even be on my 'to do' list. It was this subtle principle, hidden in Mancur Olson's argument, that distinguished his analysis from all previous thinking. Stated in isolation, it might seem a very sensible principle. Yet its implications are deeply implausible and fly in the face of how we usually think.

To begin with, if it is stupid to spend time on something when I know that someone else will do it if I don't, then I should *only* do things in which my participation is indispensable – things which won't happen unless I do them. But no one would arrange their work-ing life, or indeed their life as a whole, on that basis. Suppose I am taking my dog for a walk on the beach and I see someone in the sea who looks in distress. I am a good swimmer. But there is another person nearby on the beach, who from her physique and clothing looks like a strong swimmer who has just emerged from the water. I judge that the strong swimmer will definitely rescue the person in distress if I don't. And only I can make sure my dog does not run off. Should I stay with my dog, or help the strong swimmer to save the person who might be drowning? Free-rider thinking is clear: the per-son in the water will almost certainly be saved in any case. I should keep hold of my dog because, unless I do, no one else will. It would be irrational to prioritize the person who might be drowning.[16]

Few of us think like this. We think there are good reasons to save the person in distress, even though they will be rescued regardless of our intervention. Deciding *not* to free-ride is just like that. It can be perfectly rational to contribute to a collective activity, even if the activity will still go ahead regardless of whether or not I contribute. At work I might prioritize working on a major team project for an important client over doing the client bills, even though I am the only one authorized to do the bills. The project just matters more, even though the work on it would progress in my absence. In this situation I do not think *it makes no difference whether or not I do it*. I believe that I *have* made a difference: I have helped cause something to happen. I have done my bit for the team effort.

The argument for free-riding assumes that my contribution to some collective project or activity can make a difference only if the activity will not happen *unless* I contribute. But the story about the person who may be drowning shows that we do not think like this, at least some of the time. I believe that I can make a difference even if, without my contribution, others would have ensured the activity goes ahead. I make a difference because *my* contribution helps cause it to happen: it is *my* effort that helps bring it about, rather than just the activities of others. If I contribute, I am responsible (along with others) for the collective activity.

Obama's election in 2008 was a powerful illustration of this way of thinking. His famous line 'You are the change you've been waiting for' brilliantly exploited the desire of some voters to be 'part of' the endeavour to get him elected – to help bring that about, even if it was probably going to happen anyway. Research by pollsters at the time showed that many of the 'don't knows' shifted to supporting Obama once it became clear he was likely to win. This 'bandwagon effect' has been observed in many other elections too. Yet it contradicts free-rider thinking: if one candidate seems highly likely to win, so your vote will make no difference to the outcome, why make the effort?

It is one thing to identify behaviour where free-rider thinking does not prevail, such as election bandwagon effects or office teamwork. Perhaps these are just isolated instances. But is there any systematic rejection of free-rider thinking nowadays, even when the stakes are high?

Yes, because of how we think about responsibility. It is not just that people in distress in the sea are rescued by saintly dog-walkers passing by. More worrying for free-rider thinking is how we treat these rescuers. We honour them and praise them – you weren't surprised when I called them saintly. We do *not* say that the rescuer deserves no credit, because they are not responsible for the rescue, and made no difference, because someone else would have stepped in to save the person if the rescuer didn't. Our thinking about responsibility is especially well developed in connection with serious crimes: the meaning of criminal responsibility has been discussed over thousands of years of popular debate and legal argument, leading to a strong consensus.[17] Different legal systems agree that if two gangsters corner an enemy in a dark alley and both of them point their guns at their victim, intending to kill, but only one of them fires, then the gangster who fired is responsible for the murder. We do not say: 'Had the gangster not fired, the other gangster was certain to do so. Therefore the first gangster didn't make any difference; the murder would have happened anyway.' But this is precisely the view of responsibility behind the free-riding argument.

Once we uncover this perverse view of responsibility, a view which greatly restricts how an individual's contribution can make a difference, then free-rider thinking itself begins to seem equally perverse. Mostly in life we do not restrict our efforts to activities where our contribution is absolutely essential for the success of the activity. Yet the free-riding argument says we are irrational unless we focus on being indispensable in this way. So at the very least, the free-riding argument is shaky: often it is not irrational to contribute to a collective activity, even if the activity will happen anyway. Buried inside free-rider thinking is a view about what it means to 'bring something about' or 'cause something to happen' – a hidden assumption about the meaning of cause and effect.[18]

What should we conclude from all this?

On the one hand, free-rider thinking doesn't just run counter to our common sense, our ideas about responsibility and so on, it also runs counter to the arguments of generations of thinkers before Olson, including Socrates, Adam Smith, David Hume, John Stuart Mill and Karl Marx. They thought that if you benefit from a collective activity, then that alone is reason enough to contribute to it (providing that your benefit from the collective activity exceeds the cost of contributing). And, it's worth noting, their argument for doing your bit appeals purely to self-interest, rather than expecting individuals to make sacrifices for the sake of the common good.

On the other hand, the logic of the free-riding argument has not gone away. If you avoid paying tax, don't vote or don't do your bit to reduce carbon emissions, you are unlikely to have been persuaded to give up free-riding just yet. Why *exactly* should you contribute to some collective activity, if the activity will happen in any case?

One reason has been mentioned already: you might contribute because you want to be involved – you want to be 'part of the change', you want to belong, rather than watching from the sidelines. Many economists snigger at this possibility, dismissing it as a desire for 'warm glow'. As so often, economists' language used to describe virtuous behaviour subtly belittles it. 'Warm glow' suggests a narcissistic smugness, self-centredness rather than altruism, insinuating that an altruistic or political act is really all about you. Yet wanting to help bring about some collective goal – actively contributing to it – makes sense only if you identify with and value the outcome as an end in itself. Desiring the outcome is the reason for your contribution; any warm glow you feel is just a by-product of your involvement. Of course, the sense of fulfilment associated with helping bring about some collective goal may be outweighed by the drawbacks of making a contribution. Many blood donors get this kind of fulfilment, a sense of doing their bit, from giving blood – but still not enough satisfaction to give blood every time they are invited to do so, because of the time and inconvenience involved. And not many people get a deep sense of fulfilment from paying tax.

However, there are two more general reasons for doing your bit. First, there is uncertainty. For the sake of simplicity, we have assumed so far that the collective project or activity will *definitely* still happen, regardless of whether you contribute. But in reality there is always uncertainty. I am never absolutely sure that other people will step in if I don't do my bit. Even with the best intentions, few work colleagues are a completely reliable back-up if I don't get things done. Perhaps the election will be decided by one vote. And perhaps the other person on the beach – the strong swimmer who has just emerged from the sea – is in fact to blame for the person in distress in the water and I have stumbled on the scene of an attempted murder by drowning. Second, in many cases when I am tempted to free-ride it *will* make a difference if I do so: the final outcome will not be exactly the same. If I evade paying tax, there is a real loss of tax revenue to the government. It may be small, but it is not zero. Free-riding makes a difference whenever a collective endeavour or project is made up of the sum of individual contributions, and more contributions imply a more successful project. When I do not bother to recycle my household waste or give blood but rely on others to do so I make a small difference to the success of these socially valuable activities. Yet there is a widespread belief that my tiny contribution to a large project is so negligible that it can be ignored.

These points may seem minor, but their implications are major.

CLIMATE CHANGE and me

I am worried about climate change. I really am. But what can I do? It is absurd to believe that the car I drive, or the number of flights I take, or whether I fit solar panels on my house, can make any difference to the big picture. The UK as a whole, for instance, is responsible for only around 2 per cent of global emissions. Climate change is going to happen regardless of what we do. And the scale of the problem is barely comprehensible. Across the world in 2017, more than 170 tonnes of coal were burned *every second*.[19]

The enormity of the climate-change problem and the negligible impact of individual actions are two themes that arise repeatedly in focus groups on public attitudes and are echoed by large corporations and governments.[20] Together, they are probably the biggest obstacle to radical action to address climate change. But we should be suspicious: as ever when free-riding beckons, it is extremely tempting to let ourselves off the hook, to assume that individual contributions make no difference.[21]

The psychology of cognitive dissonance tells us that when the truth is uncomfortable, we often respond by falling into self-deception. This need not be due to selfishness: it may be that if I make an uncomfortable effort or sacrifice now, I will gain much more later. But this kind of self-control is hard to achieve. Psychologists have shown that thinking about an experience in the present will be more 'salient' – more vivid, more prominent in our minds – than the same experience in the future. So we pay more attention to an immediate sacrifice than a distant future benefit. If I pretend to myself that my contribution makes no difference, then I can avoid the vivid, immediate sacrifice.

There are other psychological forces which lead us to underestimate the difference our 'negligible' contributions make. If the context of a contribution is local, small, personal or temporary, we underestimate the impact it can have on an outcome which is global, large, public or permanent, because the two contexts are cognitively distinct.[22] This is why in 1883 Thomas Huxley, rightly regarded as one of the greatest biologists of his era, could nevertheless write: 'probably all the great sea fisheries are inexhaustible; that is to say that nothing we do seriously affects the number of fish'.[23] He simply could not imagine a permanent reduction in fish stocks, given the scale of fishing he observed and the temporary losses it implied – temporary because breeding constantly replenishes stocks.

As well as these unconscious cognitive errors, there are also flaws in our conscious reasoning about contributing to collective activities and projects. Suppose my contribution really is negligible relative to the size of the project. That fact alone is not enough to justify doing nothing. Mixing the metaphors, in order to let myself off the hook, I have to be able to pass the buck. After all, my contribution makes a difference, however small. To justify not contributing myself, I have to believe that although I cannot make a useful difference, someone else can. In the case of climate change, corporations and governments can make a difference on a scale I cannot.

This response is fine as far as it goes – but it doesn't go very far, certainly not far enough to let you off the hook. To begin with, individuals usually bear some responsibility for the large impacts of corporations and governments. When governments support fossil-fuel-based energy and corporations supply it, this is in large part because we demand cheap energy, and a lot of it. And just because governments or other powerful actors in society should act, it does not follow that I need not bother.

It bears repeating: small contributions are small, not zero. When I donate money to famine relief and my donation pays for food which saves the life of one child, that donation is clearly a worthwhile contribution. It remains worthwhile even if many people still die from the famine, lives which could have been saved through more donations from me or others.[24] There is a psychological dimension here as well as a moral one. Excessive focus on the enormity of the total task leads us to ignore the value of completing part of the task, even a small part. To overcome this 'focusing illusion', we must frame the task or problem differently. Saving single lives is worthwhile; so, too, is reducing carbon emissions in my household, city or country. The total task is no more than the sum of these smaller gains and cannot be completed without them.

Another problem with our fixation on the enormity of the total task is that we overlook the contributions already made by others, contributions which diminish the task remaining – and so my individual contribution becomes more significant. My judgement that my contribution is negligible often assumes that no one else is contributing. Governments and large corporations often assume this too, whether through self-deception or deliberately seeking an excuse for inaction. In Britain, the individual contribution of the aviation sector to total UK emissions is currently around 6 per cent – a figure which is repeatedly used by aviation lobbyists to argue that the sector's contribution is relatively minor and so government intervention is unwarranted. But because of the efforts being made elsewhere in the economy to adopt green technology and reduce consumption, the contribution of aviation will rise to around 21 per cent by 2050. The negligibility of the aviation contribution rests on ignoring these efforts. And there is more: the 21 per cent estimate is based on business as usual: it assumes that emissions reductions elsewhere in the economy will simply maintain current trends. If we assume instead that these other emissions will be in line with what they *should* be (according to the UK's official national carbon budget), then aviation's contribution rises to somewhere between 50 and 100 per cent of total emissions by 2050.

Finally, and most importantly, we have so far looked only at the direct effects of individual contributions, but there are usually indirect effects too. We've seen how Buchanan and the other public choice theorists were puzzled by rational people bothering to vote, because in many electoral systems your vote has no direct effect on the candidate elected – unless the election is decided by one vote, which is extremely unlikely. But this so-called 'paradox of voting' is in truth not paradoxical at all. I vote because my vote has the indirect effect of increasing my preferred candidate's mandate. With more votes cast in her favour, my preferred candidate can demonstrate greater support for her policies; in a democracy this should increase the chance of these policies being put into practice. Similarly, when I fit solar panels on my roof at home, the indirect effects may be more important than the direct reduction in carbon emissions: my action may stimulate friends and neighbours to fit panels; it may help market demand for panels reach the level where economies of scale in their production kick in, reducing panel prices; it shows a willingness to incur a large upfront cost to obtain renewable energy, which may change politicians' views about popular support for renewable energy. These indirect effects arise in many contexts. My individual contribution can often influence others, raise market demand or change politicians' perceptions of public support – and indirect effects such as these can help cross-cultural, economic or political 'tipping points', in turn triggering wider change. The tipping point can have political and social consequences as well as economic ones. Once enough people do their bit – diligent household recycling or installing solar panels – this behaviour becomes 'normal' rather than restricted to the lone Green Warrior in the neighbourhood.

Even when free-rider thinking pays attention to indirect effects, it assumes we know their size, and the location of the tipping point, so the probability of your contribution crossing the tipping point can be calculated. But usually in reality, none of this is known. Tipping points are often entirely unexpected, their existence becoming clear only with hindsight.

The upshot of all these possibilities is that the overall effect of your contribution to some collective effort can often be significant, because you can influence the thinking and behaviour of others. Much of the blame for our believing otherwise lies with economists, not just for their advocacy of free-riding as the smart choice but for the world-view influenced by their 'physics envy': each of us is like an atom, having negligible effect on the system around us. However, part of the blame lies with us, because the belief that each of us has a negligible effect on the world around us is just the flip side of our cherished belief that *others* have no effect on *us*. Most of us, consciously or not, embrace some kind of sovereign fantasy: we assume that we are completely autonomous, even though the evidence against this is overwhelming. Humans are social beings to their core and our beliefs and behaviour are heavily influenced by observing and learning from others.

The dark side of the sovereign fantasy is the belief that I cannot influence others because they are sovereign decision-makers too. This idea, together with the belief that individual contributions are negligible, constitutes the cornerstone of individualism, implying that I can forget any wider social consequences of my actions and focus just on my own interests. I can act with impunity because my actions make no difference to society. But if my actions make no difference, I am also powerless to effect social change. A belief in the negligibility of your contribution doesn't just license free-riding. It encourages a fatalistic view of the world in which individual action to bring about social or political change is pointless. Powerful people who seek to discourage the rest of us from challenging the status quo have good reason to promote the belief that you can't make a difference.

HEAPS, HARMLESS TORTURERS AND HESITANT POLITICIANS

Try this experiment. Take a clean sheet of paper. Add a small amount of sand, say the amount you can pinch between two fingers. Then add roughly the same amount of sand again, dropping it on top of the rest. Do you have a heap of sand? Not yet. Keep adding sand, a pinch at a time. Do you have a heap now? It seems unlikely, because a pinch of sand is not enough to turn a non-heap into a heap. If you don't already have a heap, adding another pinch makes no difference. Unfortunately, this logic always holds: another pinch is never enough to make a difference, so you can never make a heap of sand in this way. And yet if you add sand for several hours, surely you have a heap? Philosophers have been teased and tortured by this paradox ever since the ancient Greek philosophers first identified it; they label it the Sorites paradox, after the classical Greek for 'heaped up'. There is no straightforward solution to the Sorites paradox.[25] The problem is inherent in the meaning of 'heap'. There seems to be no distinct threshold between a non-heap and a heap, one which can be crossed by a pinch of sand. Instead there seems to be a vague range of piles of sand which are just about big enough to qualify as heaps.

This kind of vagueness is very common. If a man loses all his hair little by little over time, each hair lost does not make enough difference to turn him bald, so how does he go bald? Here is a refutation of free-riding and bogus ideas about negligibility: each individual contribution seems to make no difference, yet together they bring about a significant change. This argument against free-riding is so important that it's worth looking at another thought experiment which focuses explicitly on how small acts by different people can together make a big difference – the *Puzzle of the Harmless Torturers*.[26]

In the Bad Old Days, a thousand torturers each had a different victim. Each torturer pressed the button on a torture device a thousand times. Their victims could not perceive the extra pain from each button press but the cumulative effect of a thousand presses left them in horrendous pain. All the victims suffered in the same way, from separate but identical devices.

But now the torturers develop moral scruples. They change how they work. Each torturer now presses the button on a torture device just once, but they do this for every device: they press once on each of a thousand torture devices. The victims suffer the same horrendous pain. But none of the torturers makes any single victim's pain perceptibly worse, so each torturer sleeps peacefully, pleased to be a harmless torturer.

Such thought experiments are nice puzzles, but it is hard to believe they help us make decisions in the real world. Yet the Puzzle of the Harmless Torturers may be an exception. It has, arguably, led to a rare thing: progress in moral philosophy. Most philosophers are now convinced that a series of negligible harms can add up to something substantial, *even if each harm is truly imperceptible*. The same goes for benefits. This surprising conclusion matters to the rest of us because – as we've seen with climate change and fishing – many real-world situations have an analogous structure. Imagine some large area of land which you perceive as 'unspoilt' – perhaps a national park. Bit by bit the park is developed, with a few sensitively designed houses spread about and some small access roads. Slowly, the houses and roads accumulate. Eventually, most visitors decide the park is 'spoilt', but exactly when did that happen? How much development is compatible with leaving the park unspoilt?

The Puzzle of the Harmless Torturers and the Sorites paradox show us that these are hard questions. The park really does end up spoilt; it is not an optical illusion. The problem lies in the vagueness of concepts like 'spoilt', which allows developers to argue that small developments make no difference. Elsewhere, free-riders can exploit vagueness to justify their claim that individual contributions make no difference.

But any simplistic attempt to make vague concepts precise is clearly doomed to failure. It is not just that no one has the power to meddle with our use of ordinary language. The vagueness is inherent in the concept. A 'heap' just *is* a vague thing – it would be absurd to assume instead that there is a clear threshold, a precise number of grains of sand, that differentiates a non-heap from a heap. And yet this absurd imposition of sharp thresholds is just what free-rider thinking requires of us.

To see why, let's return to the common-sense objection to free-riding: what if everyone did it? According to Mancur Olson's analysis, there are three cases to consider. The first two are straightforward: (i) If everyone free-rides, the collective project will not happen, so my non-contribution makes no difference; (ii) If no one else free-rides, the collective project *will* happen, so again my non-contribution makes no difference. In both cases, the conclusion is that I should free-ride.[27] But what about the intermediate case (iii): Some people free-ride and some people contribute? Then, according to Olson, I should free-ride only if other people are contributing enough that the project can go ahead without my contribution.[28]

The problem here is not quite the obvious one – how much is enough? – but the assumption that there is an answer to that question. Olson's analysis assumes that there *is* a threshold or tipping point, beyond which there are enough contributions for the project to go ahead. But life is not like that. The collective project or goal may be defined in terms of inherently vague concepts, like the goal of retaining an unspoilt national park. And even if the goal can be precise in principle, in practice it may be impossible to identify where the threshold or tipping point lies. One of the big difficulties with securing global agreement on substantial measures to tackle climate change is the disagreement over how much climate change is tolerable and, prior to that, how to define and measure the extent of change. Against this background, free-riding is especially tempting, because there is no tipping point triggering drastic climate change to worry about. Or rather, if such a point exists, there is uncertainty or disagreement concerning where it lies. And this kind of uncertainty can arise even in circumstances, like voting, where the tipping point seems absolutely clear.

The Great Reform Act of 1832 began the process of extending the franchise towards universal suffrage in Britain. Although its effects were modest – even after the act, only one in six adult men could vote (and no women) – the act was passed only after the country became virtually ungovernable because of huge political unrest. There were riots across England, with mob rule over Bristol for three days. Protesters urged a run on the banks: £1.5 million (about £160 million in modern terms) was withdrawn from the Bank of England. In this atmosphere, an important vote in Parliament was won by just one vote. That decisive vote was cast by John Calcraft, who spoke fiercely against reform, then changed his mind at the last moment. Given the strength of feeling on both sides, this did not go down well: 'He killed himself six months later, correctly imagining himself to be hated by both sides equally.'[29]

As we have seen, free-rider thinking implies it is worth voting only if your vote is decisive – if the election hangs on one vote. In elections, there *is* a sharp threshold, so in principle free-rider thinking makes sense. If your vote will not cross the threshold – if you are sure that one side will win by a large margin – then it seems pointless to vote. At least in terms of its direct effects, your vote will make zero difference to the outcome. Free-riding seems more compelling because your contribution truly makes zero difference.

But in practice free-rider thinking here faces the same problem as in the climate change example: the difficulty of identifying the threshold. Even in the extremely rare case where your vote might be decisive, your decision is upset by people like John Calcraft who change their minds at the last moment. While having the chance to cast the decisive vote might sound like a great power trip, Calcraft's ending reminds us that most people do not want to be in that position. Suppose Obama had been elected by just one vote: would you want to be known publicly to Republicans as the one who elected him? The closest modern US result was in Florida in 2000; again, a sharp threshold for electoral success was hard to identify, lost in a haze of 'hanging chads'. In Britain, the recount process is no clearer: it continues until one side gives up in despair or exhaustion. In the 1997 general election, Mark Oaten won the seat of Winchester by just two votes, after multiple recounts. Then the loser got the result declared invalid in court on a technicality, so the election was re-run. Oaten won again, this time with a majority of 20,000.* The evidence of closely contested real elections, then, suggests that theoretically clear thresholds are hard to identify in practice – one more reason why it is foolish to use free-rider thinking to decide whether or not to vote.[30]

And even in cases where a sharp threshold can be identified, there is yet another problem with free-rider thinking. It implies that I should contribute only if we are just below the threshold – only if my contribution adds enough to lift total contributions above the threshold. Unfortunately, if everyone thinks like this, the result will be a giant game of Chicken. Everyone is trying not to contribute until the last possible moment, in the hope of avoiding doing so. But if just one person miscalculates, the collective project collapses and everyone loses. In most contexts, this is a stupidly risky way to live. And it leads to a highly unstable society.

The rise of free-rider thinking is not a straightforward story about a crazy idea wreaking havoc. Or a sensible idea distorted and deformed so that it begins to do more harm than good. Instead there has been a small but profound shift in our thinking about how, as individuals, we can or cannot 'make a difference' – a shift so subtle that it has

---

* But within ten years Oaten had resigned after the revelation of his involvement in a string of bizarre sex scandals, something he ascribed to a 'mid-life crisis'.

taken some deep intellectual excavation to uncover it, even though the effects can now be seen everywhere.

Just a few decades ago it was the free-riders, not the contributors, who would have been seen as 'irrational'. According to Socrates and Adam Smith (among others), free-rider thinking departs from wise thinking in multiple ways: small contributions matter, the indirect effects of our contributions matter too, and people deserve credit (or blame) for helping make something happen, even if it would have happened anyway. Free-rider thinking relies on identifying a threshold of 'enough' contributions by others, something that may be impossible even in principle and is almost always risky in practice. And finally, we should be open to the possibility that people will behave selflessly rather than selfishly. In his working life Mancur Olson was always giving his time for free and contributing to collaborative academic projects, expecting nothing in return, rather than free-riding. All these considerations suggest a hopelessly complex approach to decision-making, but there is a simple rule of thumb which even the selfish can live by, a rule which gives the right answer most of the time: contribute if you estimate that your long-term benefit from the collective endeavour at least matches the cost of your contribution. Free-rider thinking has introduced a particular form of needless strategizing into modern life. We will all be better off the sooner we recover the ancient wisdom that cooperation generally beats free-riding.

6

The Economics of Everything

Ever wondered how the rich do theme parks? Their children want to visit Disney World like everyone else, but it is hard to imagine the global elite – or their offspring – spending hours queuing for the rides. One answer is that for around $500 an hour Disney will provide a 'VIP tour guide' who will escort you to the front of the queue for selected rides that you have pre-booked. But another solution has recently emerged, both cheaper and more flexible. For $130 an hour, DreamTours Florida will provide a black-market disabled guide to pose as a family member, allowing you to jump the queue along with them. As one Manhattan mother boasted: 'They escorted me, my husband and two children through the park in a motorized scooter with a handicapped sign on it. We waited less than one minute to get on the It's a Small World ride when the other kids had to wait over two hours. This is how the 1 per cent does Disney.'[1]

Queue-jumping is a fast-growing industry. In the US you can now pay LineStanding.com to employ someone (they often use the homeless) to do it for you. The lobbyists who work for big corporations are heavy users of this kind of service. They pay to have someone stand in line to enter Congressional hearings and Supreme Court sittings, often overnight, so the lobbyist can step in just before the session starts. In November 2016, long queues formed outside banks across India as people rushed to change high-denomination notes before they ceased to be legal tender; the rich employed the poor to queue for them. Queue-jumping is one among many things in which trade used to be socially taboo, or even illegal. A Chinese teenager (known as Little Zheng to his friends) sold his kidney to pay for an iPad. Convicts in some US prisons pay an upgrade for a better class of cell.

Companies routinely take out insurance policies on their employees' lives, policies which they then sell on to investors: there is a multibillion-dollar market in these bets on death, originally known as 'dead peasants insurance'.[2]

Many of us disapprove of these kinds of trades – but what exactly is wrong with them? Media outrage over Little Zheng's sale of his kidney seemed more than anything due to his purchase of an iPad with the proceeds. (Presumably, if he had sold his kidney to pay for hospital treatment for his sister, that would have been okay.) A market in kidneys or other organs seems distasteful but, if it increases the supply of organs, then lives will probably be saved. Academics express horror at the idea of richer students buying their way into elite universities. But a simple auction of elite university places might help open them up to ambitious but poor students who value the opportunity highly. Still, almost all of us agree that *some* things should not be for sale. Yet as soon as we contemplate something which might be on that list, there seem to be powerful arguments for opening it up to the free market after all.

It wasn't like this in the olden days, they say. But the historical trend is not a simple slide towards everything for sale. The lively market in child labour in Victorian Britain has, thankfully, become a taboo trade in most modern societies. What distinguishes twenty-first-century life from all previous eras is not that 'more' things are traded in markets nowadays (what would that mean? how would we count up?) but a change in the way we think: our growing willingness to apply economic thinking to all aspects of life. The arguments we hear nowadays for markets in art, education, kidneys, procreation, queue-jumping, and so on, were unheard of as recently as the 1960s.

This change did not happen by accident. From the late 1950s a handful of economists began to apply economic analysis to areas of life hitherto beyond the realm of economics. The door to this profound expansion of the scope of economics was opened by game theorists like John von Neumann and Oscar Morgenstern, and avowedly mathematical economists like Ken Arrow. In their work, humans were single-purpose robots, constantly calculating in order to maximize their 'payoff' (in game theory) or their 'preference satisfaction' (in Arrow and most mathematical economics). With this astonishingly limited representation of humanity in hand, there is no reason to restrict attention to the traditional economic realm of producing and consuming stuff. If humans are neither more nor less than robotic maximizers, their maximizing behaviour in other areas of life can be just as readily studied. This was an extension of economic thinking entirely consistent with von Neumann's dream to create an all-encompassing science of society.

The Chicago economist Gary Becker was the pioneer and leader of this new adventure to expand the scope of economics. At first Becker's efforts were ridiculed. When he first spoke of children as 'durable consumer goods' his audience of economists just laughed. Later, this colonization of the rest of our lives by economic thinking was derided by critics as *economic imperialism*. Their mockery soon backfired, with Becker and his followers cheerfully adopting the moniker as a description of their project. By the time Becker won the Nobel Prize in 1992, many of his ideas had become part of mainstream economic thinking and had begun to filter into everyday life. Where Becker led, governments followed. In 1987 Becker caused uproar when he proposed that the right to immigrate to a country should go to the highest bidder. This idea, far from shocking us, now shapes immigration policy in the US and many EU countries: anyone can immigrate if they buy enough assets in the host country. In 2019, buying £2 million of UK bonds or stocks gives you the right to live in Britain. Spend £3 million more to cut the waiting time for permanent residence (and once you have that, you can have your cake and eat it by selling your assets and getting your £5 million back).

For many people over forty, with distant memories of the Nanny State, the free market still seems like an exhilarating freedom, a kind of voting machine: it gives us what we want, and more of it, the more we are willing to pay. But where to draw the line with our economic thinking? Globally, we are willing to pay more for anti-wrinkle treatments than for malaria treatments. Does that mean anti-wrinkle treatments are more valuable? And if meaningful access to political and legal systems can be obtained only by those with enough money to pay for good lobbyists, line-standers and lawyers, what does that imply for democracy and justice? And, given that the scope of economic thinking has expanded so dramatically and rapidly in recent decades, where will it take us in the future?

THE NEW ECONOMICS OF EVERYTHING

Ironically, given that he would become notorious for analysing all human behaviour through the lens of selfish *homo economicus*, the thing that first got Gary Becker thinking about economics seems more altruistic than selfish. As a teenager in 1940s Brooklyn, Gary started reading the financial pages of newspapers, not out of interest – 'I was rather bored by it,' he confessed – but to help his businessman father, whose eyesight was failing. Soon, young Gary was transformed: 'Entering Princeton, I was a socialist,' he explained. 'Two years or so later I was no longer a socialist.' Becker pinpointed the catalysts for his transformation: 'two things: Milton Friedman and economics'.[3] Becker would go on to embrace economics as a universal way of thinking, arguably to a greater extent than any economist before him.

The genesis of big shifts in how we think is often obscure. But here there is no doubt. Becker was the first to extend economic reasoning to aspects of life seemingly far removed from the economy itself. This single-minded, lifelong project began with his PhD thesis, *The Economics of Discrimination*. Becker focused on the idea that bigotry is financially costly to the bigot: an employer who hires a white worker rather than a black one who is better qualified for the job incurs a cost in doing so. Discrimination is in fact defined by this cost, Becker reasoned, because there will be a financial cost to the employer if and only if the best person for the job is *not* chosen – which seems a good way of defining when discrimination has occurred. This definition ignores the employer's motivation. It does not matter, Becker argued, whether the black best candidate for the job is not hired because their employer is a pure bigot, or because other employees refuse to work with a black, or because customers don't want to look at a black face. Whatever the appalling explanation, the black candidate who should have got the job did not – and this fact alone is sufficient to alert us to discrimination.

Becker's analysis leaves most of us feeling uneasy, even if we can't immediately spot what's wrong with it. The problems begin with Becker's definition of discrimination: that discrimination occurs *only if* there is a financial cost to the discriminator. In reality, a firm might refuse to hire the best job applicant for bigoted reasons without incurring a financial cost – missing out on the best applicant is unlikely to affect profits if that employee would be just one among many. In these circumstances, there is no discrimination, according to Becker's definition. And a landlord may suffer no financial loss if they select only white tenants on racist grounds, so long as those tenants pay their rent and maintain the property. Again, Becker's theory is blind to this discrimination.

But even behaviour which does satisfy Becker's narrow definition of discrimination is less of a problem than we might imagine, because the free market will fix it. Or so Becker argued: in the textbook world of competitive markets, any firm with higher production costs than its rivals (whether due to discrimination or not) must either lower its costs (cease discriminating) or be forced out of business. Becker concluded that in competitive markets discrimination cannot exist – it is at most a fleeting phenomenon. Despite being ignored for many years after its first publication in 1957, *The Economics of Discrimination* has since become much, much more than an ivory-tower exercise. Richard Epstein, a highly influential American legal scholar, has argued that the US Civil Rights Act should be repealed on the basis of Becker's arguments: since discrimination does not exist, Epstein reasons, anti-discrimination laws are intrusive and unnecessary.

Today, Becker's ideas have become impossible to avoid – and they remain deeply controversial. Becker doesn't so much divide opinion as dynamite open a vast chasm with his ideas, forcing people to jump one way or the other. Among *Financial Times* writers alone, one long-established contributor wrote enthusiastically about Becker's approach to discrimination, while another regards him as beyond parody.[4] Evidence for the latter view is not hard to find. Take perhaps Becker's most famous work, which he laboured on for many years, *A Treatise on the Family*.

The *Treatise* argues that it is efficient for two people to marry and 'specialize', as Becker put it, meaning one person works for pay while the other stays at home doing housework and raising children. Becker's argument was an attempt to apply Adam Smith's idea about division of labour: if workers specialize in particular tasks, they will be more productive overall. Becker reasoned that marriages with one earner would be more common than other household arrangements because this kind of specialization raised the household's productivity and in turn its standard of living. Believing that women have a 'comparative advantage' in raising children, Becker concluded that women should stay at home while men take paid work. The *Treatise* was published in 1981 – just as the evidence turned overwhelmingly against Becker, with many more women in Western countries taking paid work. But it's not just the mismatch between Becker's stories and the facts; it's the way he tells them. Here's Becker on love:

> It can be said that M_i loves F_j if her welfare enters his utility function, and perhaps also if M_i values emotional and physical contact with F_j. Clearly, M_i can benefit from a match with F_j, because he could then have a more favourable effect on her welfare – and thereby on his own utility – and because the commodities measuring 'contact' with F_j can be produced more cheaply when they are matched than when M_i has to seek an 'illicit' relationship with F_j.[5]

In case you were wondering, the 'commodity' in the last sentence is children. As for women who take paid work outside the home, they are repeatedly labelled 'deviant' by Becker. In a footnote he states 'that "deviant" is used in a statistical, and not a pejorative sense' – although even in 1981 working women were hardly a statistical outlier. Elsewhere in the *Treatise*, Becker argues that women would generally benefit from the legalization of polygamy, approvingly citing Ayatollah Khomeini of Iran – not an authority famous for his understanding of women's interests – in support of his argument.[6]

Becker's disregard for the facts was not limited to his work on the family. During the 2007–10 financial crisis he was asked whether low-waged and unemployed people who took out huge mortgages which they could not possibly hope to repay were rational. Becker answered yes, they were perfectly rational, since any default was on the lender's capital, not their own.[7] True, but the defaulter still ends up homeless – and being rational surely requires that you prioritize keeping a roof over your head over taking risks with other people's money.

All this begs a question: if Becker's own work epitomizes the absurdity of applying economic thinking to manifestly non-economic aspects of life, why is economic thinking nevertheless being extended into more and more areas of contemporary life? More bluntly, how has Becker been so influential on twenty-first-century life if his theories are so obviously flawed?

THE ELUSIVE FREAKONOMICS OF GARY BECKER

One reason for the influence of Becker's work is, quite simply, its accessibility for other economists. Much cutting-edge research in economics has become like theoretical physics or avant-garde poetry: only intelligible to a small group of insiders. Even for economists, some economic theory outside their specialist field is as unapproachable as James Joyce's *Finnegans Wake* – while most of Gary Becker's work reads more like Dr Seuss.

But a bigger part of the answer is that Becker's theories are in many respects quite subtle – or perhaps 'slippery' would be a better word. Becker's critics have repeatedly portrayed his approach as selfish *homo economicus* on the rampage. This is a basic misunderstanding. In the third sentence of his Nobel Prize lecture in 1992, Becker denied any assumption of selfishness in his work. On the contrary, he 'tried to pry economists away from narrow assumptions about self-interest'. But if applying economic thinking to non-economic aspects of life is not about assuming selfishness, what is it about? Becker described his approach as assuming 'that individuals maximise welfare *as they conceive it*, whether they be selfish, altruistic, loyal, spiteful, or masochistic'.

As with von Neumann, Morgenstern and Arrow before him, Becker's focus was on the mathematical representation of human thinking – as maximization – rather than on *what* they maximize. The exact meaning of 'welfare' was not important. For Becker, then, our behaviour is driven by the desire to maximize something – get as much of what we want as possible – but our goals can be varied and need not involve money or any materialistic goal.

As Becker put it in an assertive summary of his way of thinking in 1976, *The Economic Approach to Human Behavior*, the twin assumptions that people are maximizers, and markets are mostly free and competitive, 'used relentlessly and unflinchingly, form the heart of the economic approach.'[8] To say this definition of the economic approach proved influential is an understatement: it has become many economists' favourite way of defining economics. The main reason why was clearly stated by Becker: 'the economic approach is a comprehensive one that is applicable to all human behaviour'.[9] Economists were liberated from the mundane study of the economy; they could now claim expertise in all aspects of life. This was the moment economic imperialism emerged, all guns blazing, into the limelight. The movement begun by Becker in 1976 led to economists doing research on a vast range of new topics, later popularized in books such as *Freakonomics* (2005), *The Undercover Economist* (2005) and *The Logic of Life* (2008).

This new kind of economics is puzzling. It claims to say something about everything yet relies on almost nothing in terms of assumptions. This is surely a con. In fact, on closer inspection, Becker's work assumes more than just that people maximize something. That is an assumption which could be used to describe the behaviour of almost anyone. Yet Becker's theories about the family do not seem to be about anyone: they seem to be about people who think in very peculiar ways. There must be more to the elusive economics of Gary Becker. We need to dig deeper to uncover the hidden assumptions.

Becker's approach can be used to explain everything after it has happened, since almost any human behaviour is consistent with the idea of maximizing something. But to make predictions, Becker's theories need filling out with specific assumptions. And this is exactly what Becker did in practice. The *Treatise on the Family* relies on several powerful assumptions. The core argument about specialization assumes unpaid work at home – cooking, cleaning, childcare, and so on – is a *more* specialized job than the paid employment which might be available. But the reverse assumption seems more plausible. Becker assumes one family member is the altruistic 'head of the household', deciding who should do what in order to maximize the welfare of household members overall. Other ad hoc assumptions are casually slipped into the analysis too. In discussing divorce, Becker claims 'the average divorced person can be presumed to be more quarrelsome and in other ways less pleasant than the average person remaining married'.[10]

Beyond these questionable assumptions, Becker's core idea of people maximizing something is not what it seems. It evokes a picture of people perpetually engaged in conscious calculation, yet Becker and those who follow him often deny this. As the story goes, a distinguished academic economist was offered a prestigious job, but in a faraway university. His (non-economist) friend remarked, 'Well, at least you can use your economics to make the decision – you can quantify all the possible consequences, and weight them by their probabilities.' The economist replied, 'Come on, this is serious.'

This story would not make Becker uncomfortable. Becker was once asked whether he had used his own theories when deciding whether or not to become an economist. He summed up his answer as follows:

> I believe, rough as it was, my decision to enter economics was a 'rational' decision, but people do not literally make a fine-tuned calculation. How many people sit down before they marry and say, oh these are the reasons I should marry this woman, these are reasons why I should not marry her, then weigh these and see if the pluses exceed the minuses? Very few people do that. If your girlfriend knew you did that, she probably would not want to marry you.[11]

So Becker seems human after all. But how does he reconcile his core assumption that people are maximizers with his awareness that people don't literally calculate the costs and benefits of every decision?

Becker assumes instead that people behave *as if* they make these calculations: their behaviour will be akin to that predicted by the theory, even if they don't actually think in the way the theory describes. Becker's thinking came direct from 'by far the greatest living teacher I ever had' – Milton Friedman.

Friedman's influence is woven in cross-cutting ways through

modern economics. He was a founder member of the Mont Pèlerin Society and rapidly emerged as a force within it comparable to Hayek. Of all the formidable intellects in Chicago economics, Friedman was dominant – it was inevitably Friedman who led the interrogation of Ronald Coase over dinner at Aaron Director's house. More importantly, Friedman revived monetarism to challenge the Keynesian orthodoxy that had reigned supreme over macroeconomics since the late 1930s. Indeed, many historians cite Friedman's Presidential Address to the American Economic Association on 29 December 1967 in the Sheraton Hall, Washington DC, as the key moment when monetarism became intellectually respectable again. This respectability encouraged the Reagan and Thatcher governments to adopt monetarist – not Keynesian – economic policies a decade or so later at the start of the 1980s. Naturally, both governments turned to Friedman for advice – by which time the new status of monetarism in economics had been further enhanced with the award of the Nobel Prize for economics to Friedman in 1976.

And yet, despite the huge impact of Friedman's work on monetarism and related macroeconomic issues, his most enduring influence on modern economics looks set to be his 1953 essay about how economics can be a science, entitled 'The Methodology of Positive Economics'. Friedman argued that, although many economic theories were obviously at odds with reality, that did not prevent them being scientific. For Friedman – and then Becker – it does not matter if the description of human behaviour in an economic theory is obviously unrealistic: the theory still qualifies as sound science if it makes accurate predictions. 'Consider the problem of predicting the shots made by an expert billiard player,' says Friedman.[12] Suppose we assume that the player uses complex mathematics to calculate where to aim the ball and how hard to hit it, makes all the calculations correctly and hits the ball perfectly. Using these assumptions, we will generally make good predictions of which shots the player will make, even though the assumptions are obviously false. In other words, the player acts *as if* they use sophisticated mathematics. Similarly, Friedman argued, consumers and businesses act as if they maximize satisfaction and profits, respectively. Even if they don't consciously do this, our assumption of maximizing behaviour will give us good predictions.

Economists fell in love with Friedman's argument because it freed them from the bother of finding realistic assumptions to underpin their theories: the realism of assumptions is not important, Friedman emphasized, as long as the predictions are accurate. Adopting Friedman's argument, Becker and his followers saw no need to apologize for the caricature of *homo economicus* that inhabited their theories: the resemblance to actual human beings was tenuous at best, but it didn't matter.

Despite its influence among economists, however, Friedman's argument is not taken seriously by philosophers of science. During the 2010 FIFA World Cup, Paul from Germany correctly predicted the outcomes for all six of the German team's matches. But Paul was an octopus (a shame he wasn't called Milton). Paul's success reminds us that correct predictions can be made repeatedly, against the odds, even though there is no basis for them.

Another problem with Friedman's argument is his flawed analogy of consumers and firms with billiard players. We are confident in our predictions about an expert billiard player because the player's objective is usually clear (to pot the ball); our prediction is based on the mathematics that, in theory, enables the billiard player to achieve this objective; and we know the player is skilled enough to get close to playing this theoretically optimal shot in practice. Real-world economic decision-making is different. We don't know the objectives of the economic actor (consumer, worker, manager, and so on); there is no reliable theory to guide them (or us), even if their objectives are clear; insofar as a theoretical guide exists, it is hard for the actor to pursue it due to practical problems such as lack of information, the complexity of the choice, uncertainty about the future, and so on. So we have no understanding on which to base predictions – and that does not change even if, like Paul the octopus, we fluke a run of successful guesses. To begin to understand, say, consumer behaviour, we need realistic assumptions about how consumers think about their goals, how they perceive the choices facing them, what information is available to them, and so on.

We've seen how Becker's theories of discrimination and the family rely on controversial assumptions and definitions which are not immediately obvious. Such hidden assumptions, along with the slippery *as if* idea of maximization, have together helped Becker and his Freak-onomics followers evade criticism. But that alone cannot explain the widespread influence of their economic imperialism.

Perhaps their assumptions are broadly realistic after all. Becker concedes that people don't engage in elaborate calculations when deciding who to marry, but perhaps they do in other contexts – or at least go through some kind of rough weighing up of costs and benefits. Becker refers to 'a rise in the shadow price of children reducing the demand for children.'[13] Stripping away the jargon, we find a simple idea: when having children involves a bigger financial sacrifice – such as higher rent, because of the need to find larger accommodation – then people are less likely to have them. Yes, this is generally true (there is supporting evidence from a variety of times and places), but we did not need Beckerian economics to reach such an obvious conclusion. Or any kind of economics. Consciously, delib-erately, weighing up the pros and cons of alternatives before making a decision is hardly a new idea, even in 'non-economic' decision-making. The novels of Jane Austen are full of characters who carefully weigh up the pros and cons of marriage, or taking on the responsibili-ties of parenthood (even when not the biological parent). In short, as another Nobel laureate in economics put it, Becker's theories seem to 'oscillate between the obvious and the false'.[14]

But the influence of Beckerian economics went far beyond any spe-cific theories he had developed on discrimination, the family, and so on. A confident individualism had begun to emerge across society by the late 1960s. Becker's broad approach, as summarized so clearly by him in 1976, fitted in perfectly with the new mood. Let's explore this new Beckerian individualism.

THERE'S NO ARGUING OVER TASTES

First, please lie on the couch. If your economic reasoning process is analogous to that of an expert billiard player, as Becker implied, then the message is an empowering one: you are smarter than you think – you just aren't aware of the unconscious calculations driving your behaviour. This is Beckerian economics as pop psychotherapy. As one university teacher explains it: 'I try to teach it as a tool that says "a lot of things that you've done are really clever, and you don't even know why, and let me explain to you what I think is driving you, and tell me if it resonates with you once we make it explicit".'[15]

Second, Becker provided an intellectual framework to attack the moral rules, social norms and government interventions that seemed opposed to individualism. On government intervention, Becker and the economic imperialists who followed him typically conclude that government policies are not needed, and existing government interventions should be abandoned. Regardless of the circumstances, their argument for small government is essentially the same: there is no problem for government to fix. The argument is simple but powerful. Since everyone is rational, they will already be making the best possible choices, so there is no scope for government being able to improve matters. The argument combines a fantasy about human rationality with the subtle falsity that improvement is only possible if individuals acting in isolation can make better choices. In reality, progress often requires coordinated change across many groups of people, and government intervention is one way to achieve this coordination. Becker argues, for example, that the early death of smokers or the obese is not a social problem: it simply reflects the preference of some people to forfeit lifespan for the sake of immediate pleasures. Then Becker extends the argument: 'therefore *most* (if not all!) deaths are to some extent "suicides" in the sense that they could have been postponed if more resources had been invested in prolonging life. This . . . calls into question the common distinction between suicides and "natural" deaths.'[16]

At a stroke, the rationale for much public health policy is dismissed. Even terms like 'premature death' are misleading, according to Becker, because there is no such thing as a normal or natural age of death. And poor health is a just a preference.

This brings us to *De Gustibus Non Est Disputandum* – there's no arguing over tastes – the title of a highly influential paper published in 1977 by Becker and his Chicago colleague George Stigler (who would win the Nobel Prize in 1982). Highly influential? It hardly seems like news. Most of us see little point in arguing over tastes between apples and pears, chocolate and strawberry ice cream,

Mozart or The Beatles. But Becker's assertion the year before that the economic approach applies to all human behaviour implies that people can have tastes or preferences about anything. In short order the academic literature began to bulge with talk of people's 'taste' for discrimination, immigration, nationalism, suicide, and so on. And if there's no arguing about those either, much moral and political debate is silenced.

Again, you have to admire the ability of Becker to wrongfoot his critics. Economist Alan Blinder (a future Vice-chairman of the US Federal Reserve) was so exasperated by Beckerian arguments about suicide that in 1974 he published a spoof piece of Beckerian economics, *The Economics of Brushing Teeth*. But satire only works if the victim recognizes it. Becker didn't: he thought Blinder's *Teeth* paper was interesting and recommended publication in the leading journal of Chicago economics.[17]

The critics make the obvious point that Becker's approach ignores our moral values, social norms and religious convictions. But it doesn't. What it does is collapse them into mere tastes: our cherished values are understood as preferences neither more nor less than our taste for chocolate or strawberry ice cream.

This distinction between values and tastes is much more than wordplay. Arguments about discrimination or premature death from smoking are arguments about values because there is something to argue about, reasons to be given, for and against. This possibility of reasoned argument extends beyond the traditional sphere of morality, not least because the argument can be with myself rather than others: so the scope of mere tastes is more restricted than it first appears. I can have a taste for another slice of chocolate cake, glass of wine or cigarette but at the same time a value, a personal commitment not to have these things. That is why real people sometimes say, 'If I ask for another one, don't let me have it.' Becker's *homo economicus* would never say this. Yet it is a uniquely human trait, the ability to step back from our expressed preferences and existing behaviour and ask ourselves whether this is really what we want. Despite their fixation on 'rationality', the economic imperialists ignore this possibility of stepping back and reflecting – which is a defining part of what it means to be rational.

If the economic imperialists had *banned* values from economics, the PR would not have been good – economists as amoral scientists beholden to materialism, and so on. Instead, by treating values as tastes, the imperialists have smothered moral debate with a blanket of welfare calculations and trade-offs, with everything up for grabs, everything for sale. And subtly, largely unnoticed, they have closed off a primary route towards changing people's behaviour for the better: because there is no arguing over tastes, there is less scope for influencing behaviour through education, whether formal or informal.

The economic imperialists do not recognize the scope for influencing behaviour through the law either. Becker doesn't get crime. No, really. As he explained in his Nobel Prize lecture: 'I was puzzled by why theft is socially harmful, since it appears merely to redistribute resources, usually from wealthier to poorer individuals. I resolved the puzzle by pointing out that criminals spend on weapons and on the value of their time in planning and carrying out their crimes and that such spending is socially unproductive . . .'[18]

Not quite. Even if the weapons were free and criminals had nothing better to do with their time, theft would still be 'socially harmful' – the anger, fear and sense of violation felt by victims, as well as the violence and property destruction which often accompanies theft. Unsurprisingly, given his amoral understanding of crime, Becker completely overlooks the role of publicly proclaimed laws in stigmatizing immoral behaviour. For Becker (and his Chicago judge and lawyer friend Richard Posner, who took 'justice' to mean 'wealth maximization' in Chapter 3), law discourages crime just by raising its price. Potential criminals calculate the price of crime as the punishment they might face, multiplied by the probability of getting caught. Becker and the Chicago lawyers concluded that a cheap way to discourage crime is to reduce expenditure on law enforcement yet keep the price high by introducing very long prison sentences. In parts of the US which followed this prescription in the 1970s and '80s, a well-documented crime wave was the result.

In the twenty-first century, although we have wisely begun to listen to criminologists more than economists when it comes to tackling crime, economic imperialism still holds sway over other areas of

LICENCE TO BE BAD

social policy: too often, we unthinkingly assume that the best response to unethical or antisocial behaviour is to raise its price.

But Becker's greatest influence on us lies elsewhere. Once values are boiled down to mere tastes, then Becker can conclude that there is no distinction between 'major and minor decisions such as those involving life and death, in contrast to the choice of a brand of coffee', or between decisions such as 'choosing a mate or the number of children in contrast to buying paint'.[19] And of course we have markets for coffee and paint. So why not have markets for more life-and-death decisions? Perhaps a market for babies, as Posner proposed in 1978. From the perspective of Becker, Posner and their followers, the presumption is clearly reversed: why wouldn't you?

We will come back to the baby-market idea, but for now we turn to another kind of economic imperialism, from someone operating entirely independently of Becker. And sometimes highly critical of Becker's thinking too.

THE NOBEL CONSOLATION PRIZE FOR ECONOMICS

It is easy to pigeonhole Tom Schelling. His career reads like that of a Grade-A Cold War defence hawk. From 1948 to 1953 he worked for the Marshall Plan and then the White House; after that he had stints at RAND and various consultancy jobs in Washington drawing on his expertise in military strategy. Although it was John von Neumann who invented the infamous nuclear war jargon 'mutually assured destruction' (largely because he liked the acronym MAD), it was Schelling who became a MAD expert. Schelling was close to some of the most influential figures in the Cold War. In his day job as an economics professor at Harvard he co-taught a course on foreign policy with one of the dominant minds behind post-war US foreign policy, Henry Kissinger. And Schelling was reputed to have more influence than anyone else on the thinking of Secretary of State Robert McNamara. Schelling received the Nobel Prize for economics in 2005 'for having enhanced our understanding of conflict and co-operation through game-theory analysis'.

But this pigeonholing is too simplistic. Schelling did not see himself as a game theorist: his bemused response to the Nobel Prize announcement was 'I must have been doing game theory without knowing it.'[20] This reply was partly motivated by Schelling's view of mathematics. Unlike most game theorists and RAND analysts, Schelling did not assume maths was the best tool for every task – he thought maths was 'used too much to show off'.[21] There was minimal mathematics in Schelling's work, while game theory played only a supporting role, used creatively and flexibly to gain insights into military strategy.

Schelling, too, was arguably as much a dove as a hawk – albeit a dove immersed in realpolitik. No other recipient of the Nobel Prize for economics has been talked about as a candidate for the Nobel Peace Prize instead. Schelling's economics prize came late and unexpectedly – he was eighty-four – and many commentators saw it as a consolation prize for having not won the Nobel Prize for Peace.* Schelling's Nobel lecture even reads as if it could have been written with the peace prize in mind. It begins, 'The most spectacular event of the past half century is one that did not occur. We have enjoyed sixty years without nuclear weapons exploded in anger' – and proceeds, not unreasonably, to claim some credit for this outcome.

Schelling certainly deserves credit for his obsession with the possibility of accidental nuclear war. In 1959 he wrote a magazine article outlining scenarios for accidental war. After reading it, Stanley Kubrick was inspired to make *Dr Strangelove* – with advice from Schelling on the plot. In 1961 Schelling was made chair of a White House committee on 'War by Accident, Miscalculation, and Surprise'. He discovered that, astonishingly, there was no means of speedy, reliable communication with the Kremlin: 'I could direct dial my mother three thousand miles away to wish her happy birthday [but] Kennedy had no way to get in touch with Khrushchev.'[22] Schelling persuaded President Kennedy to install what became known as 'the hotline' to solve the problem. With this single, simple act, Schelling may have made more difference to humanity than all the other

* The prize came late to Schelling in another way too. He was notified only moments before the public announcement, because the prize committee did not have Schelling's correct phone number. Schelling pointed out he was in the phone book.

thinkers in this book put together – although, with disturbing hindsight, the hotline was not fully operational until after the nuclear near-miss that was the Cuban Missile Crisis. It took until 1963 to persuade Soviet diplomats that the hotline was their idea, and to get special Cyrillic teletypewriters installed in the White House.

As for Schelling's economics, much of his work has a realism missing from Gary Becker's world. Like Becker, Schelling studied discrimination. But Schelling was more interested in how discrimination spreads. One evening he played around moving coins on a black-and-white checkerboard according to simple rules. Based on the patterns which emerged, Schelling realized that neighbourhoods can become totally segregated along racial lines if residents seek merely to avoid living in an area where all their neighbours are from another race. A seemingly 'mild' preference can have extremely divisive consequences.

Schelling turned his attention back to war, but this time war with yourself. As we have seen, Gary Becker and his followers have a naïve view of our addictions to alcohol, nicotine and some foods: 'rational addictions', Becker called them, arguing that they reflect a carefully considered balancing of pleasure against health risk. Schelling was unimpressed: 'they don't know what they're talking about.' In a 1980 essay, 'The Intimate Contest for Self-command', Schelling sought to understand the smoker 'who in self-disgust grinds his cigarettes down the disposal swearing that this time he means never again to risk orphaning his children with lung cancer and is on the street three hours later looking for a store that's still open to buy cigarettes'.[23] (You can tell that Schelling spent fifteen years trying to quit.) Schelling outlined 'self-command' strategies that addicts can use to help win their private war – strategies revolutionary at the time, which are now familiar to behavioural economists and psychologists around the world.

Given Schelling's nuanced understanding of how we think, far removed from *homo economicus*, it is perhaps surprising that he was also largely responsible for another form of economic imperialism, another way of replacing ethical considerations with preferences expressed in markets. But necessity is the mother of invention.

HOW MUCH ARE YOU WORTH?

Shortly after the USSR detonated its first atomic bomb in 1949, the US air force asked RAND for help in designing a first-strike attack on the Soviets. The analysts at RAND considered over 400,000 scenarios involving different combinations of bombs and bombers in their attempt to find, almost literally, the biggest bang per buck. They concluded that the US air force should attempt to overwhelm Soviet air defences with huge numbers of planes, including cheap and vulnerable propeller planes carrying no nuclear bombs that would act as decoys to reduce attacks on the planes which did carry bombs. RAND was proud of its work, but the air force generals were furious.

The generals, many of whom were former pilots, rejected the proposal outright and told RAND bluntly that their analysis needed a complete rethink. In calculating the cost of different strategies, RAND had simply ignored the human cost: the air force personnel who would die. So their proposal of a strategy involving cheap planes but high casualties was almost inevitable. RAND's omission of the human cost was because of internal disagreement over how to value human life. As one senior RAND analyst admitted, 'factors which we aren't yet in a position to treat quantitatively tend to be omitted from serious consideration'.[24] RAND economists could not even agree whether this was an economic question, for economists to decide. On the one hand, putting a dollar value on pilots' lives seemed beyond the scope of economics: RAND could do no more than present the Pentagon with different strategies involving various 'efficient' combinations of dollar cost and lives lost – it would be up to the Pentagon or the president to make the ultimate trade-off. On the other hand, perhaps the financial investment in pilots (training costs, and so on), while not a full measure of their dollar value, was at least a starting point for such a calculation.

It would take over a decade for a possible resolution to emerge – from the creative mind of Tom Schelling. Schelling's work on the value of human life was triggered by research undertaken by his PhD student Jack Carlson, a former fighter pilot. They began by looking at military decision-making, although it was soon clear that their ideas had wider applicability. It was surely wrong to value a pilot's life in terms of the air force's financial investment in him. Similarly, most economists were uneasy with valuing a civilian life in terms of the person's earnings (as courts did when determining compensation after industrial accidents). Schelling argued that the most fundamental problem with this approach was that it valued your life in terms of its value *to other people*, not yourself. Yet, as Schelling acknowledged, the value of human life (to that human) was too 'awesome' a question for an economist to address. So he changed the question: 'Where life and death are concerned, we are all consumers. We nearly all want our lives extended and are probably willing to pay for it. It is worthwhile to remind ourselves that the people whose lives may be saved have something to say about the value of the enterprise . . .'[25]

Schelling shifted the question from valuing life to valuing keeping people alive – the value of a reduced risk of death. These were not the lives of particular, named people, but 'statistical lives'. If a regulation for drinking water will reduce the risk of death per year by just one in 1 million, but the entire population of a large country is affected (say, 100 million people), then the regulation will statistically – on average – save the lives of a hundred people a year. A hundred 'statistical lives' are saved. Schelling had a gift for rhetoric (at least by modern economists' standards) and titled his landmark 1968 essay 'The Life You Save May be Your Own'. But it was more than just wordplay. Schelling saw a way to infer from someone's behaviour how much a reduced risk of death might be worth to them.

Here was a new front on which economists could push forward with their imperialistic ambitions, far beyond the decision-making of the US air force. Governments and businesses often face decisions between alternatives which lead to loss of life (or lives not being saved), such as choices involving healthcare, environmental protection or product safety. If a credible money value for human life is available, then decision-makers can simply throw it into their calculations, along with the other costs and benefits of different alternatives – all measured in terms of money, of course. While many people strongly object to this way of thinking, most economists see their complaints as nothing more than irrational squeamishness, a gut 'yuk' reaction. Decisions have to be made; resources are finite. As individuals, there is a limit to how much we spend on making our car safer to drive, or on helmets and other equipment for protection when playing dangerous sports. Similarly, there is also a limit to how much a government should spend making drinking water safer, or businesses should be required to spend in minimizing the risk of dangerous side-effects from drugs. All this is unobjectionable. And Schelling's approach was a big improvement on valuing someone's life in terms of their earnings.

Today his approach lies at the heart of policy-making in many countries, with a standardized value of statistical life used across much of government. In the US, the value of statistical life is around $10 million (in 2019 prices), and government agencies are compelled by law to decide policy by putting monetary values on the benefits and costs, including the value of life.

Yet there is more to concerns about the value of statistical life than naïve squeamishness. Consider the following thought-experiment-style argument. Suppose there are two jobs, identical in every respect, except that one involves some dangerous task (perhaps handling harmful chemicals or serving on active duty in the army) which implies a one in 10,000 risk of death each year. Textbook free-market economics asserts that any observed difference in wages between these two jobs must be entirely due to this extra risk. Wages in the riskier job are higher only because the employer must offer more money to persuade workers to tolerate the risk. Suppose this 'wage differential' between the two jobs is about $1,000. This implies workers will tolerate a one in 10,000 risk of death for $1,000. If there are 10,000 workers each facing this risk, then the total extra wage paid out by employers will be $10 million ($1,000x10,000). And on average one worker will die per year. Workers collectively tolerate the loss of one statistical life, in return for $10 million extra pay.

Incredibly, this is not just a thought experiment. It is Schelling's method. Using exactly this reasoning, real governments around the world arrive at a monetary value for statistical life via estimates of wage differentials. But there are basic problems with Schelling's method. When choosing between different, more-or-less risky jobs, real people usually have little knowledge of the probabilities and magnitudes of the risks they face – and even if they have this knowledge, the exact wage on offer is unlikely to be the only factor determining which job they take. What's more, it is far from obvious that people who take high-risk jobs are in reality expressing a genuine choice at all. Instead, poverty may lead them to take the best-paid job they can get, regardless of the risks.

Even if we set aside such problems and assume that reliable numbers can somehow be found, Schelling's approach is a misleading one. When non-economists complain that talk of 'statistical lives' is misleading, economists dismiss the complaint, again, as mere squeamishness. But the terminology *is* misleading. It was introduced by Schelling as a rhetorical device to help link government decisions involving loss of life to private decisions involving risk to life. Schelling suspected that economists would take some persuading to derive money values for the former from behaviour at best reflecting the latter. He was right: the initial reaction to 'The Life You Save May be Your Own' was deeply hostile. Nowadays, Schelling's once-controversial logical leap goes unquestioned and talk of 'statistical lives' obscures the fact that real lives are lost. If a government decides to scrap the drinking-water regulation described earlier on the grounds that it is too costly, this might be the right decision but, on average, a hundred lives will be lost. (And the laws of probability tell us that it is *extremely* likely that the actual number will turn out to be very close to a hundred). We just can't identify in advance exactly who will die. Rather than talk of 'statistical lives', it would be more honest to present the decision as 'causing the death of a hundred people on average, but we do not know who'. And it would force us to confront a hard question – whether we should spend less on saving unidentified lives. At present we spend much more on saving identified lives, such as the child who falls down a well or miners trapped underground.

This points to a fundamental flaw with this kind of economic imperialism in action: there is no single money value of life suitable for all decisions. In different decisions involving risks of death, we make different choices – for good reasons, such as the age of the potential victims, whether the risk is borne voluntarily or imposed by others, whether the risk of death is one in a hundred or one in

100,000, whether the risk is irreversible, and so on. Our laws, morals and social norms acknowledge these reasons, but economists' insistence on a single money value of life implies we should ignore them. The imperialists say we must use a single money value of life in order to be consistent. But real life is inconsistent. It is not life as *homo economicus*. And real-world economics is not science.

Schelling himself was inconsistent. He changed his mind. In 'The Life You Save May be Your Own', he had great faith in our ability to make rational and consistent choices between risky jobs. But by the time of 'The Intimate Contest for Self-command' twelve years later, Schelling had developed a sophisticated analysis of the motives behind our irrational, inconsistent behaviour – and, as we shall see shortly, an equally sophisticated understanding of the problems with expanding the scope of markets.

BABIES AND KIDNEYS

Let's return, then, to the argument for markets in babies, kidneys and most things besides – an argument which began with the work of Becker and Chicago colleagues including Stigler and Posner but which today attracts supporters from around the world. The core of their argument for new markets is easy to state: if you want something, why shouldn't you be able to have it? In other words, these economic imperialists see markets as offering an important kind of democracy. There's no arguing over tastes: markets ignore the kind of elitism that says going to the opera is more valuable than going to a wrestling match. And markets don't make value judgements about the things you are allowed to trade, or not.

Yet market democracy is not like classical democracy. It is one dollar one vote, not one person one vote: the rich have more say because they have more buying power. This may not be a problem in most markets for ordinary goods and services (and we may be willing to swallow some problems in return for the benefits markets bring). But what about when market democracy actively undermines classical democracy?

At the heart of democracy is the principle that we are all equal citizens. Market activities (lobbying and line-standing, among others) that enable the rich to buy the political outcomes they want clearly undermine equal citizenship. Markets also undermine aspects of equal citizenship beyond the ballot box – equal citizenship rights and duties, including the duty to serve on criminal juries if asked to do so, or perform military or community service. Economic imperialists have been at the forefront of campaigns to introduce markets in citizenship duties: when called to do military service or jury duty, those who can afford it could pay others to serve instead. As for citizenship rights, Becker in 1987 proposed that the right to national citizenship (immigration rights) should go to the highest bidder. In 2009 the growth in refugees led to an update. Becker argued that asylum spaces for refugees should be available only upon payment of a large fee, because this would 'avoid time-consuming hearings about whether they are really in physical danger if forced to return home'.[26]

Equal citizenship does not just give us a reason to limit the scope of markets. It *enables* markets too: for markets to work properly and benefit both parties to a trade, those parties must be trading on roughly equal terms. When one party is desperately poor, vulnerable or powerless, then they are likely to be exploited in market trades and a ban on such trades may be justified. Child labour is prohibited in most countries (albeit with widely differing age definitions for 'child') because children are often powerless in labour markets: their labour is sold without their knowledge or consent, or they lack the maturity to understand what the work involves. A woman may enter a contract to sell her unborn baby to parents seeking to adopt, because of desperate poverty or because she does not know how she will feel after she has handed over her child. A desperately poor father might agree to a loan at an extortionate interest rate, knowing he has no hope of ever repaying it, in order to buy essential drugs for his sick child. All these cases suggest, at the least, pause for thought before assuming that markets must benefit both parties to a trade, because markets involve only trades that are freely entered into. In reality, freedom in decision-making is minimal in some contexts, so we cannot assume that market choices make all sides better off.

But how vulnerable, desperate and powerless do people have to be to justify banning markets, or (which amounts to almost the same

thing) making contracts unenforceable? One reason why the economic imperialists' arguments for extending the scope of markets
have been so powerfully influential is that there is no short and neat
answer to questions like these. Since markets are *not* all the same – the
market for paint is not like the market for reproductive services –
then, unsurprisingly, the reasons for not using markets will be
different in different contexts too. And the context changes across
time and place. That is why a perfectly acceptable market in one era,
such as the market for slaves, can be an abomination in another. But
to justify restricting the scope of a particular market in a particular
time and place, we do not need timeless, universal reasons. That is
asking too much. As a society, we can decide to embrace market
democracy in most circumstances. In Becker's terms, people should
be generally free to buy what they want, maximizing welfare as they
conceive it. But as a society we can simultaneously decide to impose
limits on this welfare-maximization process, deciding that some
things are not to be traded in markets. Neither philosophy is, or can
be, a universal one.

However, it is much easier to contemplate these limits in the
abstract than to insist on them in practice. If I need a kidney and I am
willing to pay £20,000 to get one, and you are willing to sell yours
for £20,000, then not only are we both better off if this transaction
goes ahead but my desperate need for a kidney is met. My death may
be prevented as a result. This seems to be economic imperialism in
the service of a noble goal – yet selling kidneys is illegal in every
country except Iran. And the sale of body parts has been explicitly
prohibited by the United Nations, the European Union and the World
Health Organization. In most countries, there is a severe shortage of
kidneys available for transplant. The case for a market rests on the
claim that allowing kidneys to be sold will increase their supply. But
this cannot just be assumed. (As we will see in the next chapter, paying people to supply something which previously they provided for
free does not always increase the supply.)

Economic imperialists have no patience with this response. For
them the solution is obvious: as with anything else, if the price is high
enough, the supply will come. We just need to calculate how much is
enough to get people to supply kidneys. Step forward, of course, Gary

Becker: 'the reservation price of an organ has three main additive components, a monetary compensation for the risk of death . . . for the time lost during recovery . . . for the risk of reduced quality of life'.[27] In order to come up with a kidney price here (around $19,800 in 2019 prices, in case you were wondering) Becker must make fantastic assumptions, including some we have already met, such as basing his estimate of the cash you must be paid to compensate for the risk of death in kidney-removal surgery on the off-the-shelf numbers circulating among economists for the extra wage needed to get people to do riskier jobs. But setting aside the dodgy basis for the numbers, this way of thinking transforms the debate about buying and selling kidneys. We enter an argument about whether the price is right, an argument in which the economic imperialists have an advantage, because of their mastery of the techniques for generating numbers (they also have a convenient opportunity to charge us big consultancy fees for the privilege of their expertise). Almost without noticing, the wider policy debate is shifted too: can we *afford* enough kidneys? And even if the price is steep, perhaps it is still cheaper than trying to educate people to commit to donating kidneys after their death. Here, the moral issues are left behind: education becomes just an inefficient method to induce kidney supply.[28]

Kazuo Ishiguro's novel *Never Let Me Go* describes a world in which human clones are bred solely to provide replacement organs for others. Organ markets share something in common with this dystopia: their main effect will be the reallocation of body parts from the poor to the rich. Of course, the economic imperialists will argue that since the poor 'freely choose' to sell their organs, they must be better off. However, in the words of one researcher on the global traffic in human organs, 'perhaps we should look for better ways of helping the destitute than dismantling them'.[29]

Markets in cases like this clearly pose difficult moral questions. But the arguments of the economic imperialists and their Freakonomics followers are no help. First, because they try to sideline moral questions and assume they can be separated from economics. 'Morality' as the authors of *Freakonomics* put it, 'represents the way that people would like the world to work – whereas economics represents how it actually *does* work'.[30] Second, because many markets fail even against the narrow benchmark set by the economic imperialists – welfare maximization. Welfare is supposedly maximized because markets allocate goods to the buyers who value them the most, the highest bidders. But how much buyers are willing to pay is not a reliable guide to what is truly valuable for them. People try to look after their own interests, but behavioural economics and psychology have shown how often they make mistakes. Moreover, willingness to pay is often constrained by ability to pay. That is why our global willingness to pay for anti-wrinkle treatments exceeds that for malaria treatments. Yet malaria treatments are more valuable. The last sentence is uncontroversial because while there's no arguing over *tastes*, we can surely agree about some *needs*. Ultimately, the Achilles heel of markets is the one you knew all along: price is a poor measure of value.

A *TITANIC* QUESTION

The assumption that price is a good measure of value has become so enmeshed in our thinking that we have forgotten how far this represents a revolutionary break from our attitudes just a generation or so ago. Take higher education – yet again, it was Gary Becker's thinking that triggered a decisive break with the past. Becker invented the now-familiar idea of *human capital*: today we see nothing wrong with talk of investing in yourself, marketing yourself, defining yourself as a financial asset whose worth is measured by the returns it can generate in the future. With this in mind, he argued that university places, like every other commodity from carrots to kidneys, should go to the highest bidder. Potential students know more than anyone else about how much they stand to gain in human capital from a university place, Becker reasoned, so auctioning places ensures that the human capital gain across society is maximized.

As with the sale of human organs, we can object to this market on grounds of fairness: many of us are no keener that the rich should be able to outbid the poor for access to university than for access to kidneys. But suppose we are not worried about unfairness (or live in a society akin to Norway, with relatively little inequality). We might still be uneasy about selling university places to the highest bidder. Is our unease justified? Yes, because selling places misses the point about university education. We may disagree about the exact purpose of university education, but generally we agree that places should go to those with suitable aptitude, interest and knowledge. This reminds us that, rather than market-based measures of value, education has its own internal values. None of these values – aptitude, interest and knowledge – can be measured by the amount a student is willing to pay to get a place. Some students who pay a lot of money for their university education feel they are buying a good degree result or grade. But obviously they are wrong: internal values (student performance), not price paid, determine the grade awarded. If we use market values to select or evaluate students, it's not education anymore.

Clearly, then, the problems with the ever-expanding scope of markets go beyond the poor getting a raw deal. Nevertheless, if you aren't poor, the case for constraining markets seems to rely on your altruism – giving up some of your freedom of choice so that the poor are less excluded. But the interesting thing about protecting the vulnerable, desperate and powerless is that it can help the rest of us too. When the *Titanic* went down in 1912:

> There were enough lifeboats for first class; steerage was expected to go down with the ship. We do not tolerate that anymore. Those who want to risk their lives at sea and cannot afford a safe ship should perhaps not be denied the opportunity to entrust themselves to a cheaper ship without lifeboats; but if some people cannot afford the price of passage with lifeboats, and some people can, they should not travel on the same ship.[31]

Agree or disagree, there are several surprises here. To begin with, these words come not from a philosopher speculating about moral dilemmas but from the pragmatist Tom Schelling. Schelling begins by noting that we demand that all passengers have access to lifeboats, even if some passengers would rather not pay for them. Yet we don't make the same demand more generally: in many contexts we allow people to choose different levels of safety depending on how much they pay. Some people buy safer, more expensive cars; some don't.

Intriguingly, Schelling suggests that we might allow the poor to choose less safety, as long as the rest of us don't have to watch.

This might seem to license a callous disregard for fellow humans. But Schelling seems to have had the opposite reaction in mind. We can't watch because we care. Imagine finding yourself on a sinking ship with no lifeboat spaces for holders of the cheapest tickets because society has allowed such boats to be built. Imagine not just the fights, but the desperate begging as those without a space plead that they be squeezed in. To prevent lifeboats sinking, the rich will have to push the poor overboard. This is what a society with extreme inequality of citizenship looks like. In a market society, if two parties interact with each other on extremely unequal terms, the results are horrific for the poor but they are painful for the rich too. Schelling the pragmatist identifies an argument for preventing extreme inequalities, relying on nothing more than the self-interest of the better-off members of society. Of course, we can go further. Ultimately, the case for restricting markets to parties trading on roughly equal terms comes from a respect for our common humanity. Lifting up the vulnerable, desperate and powerless enables respectful trade. But if we cannot or will not eliminate extreme inequalities, then it may be best to ban some markets altogether, rather than tolerate trade between extreme unequals.[32]

We have come a long way from the view that all behaviour can be explained and justified by the economic imperialists' narrow caricature of rational economic thinking. Like von Neumann before him, Becker's attempt to provide a complete science of society is a failure. But given its continuing influence, we need to reassert some old truths. Deciding which things should be bought and sold in markets raises moral questions as well as economic ones, and we cannot neatly separate the two. Markets can change the character of what is being traded – obvious in markets for sex, less obvious in markets for higher education; and, of course, price is a poor measure of value.

Meanwhile, the damage wrought by economic imperialism continues. In 2016 the big business news was the revelation that Volkswagen had for years systematically cheated its way through emissions tests for diesel vehicles. From a company with the pristine reputation of

Volkswagen, this came as a surprise. But it is hardly surprising that businesses cheat when a licence for bad behaviour is so easy to find: simply combine Becker's inability to understand that crime is morally wrong with Friedman's insistence that the only responsibility of business is to maximize profit. How many more business leaders, politicians and others in positions of power have excuses from economic imperialists being whispered in their ears?

7

Everyone Has a Price

In 1911 Frederick Winslow Taylor, an aristocratic Philadelphian, published *The Principles of Scientific Management*. Later dubbed 'the Isaac Newton of the science of work' by 1970s management guru Peter Drucker, Taylor was arguably the world's first management consultant. His book paved the way for what are now mainstream management techniques to improve worker efficiency. But Taylorism, as it became known, had a shaky start.

The Watertown Arsenal in Massachusetts was a US Army-run facility used mainly as a factory for manufacturing artillery-gun carriages. Taylor had been consulted on how to increase the productivity of the workers and stop 'soldiering', a word which in those days meant shirking or malingering. Taylor's assistant patrolled the factory floor armed with a stopwatch, until one worker refused to be timed. On 11th August 1911 this worker was fired for insubordination and everyone walked out in protest. It was the first strike against Taylorism, just months after Taylor's *Principles* was published. But without the official support of the union, the strike lasted only a week, while most of the operational changes introduced by Taylor were retained.[1] And Taylor had the last laugh on the Watertown site, because the Arsenal is today an office complex housing the *Harvard Business Review*, a leading journal of management science, much of which derives directly from Taylorism.

Yet the aftermath of the strike tells another story. Since the Arsenal's workers were federal employees, they had the right to protest to Congress directly. They persuaded Congress to launch an investigation. One result of this was the US government's ban on the use of the stopwatch to monitor workers in army workshops – to modern eyes, an astonishing political intervention. At the time, though, both supporters and critics of Taylorism saw it as a political and moral project, so the direct involvement of politicians would have surprised no one. Taylor did not see his 'scientific management' as morally neutral or apolitical. He argued that workers were simpletons whose behaviour had to be controlled by managers with superior intelligence. As Taylor explained to the Congressional committee: 'I can say, without the slightest hesitation, that the science of handling pig-iron is so great that the man who is . . . physically able to handle pig-iron and is sufficiently phlegmatic and stupid to choose this for his occupation is rarely able to comprehend the science of handling pig-iron.'[2]

The Congressional investigation concluded that Taylorism had a dehumanizing effect on workers. And Taylor's use of language like 'social engineering' and 'social control' – alongside pronouncements like 'In the past the man has been first, in the future the system must be first'[3] – did not help his cause, especially in the 1930s, with critics drawing parallels with fascist ideology. The perceived tyranny of Taylorism was perfectly captured in Charlie Chaplin's 1936 satire *Modern Times*.

By the late 1940s the battleground in the appliance of science to controlling human behaviour had moved beyond the workplace, with the emergence of behaviourism in psychology. Behaviourists did lab experiments using rewards and punishments to train animals to behave in any way required. They believed the same carrot-and-stick techniques could be applied to humans. Behaviourists had much in common with the economists at think-tanks like RAND: a mechanical view of human nature, leading to a belief in the universal effectiveness of incentives to manipulate behaviour; a desire for a science of social control; and they even developed some military applications – the leading behaviourist Burrhus Skinner designed a pigeon-guided missile for the US Navy.

Like Taylor, Skinner had a gift for garnering bad publicity. The cages inhabited by animals in his experiments (he taught pigeons to play table tennis and some of his students taught a pig to use a vacuum cleaner) became known as Skinner boxes. But at the same time Skinner invented a kind of sealed, heated crib, which looked like a large fish-tank on wheels, which he tested on his newborn daughter.

Skinner wrote about it for the *Ladies' Home Journal*, the editors titled the article 'Baby in a Box', and from then on most people seemed to believe that a Skinner box could be used for babies as well as lab rats. The crib may have been harmless, but it *looked* creepy. Despite the controversy surrounding Skinner, behaviourism became more influential and by the 1960s had moved on from rats in mazes to reward tokens for infants and hospital patients with mental illnesses. The practicality and wide applicability of the approach has enabled its gradual entry into the political mainstream.

But in the last half century something has changed. Nowadays Taylorist management techniques are mostly seen as legitimate, apolitical interventions which work with the grain of human nature: the mainstream application of management science in the service of efficiency. Outside the workplace, too, our language is peppered with talk of 'incentives'. The word has shifted meaning from a tool of social engineering loaded with moral and political significance to a neutral, objective term meaning nothing more than 'motivations'. Yet if Taylor was right in talking in terms of social control, something must have got lost in the translation. Incentives, after all, are tools for getting someone to do something they would not choose to do otherwise. Even if employed for noble reasons, incentives are still instruments for the exercise of power.

'You're sort of like a robot, but in human form.'[4] So speaks a manager at an Amazon warehouse, talking about their pickers, the Amazon staff who spend all day walking – or jogging – around their warehouses picking the stuff we ordered. The pickers wear small satnav devices which measure their productivity, instruct them on the most efficient route to take around the warehouse and send them texts instructing them to speed up if they have indulged in time-wasting activities such as talking or toileting. This twenty-first-century form of Taylorism is just as aggressive as anything Taylor advocated, but our reaction to it has been transformed. The modern equivalent of banning the stopwatch is unthinkable: no contemporary government would ever forbid Amazon from measuring its pickers' productivity. More generally, we have come to accept financial incentives in contexts which were once controversial. In several countries in Central and South America, governments have followed economists' advice and introduced 'conditional cash transfer' schemes to encourage poor mothers to be better mothers: the details vary, but cash is offered to mothers who stop smoking, have their child vaccinated or improve their child's school attendance. And incentivization pervades the education sector: universities accept donations on condition that they must offer certain courses or, at least, include particular books on the reading lists; retailers pay schools to install confectionery or soft-drink vending machines in recreation rooms; schools pay seven-year-olds cash for each book they read and fine parents if their children arrive late.

What caused this unnoticed transformation in the way we think about incentives? Perhaps it is linked to a parallel transformation in economics. Free-market economics has become dominant, and many economists are big fans of incentives. The bestselling *Freakonomics* enthuses, 'Economists love incentives ... The typical economist believes that the world has not yet invented a problem that he cannot fix if given a free hand to design the proper incentive scheme.'[5] Most economics textbooks extol the virtues of markets but increasingly define economics as the science of incentives, while in everyday life the boundary between markets and incentive schemes often seems blurred.

Yet for that great advocate of free markets, Friedrich Hayek, the boundary was clear and important. Hayek saw the problem of how to motivate workers as a question 'of an engineering character'.[6] He belittled those concerned with such issues as 'social planners', whose actions would violate the natural order of the market. From a Hayekian perspective, incentive schemes are damaging forms of social engineering which interfere with market forces rather than extending them. So this is not a straightforward story of ideas about incentives coming to prominence on the back of a shift towards free-market economics or the political Right.

The influence of modern economics on how we think about incentives has been more subtle. Economists have been at the forefront of the explosion in 'incentives' talk over the past few decades, a time in which incentives became apolitically rebranded as mere motivations. Labelling all our motivations as incentives suits some economists, because it is a sly way of reducing the rich complexity of human psychology to the one-dimensional motivation of *homo economicus*. So it is worth reminding ourselves that incentives are not just motivations: many motivations cannot be understood as incentives without distorting them beyond recognition. If I look after my dying mother, I do so out of love, responsibility or obligation. But we cannot describe these motives as my 'incentives' to care for her. Curiosity drives children to do new, sometimes dangerous, things. But we don't say that curiosity was their incentive. Barack Obama probably inspired some black children to pursue political careers. We cannot replace 'inspired' with 'incentivized' in the previous sentence.[7]

As we shall see, the orthodox economists' theory of motivation leaves us blind, unable to anticipate when incentive schemes will backfire and unable to see that alternative ways of getting people to do things are often better – alternatives involving open, honest attempts to persuade and respect for other points of view.

Their theory, though, is easy to summarize: everyone has their price.

BIG SHOT MEETS A YANKEE ACTRESS

There is an old joke about a rich and famous man who meets a woman at a party. Perhaps the earliest version, allegedly a true story, involved the British media tycoon and politician Lord Beaverbrook encountering a 'Yankee actress'. The year was around 1937. (In subsequent retellings the big shot has been, among others, George Bernard Shaw, Groucho Marx or Winston Churchill.) The conversation goes something like this.

Big Shot: 'So will you spend the night with me for £10,000?'
Actress: 'Well . . .'
Big Shot: 'How about £100?'
Actress: 'What kind of person do you think I am?'
Big Shot: 'We have already established that. We are just haggling over the price.'

As well as implying that you can get almost everyone to do almost anything if you pay them enough, this economic theory of motivation has a less obvious but equally dubious implication. Since money can substitute for all other motivations (if you pay enough), most economists see it as interchangeable with all motivations, a neutral common currency in terms of which all motivations can be expressed. It is a *one-dimensional* picture of human motivation in which money simply adds to existing motivations or replaces them when they are absent. But money, and material benefits and costs more generally, cannot play this neutral role. In the real world money comes with psychic baggage. Just in the way that a gift can trigger gratitude or resentment in the recipient, depending on how they perceive the motives of the giver, financial carrots can also trigger a range of responses in those on the receiving end of the inducement.

In early 1993 the Swiss government was trying to decide where a (low-radioactivity) nuclear-waste dump should be sited. One possibility was to locate it near Wolfenschiessen, a small Swiss village of 640 families. In hour-long interviews with over 300 residents, they were asked how they would feel if offered financial compensation to agree to the dump. Support for the local siting of the dump *fell* by more than half once the compensation was offered. Eighty-three per cent of those who rejected the money explained their rejection by saying that they could not be bribed.[8] When some day-care centres in Haifa, Israel, introduced fines to discourage parents from collecting their children late, more parents arrived late.[9] Like the Swiss villagers, the Haifa parents saw the financial incentive as trying to buy their compliance rather than persuade them. With a 'price' for lateness now established, the parents treated the fine as a fee – a fee which bought them the right to collect their children later.

Evidence such as this was greeted with shock by economists, although the possibility that financial incentives can be counterproductive is now long established among psychologists (who by the early 1970s had largely abandoned Skinner's ideas). Introducing explicit financial incentives to get someone to do something can undermine or displace their existing intrinsic motivation: in psychologists' language, the intrinsic motivation is 'crowded out'.[10] Often, this intrinsic motivation includes a sense of moral obligation or duty – to work colleagues, your employer, your community or your country, depending on the context. In occupations such as medicine or teaching careful interview-based research has confirmed beyond doubt what we surely already knew: nurses, doctors and teachers are strongly motivated by the intrinsic importance of what they do, an intrinsic motivation which can be undermined by clumsy financial incentives imposed by their employers. It is not just medicine and teaching. In Boston, Massachusetts, the head of the fire service noticed that firefighters were off sick more on Mondays and Fridays. He imposed a strict limit of fifteen sick days, with pay deductions for those taking more days off sick. Oh dear. The number calling in sick over that Christmas and New Year period rose tenfold.[11] We can see the same kind of response in occupations with less obvious intrinsic motivation. David Packard, the founder of Hewlett-Packard, described attitudes at General Electric, where he worked in the late 1930s: 'the company was making a big thing of plant security . . . guarding its tool and part bins to make sure employees didn't steal . . . Many employees set out to prove this obvious display of distrust justified, walking off with tools and parts whenever they could.'[12]

Just like more heavy-handed uses of power, financial incentives send a signal about the beliefs and motives of the people introducing them. If I feel manipulated like a puppet, tugged this way and that by the people pulling the strings, then I will respond by withdrawing cooperation, loyalty, gifts of unpaid overtime and other forms of altruistic behaviour. It is the familiar twenty-first-century tragedy we have seen in other chapters: people live down to economists' cynical, distrustful expectations of them. The belief that 'everyone has their price' becomes self-fulfilling.

But the news cannot be all bad, because in some contexts financial incentives work just as intended by the economists who designed them. In 2002 Ireland introduced a small tax (15 pence) on plastic shopping bags. Within two weeks the use of bags had fallen by 94 per cent. The UK followed Ireland with a smaller tax phased in from 2011, leading to bag usage falling by around 80 per cent.[13] Crucially, though, the financial incentive was not used in isolation. The government appealed to our sense of social obligation as well as the desire to avoid tax. A major publicity campaign explained how abandoned bags end up in waterways, damaging marine life, with the rest in landfill taking hundreds of years to decompose. And before the tax was imposed there was national debate leading to public support for the bag tax from most retailers and consumer groups as well as environmentalists.

Using a financial incentive in isolation is unlikely to be so successful. If the people pulling the strings make no attempt to engage us through explanation or reasoned debate, that sends two possible signals. Either they believe we are simply mercenary: our compliance can be bought and we don't care whether we are being asked to do a good or bad thing. Or they believe we are stupid, in the sense of being unable to comprehend the good reasons for doing what we are being asked to do. Both signals tell us that we are not respected by the people with power over us.

Yet running through this is a positive lesson. Badly designed incentives can be counterproductive – but when handled carefully, with astute communication with the target group, they can work well. This is the message of *Freakonomics* and many behavioural economists: incentives send signals about the beliefs and motives of those offering them. And economists are familiar and comfortable with the idea that actions send signals.

Unfortunately, matters are more complicated. There are additional reasons why incentives can fail to work as intended. The mere presence of money can be a problem; when the money is removed the problem remains; and even if the incentives work as intended, they may still be a bad idea. Economists are much less comfortable with all that.

THE JEWISH TAILOR AND THE BLOOD DONOR

There is an old fable about a Jewish tailor who had recently opened a shop in town. The local bigots were determined to drive him away. They sent round a group of hooligans to jeer at him threateningly. The tailor thanked them and gave them some money. They laughed at him and left. Next day the hooligans returned to jeer, but the tailor told them he could not afford to give them as much money. The hooligans grumbled, but they took the money and left. On the following day the tailor apologized and said he could afford only one cent each this time. The hooligans told him they would not waste their time for just one measly cent. They left, never to return.

When financial incentives crowd out prior motives for some behaviour, the displacement or destruction of this prior motivation can be permanent. As a result, even if the financial incentives are subsequently withdrawn, the original behaviour does not return. At the Haifa day-care centres, when the late-collection fine was abolished after sixteen weeks, the number of late parents remained above the levels seen before the fines were introduced.[14] The parents' sense of moral obligation to pick up their children on time had been eroded.

One reason why the imprint of incentives can linger long after their removal is clear enough. People remember the implicit message underlying the incentives, about being untrustworthy, or incompetent, and so on. But even if no such negative signal accompanies the explicit incentive, the crowding-out effect can persist even after the incentive has gone. Why?

If we think about gifts again, a clue emerges. True, our reaction to a gift depends on the motives of the giver – but more obviously it depends on the nature of the gift. Orthodox economic theory implies that the best gift to receive is cash, because then you can buy exactly what you want.* Yet cash gifts are uncommon because we all know that this misses the point. The best gifts express and celebrate something about the relationship between giver and recipient. They are about more than satisfying the wants of the recipient. After all, when we do receive cash gifts, many of us spend the money on nothing more exciting than household bills or a new vacuum cleaner.

Given the notable difference between cash and non-cash gifts, it seems likely that people perceive financial incentives as inherently different from equivalent non-financial ones, even if the motives of those offering the incentives are entirely benign. It is hard to test this

* The economist Joel Waldfogel has devoted a significant part of his career to arguing that non-cash gifts are wasteful, beginning with his 1993 paper 'The Deadweight Loss of Christmas' (published in probably the most prestigious academic economics journal, the *American Economic Review*) and more recently his book *Scroogenomics*.

hypothesis, not least because perceptions may be influenced by a variety of acquired beliefs. But in a recent experiment, when young children were shown coins and their function was explained in simple terms the children became less helpful towards others in their ordinary daily activities.[15] People respond to cues suggesting the appropriate behaviour in the situation they find themselves in, and financial carrots and sticks are likely to cue the behaviour people use in their financial transactions – thinking like a consumer. Although we can sometimes act as 'ethical consumers', on average our relationships with sellers are both more anonymous and more short-lived than our relationships outside the market, in our communities, families and places of work. Economists have long celebrated the advantages of our one-off, anonymized, transactional relationships in the market. In entering the transaction we don't need to look beyond the end of our nose, choosing just with our own interests in mind; and we always leave the transaction quits, with no outstanding obligations or responsibilities towards the other party. The result is that we are more likely to leave morality behind when thinking as a consumer, compared to how we think in the community, family and workplace. Psychologists call this 'moral disengagement' or 'switching your ethics off'. Short-term, anonymous relationships do not trigger the strong feelings of sympathy and reciprocity which fuel our moral behaviour. So the mere presence of money changes our moral framing – how we see our situation – and increases the risk of our moral disengagement.

There is a further reason why incentives can crowd out our intrinsic motivation – and again, the damaging effects of this crowding out can linger long after the incentives themselves have been removed.

As with some other pivotal moments in this book, 1968 was a key date. Back then, Britain was unreservedly proud of its National Health Service and fully wedded to Keynesian government intervention in the economy. So the conclusion of a report from the Institute of Economic Affairs was truly shocking: state management of the blood supply did not meet the growing demand from hospitals. Instead people should be paid to give blood, because this would raise the supply. The proposal was immediately rejected. Instead its major impact was to stimulate a book-length critique, *The Gift*

Relationship, from a sociologist called Richard Titmuss. He compared blood-supply statistics in Britain with the United States, where in some states there were various forms of financial incentive to supply blood. Titmuss found that not only did paying people to give blood reduce the supply but also that freely donated blood was of higher quality. When people were paid to give blood, they were more likely to conceal aspects of their medical history which would render their blood unacceptable.

The Gift Relationship was reviewed at length by Nobel Prize-winning economists Ken Arrow and Bob Solow. Both were somewhat puzzled by Titmuss's findings and could see no reason why offering financial incentives might reduce the amount of blood donated. Subsequent economists have responded similarly: although recent research continues to support Titmuss's view that paying for blood leads to a reduction in supply, some economists challenge the evidence simply on the grounds that it is inconsistent with textbook economic theory.[16] Yet countries that have experimented with paying people to give blood find that once the payments are withdrawn blood donation does not return to the level before the experiment. It remains lower, suggesting that at least some of the intrinsic motivation to donate has been permanently crowded out.

One reason for the puzzlement of Arrow and Solow was the signal sent to potential donors by the financial incentive: surely it was a signal of social approval, a reward for good behaviour. Why would this deter donors? Easy, said Titmuss. Because they are not donors any more. They are sellers. Even a small payment to supply blood makes it seem more like a transaction than a gift: it is harder to see yourself as doing something altruistic when you are being paid. My enhanced self-respect from an act of altruism comes partly from the sacrifice involved. It's not the same if I'm financially compensated for it.

Altruism is one thing; being a lone altruist is quite another. Acting altruistically can enhance your self-respect, but having that generosity exploited by others often has the opposite effect. Moreover, at a more unconscious level, psychologists agree that we learn social behaviour principally by copying others (just watch young children if you're not convinced). We become more altruistic if we observe altruism in others. But a problem with incentives is that they make it hard to read the motives of others. When I see someone being paid after giving blood, were they being altruistic or just doing it for the money? The presence of incentives, then, makes it harder to see the altruism in others, and so I am less likely to act altruistically myself. And removing the incentives does not in itself remove the problem: I would need positive evidence of the altruism of others, rather than the mere absence of incentives, in order to copy it and 'learn' to be altruistic again.

Summing up, the offer of cash can deter blood donors, because it makes it harder to see yourself as altruistic and harder to observe altruism by other people. So we learn to be more selfish instead, a selfishness that can persist in the long term. Similar effects apply when blood donors are not exactly motivated by altruism, but something closer to civic duty or public-spiritedness: financial incentives make it harder to see yourself as doing your civic duty, and harder to see public-spirited behaviour in others. So we become more selfish.

Acts of altruism or public-spiritedness enhance our self-respect. More generally, it is the freedom to act, to make our own autonomous choices, which is crucial to self-respect. This brings us to a further reason why introducing incentives can backfire: they interfere with our autonomy. Even if the motives of the people pulling the strings are entirely benign, they are still trying to control and manipulate our behaviour. The adverse effect of incentives on autonomy has been studied in detail across a wide range of skilled occupations and professions from medicine to coding. There is compelling evidence that experienced surgeons, lawyers, academics and scientists strongly resist incentive schemes which interfere with their freedom to act in line with their expert judgement or which conflict with the norms of behaviour expected in their profession. While economists have lately come to accept that incentives should be used with special care in some professions, they disagree over whether the problem is more widespread. Many economists still assume that incentives don't normally conflict with a worker's sense of autonomy, because ordinary people don't work to express their autonomy. They just do it for the money.

WHAT NOBODIES AND SOMEBODIES
HAVE IN COMMON

Meet Luke. Luke worked as a 'custodian' (a cleaner or janitor) in a major US teaching hospital. One patient was a young man in a long-term coma. One day Luke cleaned the patient's room, as normal. He cleaned it while the patient's father, who had been keeping a vigil for months, had left the room to smoke a cigarette. On returning, the father angrily shouted at Luke to clean the room. Luke cleaned it again, without a murmur of complaint. In an interview with researchers studying working practices, Luke explained the incident: 'I kind of knew the situation about his son ... He wasn't coming out of the coma ... It was like six months that his son was here. He'd be a little frustrated, and so I cleaned it again. But I wasn't angry with him. I guess I could understand.'[17]

Luke went on to explain that he saw his cleaning duties as just part of his job, which also involved making patients and their families comfortable, cheering them up and listening when they wanted to talk. Of course, none of this was in Luke's official job description, which only mentioned cleaning tasks. It is easy to imagine the effect of introducing financial incentives to encourage Luke to focus just on his cleaning. To say that Luke's intrinsic motivation might be 'crowded out' hardly begins to describe the problem. Luke's desire to help patients and their families was not just another motivation, potentially competing with financial incentives, but central to how he saw his working life.

Luke's story suggests that autonomy and identity matter not just in skilled occupations but in jobs often regarded as menial or mundane. Most of us don't want to see ourselves as working just for the money. We are also trying, like Marlon Brando in *On the Waterfront*, to be somebody. We are constructing an identity, for ourselves and in the eyes of others. Of course, this applies outside the workplace too. We want to be free to make our own choices rather than be pushed by incentives – even if done so gently, politely and for a good cause.

Luke wanted to be a somebody to the patients and families in the hospital, rather than a nobody. His philosophy would have been recognized by a somebody among philosophers, Isaiah Berlin. But before we see what the janitor and the philosopher have in common we must confront the elephant in the room. For economists have a simple solution to the problem of incentives backfiring, whether that backfiring is due to the signal sent by the introduction of incentives, the moral disengagement that incentives can encourage or the challenge to autonomy they pose: increase the money involved.

The Visit of the Old Lady, by the great Swiss playwright Friedrich Dürrenmatt, tells the story of Claire Zachanassian. Young Claire becomes pregnant by her lover, Alfred, who lives in the same small town. When Alfred denies paternity, Claire goes to court, but Alfred wins the case by bribing two townspeople to lie. Years later Claire, now an old lady, returns to the town, which has fallen on hard times. Claire, however, is now the fabulously wealthy widow of an oil tycoon. She offers the town half a billion Swiss francs, and another half-billion to be shared among the residents. But there is a catch: the residents must kill Alfred. The mayor refuses and the townspeople are shocked. Claire says she will wait. Over time the townspeople buy lots of luxury goods on credit and accumulate debts. Finally, they agree to kill Alfred. Claire, satisfied she has now 'bought justice', gives the mayor a cheque and leaves the town with Alfred's body.

Perhaps Dürrenmatt is right: financial incentives *can* work in the way predicted by orthodox economics – as long as they are big enough. If you offer enough money, people will do what you want, because the lure of the cash will outweigh any pesky moral scruples. Everyone has their price, after all. Still, for those of us uneasy about the spread of incentives, the economists' chutzpah is breathtaking: the solution to the problem of incentives backfiring is more incentives – bigger, better, longer, harder.

But does it work? *The Visit* was Swiss fiction. We need Swiss fact. Let's revisit the upstanding villagers of Wolfenschiessen, who said they would not be bribed to agree to a nuclear dump being located nearby. At the time of those interviews three other sites were being considered, but a year later the government had settled on Wolfenschiessen, whose residents were offered substantial compensation by the developer: $3 million per year for the next forty years. In July

1994 Wolfenschiessen decided in a village meeting to accept the offer and host the nuclear dump.

So is it as easy as that? Just sweep aside all need for a deeper, more realistic understanding of human motivation with a big wad of cash? Not so fast. An obvious snag is that big financial incentives are a costly way to get people to do things. Wolfenschiessen was a village of only 640 families, so $3 million per year amounted to $4,687 per family, more than a month's salary even for the wealthy burghers of Wolfenschiessen, and around 120 per cent of Wolfenschiessen's total annual tax revenue.

The real objection, though, is more fundamental. Suppose that if incentives are big enough, we can be sure they will work just as intended. Does that mean they are okay? And if so, how did we slip from Taylor's vision of incentives as an instrument of social control to incentives as okay? Most economists and other supporters of incentives answer 'yes' to the first question. Incentives are morally irreproachable, they argue, because they involve voluntary exchange. No one is forced to do anything against their wishes. But this brings us to a contradiction at the heart of the argument for incentives. On the one hand, supporters recommend incentives over other forms of social control, such as regulation or coercion, on the grounds that they preserve freedom of choice. On the other hand, the successful use of incentives depends on the ability to control people's behaviour – to induce them to respond to the incentive in a predictable way. In essence, then, the argument for incentives claims that people can be controlled while being free.

Like most seeming paradoxes, things are not what they seem to be. If a person can be readily, predictably, led to do something they would not otherwise do, we say that they are being controlled or manipulated. We do not describe them as 'free', even if they could have chosen to do otherwise. Real freedom requires more than the superficial ability to choose.

Enter the great philosopher Isaiah Berlin with the classic modern analysis of freedom, heavily influenced by his personal experiences. In 1920 the eleven-year-old Berlin left Bolshevik Russia with his family, driven away by oppression and anti-Semitism. Later, he noted the way in which totalitarian regimes equate freedom with the pretence of choice. I don't act freely, Berlin argued, 'if in a totalitarian state I betray my friend under threat of torture . . . Nevertheless, I did, of course, make a choice . . . the mere existence of alternatives is not, therefore, enough to make my action free.'[18] This provided the background for Berlin's definition of freedom (which he called liberty):

> The 'positive' sense of the word 'liberty' derives from the wish on the part of the individual to be his own master. I wish my life and decisions to depend on myself, not on external factors of whatever kind . . . I wish to be somebody, not nobody; a doer – deciding, not being decided for, self-directed and not acted upon by external nature or by other men as if I were a thing, or an animal or a slave incapable of playing a human role . . . I wish, above all, to be conscious of myself as a thinking, willing, active being, bearing responsibility for my choices and able to explain them by reference to my own ideas and purposes.[19]

And if that is too high-falutin, just remember Luke. He had his own ideas and purposes regarding his job, he wanted to be self-directed in pursuing them and responsible for his choices, judged against his own standards.

The picture of humanity which emerges from the traditional economic theory of motivation does not respect our ideals of liberty and autonomy. Since I can be predictably manipulated by incentives, it cannot be said that my decisions depend only 'on myself, not on external factors'. Nor am I 'self-directed'. Incentive schemes, then, might work just as intended by their designers, with no crowding out – but still be morally wrong because they conflict with our values of liberty and autonomy.

And incentives can be morally wrong in other ways too.

When a judge is offered and accepts a financial incentive to let a guilty person go free, this is bribery, and is obviously harmful. That both the briber and the judge might be better off is irrelevant. In the film *Indecent Proposal* (1993), a billionaire is attracted to a happily married woman. He offers the couple a million dollars if she will spend a night with him. The billionaire is not aggressive and the offer is not exploitative, so when the couple accept it is a voluntary transaction. We need older, stronger language than 'crowding out' to describe what is going on in these cases: incentives can *corrupt* us. They can corrupt both the person offering the incentive and the one accepting it. Shakespeare saw how dangerous corruption can be – and how far people will go to resist it. In *Measure for Measure*, judge Angelo offers to spare Isabella's brother's life if she will sleep with him. Isabella, a novice nun, refuses, saying that it is better that her brother die once than that her soul be sacrificed for eternity.

But is there really any likelihood of something as serious as corruption arising from the more prosaic, everyday incentive schemes devised by economists? Yes, not least because lying is another form of corruption. We've seen that when people are paid to give blood they are more likely to lie about their medical history. And when teachers' pay is linked to their students' exam scores, more teachers will lie about how well their students performed.[20]

Of course, financial incentives are not always corrupting. But sometimes they undermine the opposite of corruption – the development of good character. This is not just a worry of idle philosophers: a central purpose of school is the development of good character in young people. We want students not just to do the right thing but to do it for the right reason. We want children to learn self-discipline, the ability to resist immediate temptations. Yet schools in Dallas paid seven-year-old schoolchildren $2 per book they read. The danger of cash incentives to read is that self-discipline is undermined. Children are led to think purely in terms of immediate pleasures and pains – whether the effort of reading is outweighed by the cash payment. They begin to believe that reading is 'work' rather than pleasure, something not worth doing for its own sake. Rather than learning to read, money becomes the goal, so inevitably children focus on maximizing financial rewards, trying to cheat the system by picking shorter, easier books. With this way of thinking ingrained, it is not surprising that if the financial incentive is withdrawn, children respond by withdrawing their effort. And incentives do not encourage older children to take responsibility for their reading either. Just imagine the tweeny sneer: 'If you're not paying me, how can you expect me to read a book?'[21]

This is another illustration of why autonomy matters. It is the difference between doing something for its own sake or for your own internal reasons and doing it because of an external incentive. Children who choose autonomously, wanting to learn to read, will never stick with the easier books they can already read. It becomes boring – and there is no point in cheating if you are just cheating yourself.

THE WEIRD WORLD OF NUDGE

A widely discussed development in economics in recent years has been the emergence of behavioural economics. In essence, behavioural economics tries to study how people actually behave – in contrast to fantasies such as *homo economicus* which dominate orthodox economics. It uses ideas and methods from psychology, and it was two psychologists, Daniel Kahneman and Amos Tversky, who perhaps did more than anyone else to dislodge old orthodoxies in economics about how we think and choose. One big idea in behavioural economics began with Kahneman and Tversky's Asian disease problem:

> Suppose you are told that an unusual Asian disease is expected to kill 600 people in your country. Two alternative policies to combat the disease have been proposed. If Policy A is adopted, 200 people will be saved. If Policy B is adopted, there is a 1/3 probability that 600 people will be saved, and a 2/3 probability that no people will be saved. Do you favour policy A or B?
>
> But suppose instead the response to the same disease involves a choice between the following two policies: if policy C is adopted, 400 people will die. If policy D is adopted, there is 1/3 probability that no one will die, and a 2/3 probability that 600 people will die. Do you favour policy C or D?[22]

Kahneman and Tversky discovered that a large majority favour A when asked the first question, while a large majority favour D in answer to the second – even though the two questions are essentially the same. Policy A has the same outcome as policy C, and B has the same outcome as D. The exact wording or framing of the alternatives alters people's choices; these *framing effects* turn out to be ubiquitous in a wide range of decision contexts. For psychologists, this was not surprising: *of course* our decision-making is affected by how the alternatives are described. But it was shocking news for orthodox economists. With their careful, meticulous experiments, Kahneman and Tversky forced economists to accept the reality of framing effects. And they had an equally powerful impact on how most economists thought about incentives.

First, Kahneman and Tversky made economists much more accepting of the possibility that incentives can be counterproductive. Until they came along, the evidence for crowding out and the possibility that incentives can backfire was a huge embarrassment to economists. What could be a more basic idea in economics than that people respond predictably, obviously, to money? Once there was too much robust evidence of crowding out to be able to ignore it, the only remaining possibility was to label this kind of behaviour 'irrational': a feeble response, but a correct one, if 'rational' is defined as what *homo economicus* would do. Kahneman and Tversky's crucial contribution was to develop an explanation for what economists had previously called irrationality, in effect an entire theory of irrationality. This rescued crowding out from being an embarrassing anomaly: now it was just one among many types of 'irrational' human behaviour.

Second, some economists saw in Kahneman and Tversky's framing effects an explanation of how incentives sometimes backfire and sometimes don't. Incentives which are identical as far as economic theory is concerned – the same monetary value, and so on – can produce different results, depending on how they are described or framed.

Third, accepting the reality of counterproductive incentives suggested that another approach to policy-making was needed. But as the new behavioural economics began to filter through to policy-making circles, something strange happened. The central lesson of behavioural economics is that people make poor decisions – yet the policy innovation it provoked seeks to rely on precisely those poor decisions to bring about desirable outcomes. Welcome to the weird world of *Nudge*.

Nudge began with a 2008 book of that name by economist Richard Thaler and lawyer Cass Sunstein. Both of them had worked with

Kahneman and Tversky, who had shown that real people do not act like *homo economicus*. Rather than weighing up all relevant considerations and carefully calculating the 'optimal' choice, people are guided by rules of thumb, intuition, impulse and inertia. The core idea behind Nudge is that rather than fighting these forces, we should *use* them, to steer or nudge people to make the choices they would want to make – the choices *homo economicus* would make, or at least something close. At first, Nudge looked like a passing fashion, just the latest idea from the policy wonks hanging around central government. But it didn't go away. Sunstein worked for Obama in the White House, Thaler's 'Nudge Unit' advised the Cameron government in the UK, and self-conscious Nudge policies are now being used in around 130 countries.[23] Thaler won the Nobel Prize for economics in 2017.

Nudge enthusiasts almost always point to the same policy to illustrate the Nudge approach, its flagship success story – automatic enrolment in workplace pensions. A workplace pension has two big advantages over other forms of retirement saving: tax breaks and contributions from your employer. Yet many people fail to enrol in their workplace-pension scheme, even though they need to save for retirement one way or another. Simple inertia has long been seen as the culprit. It is easier to do nothing than to think about what to do, how much to pay in, and so on, not least because those decisions trigger uncomfortable thoughts about financial insecurity and old age. To tackle the problem, Sunstein and Thaler suggested a minor tweak, a gentle nudge. Why not make a pension contribution at some appropriate level the default or do-nothing choice for employees? Those who do not want to join the pension are still free to opt out.

It turns out that tweaks like this are available for almost every choice we make. In a school or workplace cafeteria the healthy foods can be displayed prominently and attractively – while the least healthy choices can be literally kept under the counter. At Amsterdam's Schiphol Airport, each of the urinals in the men's bathrooms has a picture of a fly drawn on them. Letters reminding people to pay their outstanding taxes are more effective when they point out that most people living nearby have already paid up. In the UK, economists were mystified that government subsidies for energy-saving loft insulation had little effect. Then the government's 'nudge team' suggested that loft-clearance services should be subsidized instead. The overall cost to households increased but the demand for loft insulation rose significantly.

No wonder Nudge has proved popular with politicians of all shades: desirable social outcomes can be engineered without the heavy-handed use of financial incentives or coercion via laws and regulations. Instead, Nudge works with the grain of human nature and respects freedom of choice.

Or so it seems. The trouble with Nudge – and behavioural economics more generally – is that it still shares too many ideas with orthodox economics. Behavioural economics inspired by Kahneman and Tversky's work is often labelled research on *heuristics and biases*. That last word reveals the underlying assumption of most behavioural economics: human decision-making is biased – in other words, flawed. While Kahneman and Tversky had launched a revolution in irrefutably demonstrating that people do not behave like *homo economicus*, they left unquestioned the equally central pillar of orthodox economics that people *ought* to behave like that – leaving *homo economicus* untouched as the ideal of what it means to be rational. And the Nudge enthusiasts leave it untouched too. So at the heart of their approach is the assumption that the ideal choice, the perfectly rational choice, is what *homo economicus* would do. *Homo economicus* has just one goal – the promotion of his or her own well-being or welfare. Exactly how welfare is maximized does not matter to *homo economicus* – ends justify means – so autonomy, being the author of your well-being, gets ignored. As Sunstein insists, 'People speak in terms of autonomy but what they are doing is making a rapid, intuitive judgement about welfare.'[24] And if *their* only goal is welfare-maximization, there is an obvious role for *us*, the 'we' that appears so frequently in the writings of Nudge wonks and behavioural economists. We, the Nudge experts, needn't get bogged down in messy compromises between ethical values or wondering what 'they' really want. We, the Nudgers, already know what they should want, so we can get on with nudging them in that direction.

One practical problem here is that behavioural economics applies to elites too. Experts can mess up Nudging because they are vulnerable to the same cognitive flaws as the rest of us. Of course, experts can be incompetent in using other policy tools, including financial incentives. So Nudge may seem no worse than the alternatives in this respect. But with financial incentives, at least we know we are being 'incentivized' and can be on guard. In contrast, we often don't know we are being Nudged. More than that, subterfuge can be essential to Nudging. Nudges frequently rely on covert manipulation of our behaviour or a degree of secrecy – such as putting the unhealthy foods in the cafeteria out of sight. This example might make covert manipulation appear relatively harmless, but in general Nudge is wide open to being exploited by mendacious regulators and politicians with darker motives. At the very least, the 'harmless' aura surrounding some nudges and the sheer subtlety of others suggests that Nudging may be less subject to democratic scrutiny than traditional regulations and more vulnerable to capture by special-interest groups.

Finally, there is a more basic objection to some seemingly harmless nudges like 'auto-enrolment' in pension schemes (making 'opt in' the default): other policies may be superior to Nudge. Some US evidence suggests that auto-enrolment may have *reduced* retirement saving.[25] Default pension contributions in the US have often been set very low (around 3 per cent) and many employees who might otherwise have contributed more than 3 per cent stick with the default out of inertia. Bizarrely, many Nudgers assume that once the nudge draws people's attention to their pension, employees will adjust their contributions to the 'optimal' level. They won't stick with the default. This is an astonishing assumption from behavioural economists, who know the power of inertia in leading us to stick with the default. In any case, why not just compel people to save enough for retirement, either through private schemes, or tax-funded public ones?

Again, the culprit is the default: the default adherence of the Nudgers to orthodox economics. They assume that, once given the appropriate nudge, people will default back to behaving like *homo economicus*. The Nudgers begin their argument by essentially dividing humanity into two groups. It's us and them again. There are the slaves of impulse, inertia and rules of thumb. And then there are the smart people (guess which group the Nudgers think they are in).

Then the Nudgers revert to orthodox economics, which holds that any form of government mandate or compulsion must harm *homo economicus*, because mandates force a change in behaviour – and the prior behaviour of *homo economicus* was already optimal. Nudges, on the other hand, impose no such harm, because they leave *homo economicus* free to do his own thing. As Sunstein and Thaler conclude: 'we should design policies that help the least sophisticated people in society while imposing the smallest possible costs on the most sophisticated'.[26] It is hard not to detect a note of condescension here. So what would more respectful Nudging look like? Indeed, let's widen the question: what about the respectful use of incentives more generally?

BEYOND CARROTS AND STICKS

In several Indian cities, including Bangalore and Rajahmundry, a strange street performance can occasionally be seen. A band of drummers gathers, usually outside an office building, and beats out a fast-paced tattoo, often for more than an hour. The performances attract a large crowd, cheering enthusiastically. But the drummers don't expect the crowd to pay anything. They want the company inside the office building to pay instead – unpaid taxes. This is an Indian way of giving tax avoiders an incentive to pay up, by naming and shaming them in a highly public way in the local community. It's a method that has been successful in recouping unpaid taxes where other methods have failed.[27]

Incentives accompanied by moral messages can work well. Of course, different contexts and cultures demand different approaches to incentive design, but nevertheless there are some common ingredients. To begin with, incentive designers must not ignore the previous sentence: context and culture matter. Unfortunately, ignoring context is an article of faith for many economists, and behavioural economics suffers from that inheritance. One reason is physics envy: the desire of economists to emulate sciences such as physics. Scientists do controlled experiments, so behavioural economists prefer to do controlled experiments too. Since suitable conditions for controlled experiments almost never exist in real life, most behavioural economics research is conducted in the lab.[28] Students play games or answer hypothetical questions about contrived situations, such as how they would respond to a financial incentive. But, of course, behaviour in a lab context is at best an incomplete guide to behaviour in the real world.

Paying full attention to context and culture is about understanding not just when incentives backfire but when they might work un-expectedly well too. Given the wide-ranging evidence of crowding out, where financial incentives undermine our existing intrinsic motivations, 'crowding in' comes as a surprise: incentives can enable or encourage people to act in line with their intrinsic motivations. Yes, schemes that pay children to read books have several potential draw-backs. But in some communities, the main reason why few children read is peer pressure. Reading is just not cool. Being paid to read might give children who would like to read an excuse to tell their peers, 'I'm just doing it for the money.' There is evidence pointing in this direction from a programme paying pregnant women cash to quit smoking.[29] In private, the women told researchers that a big obstacle to quitting was peer pressure to continue smoking. The cash incentive gave them cover to quit publicly, because in this group of (mainly low-income) women, 'I'm just doing it for the money' was a badge of pride.

The moral and social meaning of our actions is never far from the surface. Unlike the pregnant women, blood donors seem unlikely to tell their peers that they are motivated by money, even if that's the truth. Behavioural economists and other incentive designers need to be able to distinguish the pregnant women from the blood donors, so moral complexity and ambiguity cannot be ignored. That means going beyond labelling different descriptions of different situations as mere 'framing effects' and going beyond welfare maximization as the definition of what people want and what is best for society.

We can get another perspective on the morality of incentives by contrasting them with rewards and punishments. There is a big dif-ference. We don't say that athletes are 'incentivized' to win Olympic medals, because medals are rewards for excellence, not incentives. The difference remains even if the rewards and punishments are fin-ancial. The power of rewards and punishments, including financial prizes and fines, comes from being seen as *deserved*. For example, the prospect of a fine levied in a court of law is more powerful than a fee or other financial incentive of the same money value. The fine embodies a moral message, a public condemnation. Clearly, in some contexts, rewards and punishments could be both fairer and more effective than standard economic incentives. However, rewards and punishments earn their legitimacy only through an ongoing dialogue between those distributing and receiving them, as well as wider society.

Such a dialogue may be more obvious in the case of rewards and punishments, but it needs to happen if any kind of nudge or incentive scheme is to succeed. What might it look like? In the case of nudges, it should include showing us the defaults and rules of thumb we unconsciously rely on to make choices, to help us overcome them if we want. For example, in one US workplace cafeteria, rather than hiding away the unhealthy foods under the counter, workers were given the opportunity to choose and pay for their lunch when they arrived at work in the morning. And just in case they didn't realize why, they were told that people who choose their lunch early in the morning are much more likely to choose healthy foods than those who wait until lunchtime. You need to pay up front, too, to avoid backsliding. This is a nudge, but an open and transparent one that seeks to help people 'lock in' their willpower, at the time of day when they have it.

Perhaps the original, more covert nudge might get more people to eat more healthily, but there are other issues at stake. It is not just a matter of 'what works'. If that were true, and all the Nudgers' arguments about our error-prone decision-making hold, then we should take them to their logical conclusion: why mess about with Nudge when you can use stealthier and more powerfully manipulative techniques such as subliminal advertising? Equally important, our decision-making may not always be as error-prone as it appears. Respectful nudging acknowledges the limitations of *homo economicus* as an ideal of rationality. Yes, our mental operating system frequently deviates from that of *homo economicus*, but this is not always a bug. Sometimes it's an upgrade.

Ultimately, in a democracy, we should cherish dialogue as a way for those on the receiving end of nudges or incentives to communicate with those pulling the strings. People on the receiving end may see incentives as the unnecessary and undeserved use of power. Workers subject to extremely intensive monitoring, like the pickers in the Amazon warehouse, have cause for complaint here. (Unlike the workers in Taylor's day, they can only dream of help from the US Congress.) More subtly, people may legitimately disagree with the aims or purposes of those pulling the strings. In many healthcare systems doctors face a range of financial incentives introduced by governments (in public systems) or insurance companies (in private systems). Doctors may resist these incentives – not because they don't care about maximizing patient welfare but because they believe the incentives steer treatment in ways which harm patient welfare. Moreover, when governments and insurers insist that the entire responsibility for treatment decisions lies with doctors, it looks like incentive schemes are being used by governments and insurers to exercise power without responsibility.

When, in the late eighteenth century, Benjamin Franklin brought back from France a diamond-encrusted snuffbox, a present from Louis XVI, the US Congress was troubled. They saw that it could change Franklin's attitude to France, possibly without him realizing.[30] Worrying about the unwelcome effects of incentives is not new. The new development is the infusion of ideas from economics: only in the last few decades have economists devoted much explicit attention to incentives.[31] And the impact of economics has been highly significant. We are finally in a position to summarize it.

It is tempting to begin by supposing that financial incentives have become more ubiquitous because of the growing influence of economics. But how would we measure that ubiquity? What would it mean? True, incentives *feel* more ubiquitous partly because, as we've seen, economists have introduced incentive talk into everyday life – including in situations where that language seems horribly inappropriate. Yet the real impact of economics has been in influencing the kinds of incentives we choose, and how we justify them. First, economists have brought along their disciplinary default assumption: that people can be assumed to be selfish, and that little is lost by ignoring their altruistic and ethical motives. This leads directly to the assumption that everyone has their price. Restricting the evidence base – for example, using lab experiments rather than interviews in real-world contexts – makes it harder to develop a richer, more nuanced picture of human motivation. Second, economists consider only one value, one measure of success, in judging incentives: individual welfare or well-being, narrowly defined. They want to avoid opening up a Pandora's box of moral questions: values of fairness, responsibility, autonomy and respect, among others. Their desire to keep the box shut may be understandable, but it's impossible: values such as these play a central role in determining whether incentives work, and whether they have benign or malign side-effects. Third, economists instead see all incentives in terms of an exchange or transaction: I do what you want me to do in exchange for the incentive. Since the exchange is voluntary, it will not take place if either side is made worse off. And so, according to economists, incentive schemes cannot harm anyone's welfare. Some economists take this conclusion one step further: incentives cannot be unethical. At the very least, their argument here attempts to silence any further ethical assessment of incentives.

Together, economists' ideas have severely limited our ability to think clearly about incentives. But as we have seen, this can be turned around. By setting aside restrictive economic thinking, we can hope to develop incentives and nudges which are both effective and respectful.

Daniel Kahneman has a strong memory from around the age of seven, when he lived in Paris. This was Paris under Nazi occupation, when there was a 6 p.m. curfew. Hurrying home after curfew one evening, young Danny was terrified when an SS soldier approached him. All the more so because Danny had the yellow Star of David inside his sweater, whereas Nazi law required him to display it prominently. The SS soldier picked Danny up and hugged him. Then he put him down, showed him a picture of a young boy in his wallet and gave him some money. Danny went home thinking that people are deeply complex and unpredictable.[32]

People are deeply complex and unpredictable, and economists' understanding of incentives has barely begun to grapple with the complexities, both of predicting how people respond to some new incentive or nudge, and of the many moral and political questions which arise in trying to get people to do things. We seem determined to preserve our autonomy as a central part of our identity, and so we resist incentives which interfere with it. Yet at the same time we yearn, childlike, for a paternalistic authority to take care of us, to make decisions for us. Sometimes, perhaps, we can square this circle by embracing autonomy when it is most precious to us, while consciously giving up decision-making elsewhere. When Barack Obama was president he noted: 'I'm trying to pare down decisions. I don't want to make decisions about what I'm eating or wearing. Because I have too many other decisions to make.'[33]

But often the contradiction cannot be avoided. We want autonomy, and we want a wise, benevolent authority figure to ensure we do what is best. The best we can do is to face this contradiction, openly and honestly. And either way we jump, as a small crumb of comfort, we still deserve respect. There is no need for incentives which deny even that.

8

Trust in Numbers

On 5 October 1960 the President of IBM, Thomas J. Watson Jr, was among three business leaders being shown around the war room of NORAD, the North American Air Defense headquarters in Colorado Springs. Above the maps on the wall was an alarm indicator connected to America's ballistic-missile early-warning system in Thule, Greenland. The businessmen were told that a '1' flashing on the alarm meant nothing much, but higher numbers were more serious. As they watched, the numbers started to rise. When the display reached '5', an air of panic descended on the room, and the alarmed businessmen were hustled out of the war room into a nearby office, without further explanation. A '5' was the highest alarm level possible. In this case it meant, with an estimated 99.9 per cent certainty, a massive incoming missile attack from Siberia. The chiefs of staff were urgently contacted and asked for immediate instructions regarding a response. With minutes left before the probable obliteration of the first US cities, the Canadian vice-commander of NORAD asked where Khrushchev was. The discovery that he was at the UN in New York was enough to justify a pause before authorizing full nuclear retaliation. And then it emerged that the all-out attack detected by the computer system was in fact the moon rising over Norway.[1]

What saved us from Armageddon was the wisdom to query what the computer model was saying, rather than simply giving in to the seemingly overwhelming force of its predictions. It could have been different: the persuasive power of that extreme number, 99.9 per cent, could have led us to set all doubts aside.

This, indeed, is exactly what happened, repeatedly, in the run-up to the financial crash of 2008. Legions of very smart people in all the world's financial centres used computer models which were producing extreme numbers, numbers that contradicted the evidence emerging from the world around them. In August 2007 David Viniar, the CFO of Goldman Sachs, was quoted in the *Financial Times*, saying, 'We were seeing things that were 25-standard deviation moves, several days in a row.' Translated, Viniar was saying that in some markets recent price movements had been so extreme that they should never happen according to the predictions of Goldman's models. 'Never happen' is a simplification: Goldman's models implied that one of these market gyrations could occur, but it was *highly* unlikely, an extreme unlikeliness which is nearly impossible to describe. I will try. A 25-standard deviation event is one which happens *much less often* than once in the history of the universe since the Big Bang. It is as unlikely as winning the jackpot in the UK national lottery twenty-one times in a row.[2]

Yet such an event had occurred not just once but repeatedly, several days in a row. But rather than abandon the models, given their falsification by reality, Goldman Sachs, along with many other investment banks, continued to rely on them to quantify various kinds of uncertainty. Maybe they thought, as financial experts through the ages have repeatedly asserted, 'This time is different.'

Why do very smart people put their trust in numerical measures of uncertainty, even when faced with conflicting empirical evidence? Most of the smart people in the world's financial sectors are familiar with modern finance theory, an offshoot of economics. And the error of trying to measure the extent of unknowable uncertainty in numerical terms has been widely discussed in economics for decades, since a RAND analyst called Daniel Ellsberg published an experiment back in 1961 (just after that nuclear near-miss the previous October). Ellsberg's experiment perfectly pinpointed the strangeness of attempting to measure pure uncertainty in numerical terms – that is, using odds or probabilities.

Suppose there are two boxes: box A holds fifty red and fifty black balls; box B also contains a total of one hundred red and black balls, but in a ratio which is unknown. A ball is to be drawn at random

from one box, but you can choose the box. You win $100 if the ball is
red. Which box do you choose?

There is no need to spend much time thinking about this: it is not
a trick question. Nor is the follow-up question:

Now suppose you win $100 if the ball drawn is black, but the boxes
are left unchanged; will you change your choice of box?

The purpose of Ellsberg's experiment was not to ridicule our ordinary thinking. On the contrary, its target was the gap between our
ordinary thinking and the intellectual orthodoxy perpetuated by
economists, decision analysts, game-theorists and other peddlers of
theories about how we ought to think. Faced with the choice between
box A and box B, most of us choose box A initially and do not change
our choice after the prize is switched to the draw of a black ball. That
people choose box A, and stick with it, seems easy to explain: we like
to know the odds we face, so we choose box A both times, rather
than the pure uncertainty of box B.

But the dominant theory of decision-making under uncertainty
holds that this is a confusing, inconsistent, irrational way to think
and choose. According to this dominant view – an approach with its
intellectual roots in economics but nowadays mainstream in a wide
variety of applied fields from finance to epidemiology – the only
rational way to choose in situations of uncertainty is to think in terms
of numerical odds or probabilities.

This seems unarguable in circumstances where the probabilities
are obvious. When I toss a coin, I should know it will come up heads
about half the time. But the dominant view is that we should
always think in terms of probabilities, even when we have absolutely
no basis for knowing what they are. When we don't know the probabilities, we should just invent them. And if people are rational, then
we can infer the probabilities they have invented by observing their
choices. So according to the orthodox view, in Ellsberg's experiment,
if you choose A in the initial choice, that *must* mean you believe it
contains more red balls than box B – in other words, you believe the
probability of a red ball being drawn is higher. It follows that you
believe box A contains fewer black balls than box B, so when the

prize is switched to black you should switch your choice to box B. The economists were so mystified by the realization that hardly anyone thinks like this that Ellsberg's experiment was dubbed the Ellsberg *Paradox*. As we will soon see, it has revolutionary implications for thinking about uncertainty, and the world would be different if the guys at Goldman Sachs, and the finance theory on which they rely, had taken these implications seriously.

Daniel Ellsberg was an unlikely source for such a fundamental challenge to intellectual orthodoxy: we would expect a RAND analyst to defend the mathematical measurement of uncertainty, rather than question it. Ellsberg's golden-boy education and early career made him a natural fit at the RAND Corporation. He graduated with highest honours in economics from Harvard, then, following graduate study and a period serving as a lieutenant in the Marines, he divided his time between RAND and Harvard. In 1964, he moved to work at the highest levels of the Pentagon. It is tempting to suppose that this reassuringly elite CV would encourage the usually cautious and conservative economic theorists at RAND and Harvard to embrace the radical implications of the Ellsberg Paradox.

But something else happened. As far as the US establishment was concerned, Ellsberg's career went terribly wrong. He became the personal target of the notorious 'White House Plumbers', the Nixon aides who would later commit the Watergate burglaries. Secretary of State Henry Kissinger publicly branded him 'the Most Dangerous Man in America'.* Perhaps it is not so surprising that the Ellsberg Paradox was largely ignored for a generation.

PROBABILITY GETS PERSONAL

Probability is not a new idea. The idea that we humans need not be passive in the face of the future but can instead take control of our fate was seen as a stand against the gods, against unfathomable nature. In Western society it is no coincidence that modern ideas of probability became

---

* There is even a film about Ellsberg with this title, one of two full-length films about him.

firmly established in the late eighteenth century, just as religion's grip began to loosen with the triumph of the Enlightenment. Probabilistic thinking stood for confident progress beyond stoical submission to uncertainty. Like so much else, that confidence ended in 1914.

The impact of the assassination of Archduke Ferdinand on 28th June that year was not immediately clear. It took a month for the financial markets to realize the implications, and the resulting panic led to the closure of the London and New York stock exchanges on 31st July. By this time, several European countries had already declared war on each other. Two days later the Governor of the Bank of England was holidaying on a yacht off the coast of Scotland. 'There's talk of a war,' he said to his friends, 'but it won't happen.'[3] Two days after that Britain declared war on Germany.

Surprises happen. With the First World War, uncertainty was back, loud and kicking. In the war's aftermath, four carnage-filled years later, when the prevailing mood oozed with unease and uncertainty about the future, two economists expressed reservations about orthodox probabilistic thinking. Chicago economist Frank Knight drew a crucial distinction between what he called 'measurable' and 'unmeasurable' uncertainty. Measurable uncertainty, he stated, includes games of chance and, more generally, situations in which probabilities can be calculated based on the relative frequency of events. Unmeasurable uncertainty is everything else: situations of pure uncertainty in which no relative-frequency information is available to us. In Britain, John Maynard Keynes drew a similar distinction to Knight, although it was embedded in an idiosyncratic and controversial theory of probability that arguably obscured Keynes's discussion. Neither Knight nor Keynes can obviously be credited as the first to draw the distinction: both published their work in 1921, and in any case the distinction has been around far longer, for instance implicit in the difference between the French words *hasard* and *fortuit*.* But both Knight and Keynes reminded economists and other thinkers interested in decision-making

* Both words can be roughly translated as 'chance', but *hasard* comes from an Arabic word used in dice games, in which uncertainty is measurable and probabilistic. This probabilistic meaning was later adopted by the French mathematician Borel. *Fortuit* is more associated with unforeseeability and unpredictability, suggesting unmeasurable uncertainty.

of the fundamental limit to probabilistic thinking: in some situations we don't have information about probabilities, so uncertainty is unmeasurable.

Yet within just a few years, the distinction between measurable and unmeasurable uncertainty seemed to be made redundant by a paper titled 'Truth and Probability' from a *wunderkind* called Frank Ramsey.

The archetypal 'Renaissance man', Leonardo da Vinci, was not just a genius but a polymath with gifts in many different fields. But the accumulation of knowledge since then has made specialization unavoidable. Renaissance man may now be extinct but, arguably, Frank Ramsey was one of the last of them. He moved in circles of genius: his major intellectual interactions were with Keynes and Ludwig Wittgenstein. Both of them learned from Ramsey, who made profound and original contributions to philosophy, economics and mathematics (a branch of which is now called Ramsey Theory). Take philosophy. Thinking he had cracked the major problems of philosophy with his first book, *Tractatus Logico-Philosophicus*, Wittgenstein abandoned the discipline to become an elementary-school teacher in a small village outside Vienna. It was Ramsey who persuaded Wittgenstein that the *Tractatus* did not in fact solve everything. Wittgenstein returned to England and Cambridge so he could work with Ramsey (even in preference to working with the greatest philosopher in Cambridge at that time, Bertrand Russell). Ramsey had got to know Wittgenstein in the first place because he had produced the first English translation of Wittgenstein's *Tractatus*, a book that several leading philosophers had declared impossible to translate, given Wittgenstein's abstruse and compressed German. Ramsey simply dictated the translation directly to a shorthand writer in the Cambridge University typing office. Ramsey was eighteen at the time.

A few months later Ramsey turned to thinking about probability and uncertainty. He began by criticizing Keynes's theory of probability. Keynes doggedly defended his contentious theory for ten years, until he reviewed Ramsey's paper 'Truth and Probability' in 1931, after which Keynes changed his mind: 'I yield to Ramsey – I think he is right.' But in one sense it was too late. Ramsey's intellectual triumph was lost in a far greater tragedy: in January 1930 he died unexpectedly of complications after routine surgery, aged twenty-six.

In 'Truth and Probability', Ramsey took theories of probability in a completely new direction. Instead of defining probability in a backwards-looking way, in terms of observed frequencies (a coin comes up heads about half the time), Ramsey saw probability as forwards-looking, a quantitative measure of the strength of someone's belief in a future event. If I believe an event is 100 per cent certain to happen, this is equivalent to saying that, for me, the probability of the event is one; if I believe it is certain not to happen, the probability of the event for me is zero. And, analogously, for all beliefs between these two extremes: for example, if I believe an event is as likely to happen as not, the probability for me is one half. Ramsey explained how these beliefs-as-probabilities ('personal probabilities') could in principle be measured – essentially, by finding the least favourable odds a person would be willing to accept in a bet over whether the uncertain future event will happen. If Ramsey's approach works, then the idea of probability suddenly becomes much bigger: its scope is dramatically widened. Probabilities based on observed frequencies can be known only if there is data on events which have been observed frequently. Personal probabilities are freed of these constraints and can in principle be used to quantify Knight's 'unmeasurable' pure uncertainty, including one-off, non-repeatable events. But Ramsey's approach assumes that a person will be perfectly consistent in their personal probabilities – and it is just this consistency which, Ellsberg showed, cannot be relied upon. Ellsberg's experiment demonstrated that if we interpret people's choices as reflecting their personal probabilities, then those personal probabilities may be inconsistent.

However, Ellsberg's work lay decades in the future. In the meantime, Ramsey's revolutionary ideas offered obvious, tantalizing possibilities for developing a science of society and had persuaded the most influential economist of the era in Maynard Keynes. Yet nothing happened. Ramsey's ideas about probability were almost completely ignored for fifty years. Why?

To begin with, Ramsey's ideas appeared as a posthumous contribution to the philosophy of belief. They were not read by economists or others interested in practical applications towards a science of society, and Ramsey was no longer there to promote them more widely. And Ramsey was truly ahead of his time: existing theories and thinkers did not catch up with, and connect with, most of his ideas in mathematics, economics and philosophy until around the 1960s. In the 1920s, no one realized the true originality and significance of his work: it was too different, too hard to relate to existing ideas. This was not helped by Ramsey's presentational style: his mathematics used unusual notation derived from Bertrand Russell, his mathematical proofs were concise, verging on cryptic, while the modesty in his philosophical writing made his ideas seem almost light and flippant, not deep and profound. Wittgenstein's reputation was bolstered – especially among people who had no idea what he was talking about – by lines such as the momentous final sentence of the *Tractatus*: 'Whereof one cannot speak, thereof one must be silent.' Now compare Ramsey's version: 'What we can't say we can't say, and we can't whistle it either.'[4]

As for the handful of people in Cambridge who had come to grips with Ramsey's ideas about probability, their attention was distracted by Keynes and Wittgenstein, both in Cambridge at the time. And Keynes's views on probability had moved on. The virtue he had once seen in Ramsey's ideas was by the mid-1930s overshadowed by his awareness of the ubiquity of pure, unmeasurable uncertainty in practice:

> By 'uncertain knowledge', let me explain, I do not mean merely to distinguish what is known for certain from what is merely probable. The game of roulette is not subject, in this sense, to uncertainty ... The sense in which I am using the term is that in which the prospect of a European war is uncertain, or the price of copper and the rate of interest twenty years hence, or the obsolescence of a new invention ... About these matters there is no scientific basis on which to form any calculable probability whatsoever. We simply do not know.[5]

Keynes wrote these words in 1937, in response to criticisms of his *General Theory*, a book that represented unquestionably the biggest development in economics in the twentieth century – effectively inventing modern macroeconomics – and probably the most important contribution to economics since Adam Smith's *The Wealth of*

Nations over 150 years earlier. Keynes's emphasis on the importance of economic and political uncertainty was, unsurprisingly, hugely influential.

But not influential enough: the Keynesian view of uncertainty is *not* our contemporary orthodoxy. Instead the Second World War and its immediate aftermath nurtured a renewed optimism about a science of society. (Ironically, Keynesian economics may have even bolstered this optimism, with its faith in the ability to measure and manage national economic performance.) However, as we saw in Chapter 2, John von Neumann and Oscar Morgenstern's version of a science of society was very different to Keynesian economics: they thought that Keynes was a 'charlatan' and economics needed to be rebuilt from the ground up on the rigorous mathematical foundations of game theory. Uncertainty had to be captured in precise numbers. Von Neumann and Morgenstern had no time for Keynesian sentiments like 'we simply do not know'.

Literally as an afterthought, von Neumann and Morgenstern added an appendix to the second edition of their *Theory of Games and Economic Behavior* in which they described a mathematical theory of decision-making. It was based entirely on ideas sketched out by von Neumann on the back of an envelope. Von Neumann and Morgenstern's theory simply assumes that the decision-maker knows the probability of every relevant future event. They were unaware of Ramsey's work over twenty years earlier. It was not until 1951 that Ramsey's pioneering ideas were acknowledged in print in America – by Ken Arrow, who knew a genius when he saw one. However, the next major contribution was to come not from Arrow, but a mathematician named Leonard 'Jimmie' Savage.*

Milton Friedman described Savage as 'one of the few people I have met whom I would unhesitatingly call a genius'.[6] Yet Savage had become a mathematician only by accident: he was an undergraduate

---

* What's in a name? Everyone knew him as Jimmie, but that was a name given to him by a nurse, because his mother was too ill immediately after his birth to name him. Later she named him Leonard. Jimmie used the named Leonard only for his published work. And he was born Ogashevitz, changing his name to Savage only when doing 'classified war work'. See http://www-history.mcs.st-and.ac.uk/ Biographies/Savage.html.

in chemical engineering at the University of Michigan when his exceptionally poor eyesight led him to cause a fire in the chemistry lab and get expelled. He was allowed to return to study maths, which did not involve lab work. Shortly after completing his PhD, Savage's mathematical gifts caught the attention of von Neumann at Princeton, who encouraged Savage to study probability and statistics. In 1954 Savage extended von Neumann's theory of decision-making to include personal probabilities. Savage emphasized that his core ideas were essentially the same as Ramsey's and noted that Ramsey's work had previously had little influence. But the time was now ripe: von Neumann and Morgenstern's new decision theory was irresistible to economists and other wannabee scientists of society who rapidly realized that it had limitless applications, because the uncertain future could always be quantified with the aid of personal probabilities.

THE COMPUTER SAYS THAT CAN'T HAVE JUST HAPPENED

In the world beyond academia, a key impact of the new decision theory – the new orthodoxy, following Savage's work – was that it encouraged people to believe that the uncertain future can be 'managed' by inventing probabilities about it. By implying that personal probabilities were just as valid and legitimate as objective probabilities based on observed frequencies, the Savage orthodoxy blurred the boundary between beliefs and facts. It replaced Keynes's 'we simply do not know' with some comforting probability numbers, a pretence of scientific knowledge. This urge to actuarial alchemy, dissolving the incalculable into the calculable, is strongest when everything else at stake is objective and quantitative, hence uncertainty is the only remaining obstacle to a seemingly perfectly rational mathematical decision-making process. And the urge to actuarial alchemy is even stronger when people are willing to pay a lot of money for it. These urges climax in the stock market.

Nevertheless, there is still the problem of picking the probabilities. In the stock market the obvious starting point is statistics on past performance. Clearly, stock prices do not remain constant or follow a simple trend line. The next step, then, is to describe the pattern of price statistics in mathematical terms – how those statistics are distributed. The convenient final step is to assume that the future will be like the past. Assuming the statistical distribution of past prices holds in the future, we can deduce the probability of different future outcomes for stock prices and therefore the best portfolio of stocks to hold.

Somehow you can guess it doesn't quite work out in practice.

As well as the obvious problems such as assuming the future is like the past, there are some more technical difficulties. These deserve discussion because their implications are much more than merely technical. Errors in conventional thinking about uncertainty lead directly to the conclusion that catastrophes are extremely unlikely to occur. Catastrophes recklessly ignored on the basis of these errors include those affecting financial markets and the global climate.

Conventional thinking about uncertainty assumes that uncertain phenomena display a familiar pattern found commonly in nature, the bell curve. (This distribution or pattern is so natural and familiar that statisticians call it the *normal* distribution.) For example, human heights form a bell-curve distribution. There is a typical, or average, height for humans, and the number of people with other heights diminishes the further we move away from this average. If we plot these observations on a graph, with heights on the horizontal and numbers of people on the vertical, the curve through our plots would be shaped like a bell. It is not just that unusually tall or unusually short people are uncommon. They are very uncommon, while extremely tall or extremely short people are extremely rare. The odds of observing someone with some particular height fall much faster as we move further away from the average. Depending on the assumptions we make about the present population of the world, humans are about 1.67 metres, or 5 feet 7 inches, tall. The odds of being 10 centimetres taller than average (1.77 metres, 5 feet 10) are about 1 in 6.3. The odds of being 20 centimetres taller (1.87 metres, 6 feet 2) are about 1 in 44. The odds have fallen significantly, but less than sevenfold for a 10-centimetres increase in height. But when we consider a different 10-centimetres height increase, comparing people who are 2.17 metres

(7 feet 1) tall to those who are 2.27 metres (7 feet 5) tall, the odds fall
from about 1 in 3.5 million to 1 in 1,000 million, a 286-fold reduction
in likelihood.[7] Towards the edge of the bell, likelihoods fall from
'incredibly rare' to 'effectively never'. Which brings us back to the 25-
standard deviation events mentioned by the CFO of Goldman Sachs in
August 2007.

The bank's analysts and their computer models assumed that market prices follow a bell-curve distribution. Standard deviation is a
measure of distance from the average, the middle of the bell; 25-
standard deviation events are *very* far away from this, and so should
happen less than once in the history of the universe. Events with
extreme impacts, which happen completely unexpectedly (although
they may seem predictable with hindsight), have been named *Black
Swans* by Nassim Taleb, a Lebanese mathematician and sometime
hedge-fund manager. Bell-curve thinking essentially assumes that the
possibility of black swans can be ignored, because they will never
happen.

Goldman Sachs was not alone in using bell-curve thinking. This
orthodoxy dominates the financial sector and has repeatedly been
approved by regulators as a basis for judging risks. The global financial crisis beginning in 2007 did not cause banks and their regulators
to abandon bell-curve thinking, although they could hardly dismiss
the events of that period as unprecedented 'one-offs'. It is not just that
'once in the history of the universe' events happened several times a
week in late 2007. Two decades previously, on 19 October 1987 – a
day quickly dubbed 'Black Monday' – the US stock market fell almost
30 per cent. Bell-curve thinking put the odds of that at about 1 in
100000000 ... (46 zeros). The same goes for the crashes associated
with the 1997 crisis in East Asian markets, and the dot.com bubble.
Events which finance theory says will never ever happen keep happening. So why do we keep relying on this theory?

The idea that, while we don't yet know some number, we can guess
its average or typical value, is as seductive as it is reassuring. And
surely, exceptionally low or exceptionally high numbers are very
unlikely, because they would need a series of exceptional reasons or
causes to bring them about. This 'common sense' supports bell-curve
thinking. There are two contexts where it works well. First, in nature,

where internal or system constraints such as gravity make great extremes virtually impossible. There are basic features of human physiology which explain why no person has yet reached 3 metres in height or has lived to be 150 years old. It is not just chance. Natural constraints of course apply throughout nature. And for most of our evolution the risks we have faced have come from the natural world, not human society, so we may have evolved to use simplified bell-curve thinking as a generally reliable coping strategy in a natural environment.

Another valid application of bell-curve thinking is to situations where truly random independent events are repeated. In the real world, these situations arise only in games of chance. If an unbiased coin is tossed many times, the most likely outcome is an equal number of heads and tails. Slightly less likely is observing one more head than the number of tails, or vice versa. Less likely still is two more heads than tails, and so on. The eighteenth-century French mathematician Abraham de Moivre was the first to realize that repeated random events such as these generate a bell-curve distribution.*

The problems begin when we carry over these ideas to the wrong places. Again, Jimmie Savage played a key role. Savage had discovered the work of Louis Bachelier, an obscure French mathematician who in 1900 had published a 'theory of speculation' suggesting prices in financial markets move completely randomly. Savage produced the first English translation of Bachelier's theory, and Bachelier's ideas gained further attention with the emergence of the 'efficient market hypothesis' in the 1960s. According to the hypothesis (it remains a hypothesis today because there is no convincing evidence for its truth), at any given moment *all* information relevant to the price of a stock is *already* reflected in the price. This is ensured by assuming perfectly free markets and hyper-rational, omniscient buyers and sellers. If all relevant information is already in the price, any short-term movements in stock prices are random, reflecting the many independent, individual acts of buying and selling, akin to repeated

* De Moivre did not realize he should use a bell curve to predict his life span. Instead, as his health began to fail, he noticed he was sleeping fifteen minutes longer each night. He calculated he would be sleeping twenty-four hours a day by 27 November 1754. His method was flawed but his prediction was perfect: he died that day.

tosses of a coin. Given this fantasy about prices in financial markets, the bell curve is the obvious tool to describe the uncertainty – just as it can describe the outcome of repeated coin tosses. By 1999 deregulation of US banks (repealing the Glass–Steagall Act from the New Deal era) was explicitly justified by reference to the efficient-market hypothesis. The computer models were so trusted to 'manage uncertainty' that they controlled automated buying and selling of stocks. Human intervention was removed as far as possible in order to prevent error.

One simple reason why we persist with such ways of thinking is the prospect of the alternative. Bell-curve-based analysis is relatively straightforward maths, and the risk of getting extreme outcomes can effectively be measured with just one number – the standard deviation, which describes whether the bell is tall and thin, or flat and fat. The alternative involves fiendishly difficult maths, for modest reward: even using the hard maths, the risk of a black swan cannot be measured by a single number. Indeed, there are inherent limits to how far we can measure such risks at all.

'IT'S LIKE A MASSIVE EARTHQUAKE'

So said Kirsty McCluskey, a trader at the massive investment bank Lehmann Brothers on the day it went bust.[8] And so true, because the risk of both earthquakes and the financial crisis which engulfed Lehmann Brothers can be described by the same underlying maths. Not the 'never happen' events at the end of a bell curve but a 'power law' or 'fractal' distribution of outcomes. Don't worry: although much of the underlying maths is PhD level and beyond, the core ideas are more accessible. In some parts of the world earthquake activity is almost constant but at a very low level, much of it imperceptible to humans. Then, occasionally, there is an earthquake event which is hugely bigger than that background activity. We don't speak of a normal or average earthquake, because it would be completely uninformative – just silly – to add the size of the rare earthquakes to the multitude of background activity to get an average size of earthquake event. What most of us call 'earthquakes' are too rare for their arithmetic mean to be a useful number. The idea that there is no normal or natural size for some uncertain phenomena such as earthquakes is more profound than it first appears.

What is the natural size of a snowflake? Your instinct that this is a silly question is correct. If there was an answer, it would surely be revealed by the physical properties of snowflakes. But if we look at snowflakes under a magnifying lens we find a different kind of property. Snowflakes are called 'scale-invariant' by physicists because their crystal structure looks the same no matter how much we magnify them. Snowflakes are an example of what the mathematician Benoît Mandelbrot calls fractals – structures with no natural or normal size and which recur at different scales. (Another example is trees: the pattern of branches looks like the pattern of leaves on a branch, and also the pattern of veins in a leaf). Mandelbrot noticed that prices in financial markets have this property: a graph showing the price over time of some stock or market index will look much the same, whether the time period covered is several decades, a few seconds, or anything in between. The same is true of a graph of earthquake activity.

Scale-invariance arises where there are no inbuilt system limits which prevent extreme outcomes or changes. Unlike the height, weight or lifespan of humans and most other animals, there are no physical limits to the size of earthquakes. In fractal distributions there is just a fundamental relationship describing how large events or changes are less likely than small ones. As earthquakes double in size, they become about four times less likely.[9] But scale-invariance means that this relationship *always* holds: it does not vary with the scale of the earthquake. Unlike bell-curve phenomena such as human height, the likelihood falls at a constant speed: it does not decline faster once we consider more extreme outcomes. This technical detail is crucial. It implies that in fractal distributions extreme events are realistic possibilities, albeit extremely unlikely. They are not the 'never happen in the history of the universe' events at the extremes of the bell curve.

Returning to the world of finance, research suggests that as the movement in a stock-market index doubles in size it becomes approximately eight times rarer. However, this is not especially useful knowledge. It does not enable us to predict the timing of stock-market crashes, any more than we can predict the timing of earthquakes. The relationship is based on past data; we should not assume it will hold in the future. And there is a deeper problem. Although we are no longer using bell-curve thinking, we are still trying to estimate the likelihood of extremely large, extremely rare events using past data. But to estimate the frequency of events which occur extremely rarely we need an extremely large number of observations. In the case of stock markets, we have had only a few crashes over many decades, far too few data points to estimate the probability of future crashes with any confidence. The lessons of applying Mandelbrotian mathematics to stock markets are all negative: you can't calculate the probabilities of the market moves you most want to know about (the big ones); and don't treat the absence of a market crash for several decades as evidence that bell-curve thinking works after all. These lessons are valuable, but not valuable enough to enable people to make a career out of explaining them to investors. The delusions of quantitative 'risk management' based on bell-curve thinking have proved much more lucrative.

According to the risk managers and their models in the run-up to the financial crisis, various arcane financial products linked to the housing market were safe investments: the models implied that a fall in house prices of more than 20 per cent or so had a probability equivalent to 'less than once in the history of the universe'. Yet the people selling these products must have known that a 20 per cent fall in house prices was a realistic possibility – unlikely, perhaps, but not a 'never happen' probability.[10] It is hard to deny the obvious explanation for their wilful blindness to this reality. Greed.

Greed works in subtler ways too. People will pay handsomely if you offer to measure and manage the financial risks they face. Hopefully, they won't notice that you can achieve this feat only by redefining 'risk'. This redefinition of risk began with Harry Markowitz, a Chicago student waiting to see his professor to discuss a topic for his PhD, chatting with a stockbroker sharing the waiting room.[11] That chance conversation led to Markowitz using bell-curve thinking to publish a paper in 1952 which (twenty years or more later) became the basis of financial orthodoxy on risk. Our everyday understanding of financial risk is clear: the possibility of losing money. Modern financial orthodoxy defines risk as *volatility*. A non-volatile investment is therefore a non-risky or 'safe' investment – even though its modest fluctuations may be consistently bigger and more frequent on the downside, so you lose money.

Of course, we cannot blame decision theorists and thinkers for the greedy, wishful thinking of bankers, financial economists and others in assuming that uncertainty can always be represented by a bell curve. But Savage's followers *are* responsible for the underlying idea that turning pure uncertainty into probability numbers is a kind of alchemy for generating the best decision. It was exactly this idea that Daniel Ellsberg rejected.

CALL IN THE PLUMBERS

As a child, Dan Ellsberg was obviously academically gifted. But he focused on playing the piano – and his mother was even more focused on a musical career for him. On 4th July 1946 fifteen-year-old Dan, his sister and his parents were driving through Iowa cornfields on their way to a party in Denver. They had been driving the previous day, too, but reached their overnight accommodation too late, arriving to find the reservations cancelled and the room taken. So the family slept in the car or outside, on the dunes at Lake Michigan. Dan's father got almost no sleep and was exhausted at the start of another long day's drive the following morning. Just after lunch he fell asleep at the wheel. The car crashed into a wall and Dan's mother and sister were killed instantly.[12] After his mother's death Dan's musical ambitions soon faded. But music left its mark: Dan Ellsberg was not the narrowly focused military strategist that his Harvard-Marines-Harvard again-RAND CV might have suggested.

Returning to Harvard as a young academic, he wondered about spending most of his fellowship learning all the Beethoven piano sonatas rather than doing economics. Beyond music, Dan was still a performer in everything he did. He was much less of a geek than his Harvard and RAND colleagues. By most accounts, he was an arrogant, egotistical, flirtatious party animal. He knew how to get noticed in his academic work too. Ellsberg worked with Tom Schelling on applying game theory to nuclear strategy. Ellsberg provocatively titled one of his lectures 'The Political Uses of Madness' and argued that Hitler had been a successful blackmailer because he was 'convincingly mad'.[13] Ellsberg explained his ideas to Henry Kissinger, then at Harvard; Kissinger later advised Nixon, who boasted of his 'madman theory' of waging war in Vietnam.

Even those who found Ellsberg difficult praised his intellect. The most talented people felt privileged to work with him: Schelling regarded Ellsberg as 'one of the brightest people I ever knew'. But Ellsberg often struggled to finish academic work, to commit it to paper. He was too easily distracted by new interests, academic and otherwise. He moved on from game theory to the infant field of mathematical decision theory, in which Jimmie Savage's work encapsulated the state of the art. The emerging orthodoxy in decision theory began with some abstract mathematical assumptions ('axioms') about rationality. The theory then made deductions about how a rational decision-maker ought to choose in any decision context, given their initial beliefs. The logic can be applied in reverse: given some facts about how someone *does* choose, their beliefs can be deduced from those facts, assuming that they are 'rational' in the sense defined by the theory. So, when choosing between box A and box B in the experiment described by Ellsberg, the fact that someone chooses box B allows us to deduce that the person believes it contains more balls of the colour which qualifies for a prize.

Or not, as Ellsberg argued in his ground-breaking 1961 paper 'Risk, Ambiguity and the Savage Axioms', which introduced his experiment to the world.[14] Ellsberg argued that when people are invited to choose a ball from a box containing an unknown mixture of red and black balls they do *not* attribute numerical likelihoods or invent their own personal probabilities for red and black. Their first response is to try to avoid this kind of pure uncertainty altogether – choose the other box, for which the mixture of reds and blacks is known. More generally in life, we try to avoid pure uncertainty: we are reluctant to make decisions if we have no idea of the relative likelihood of the different possible outcomes (unless of course the decision is a trivial one – in which case we don't care much about the outcome).

However, from the beginning, orthodox decision theory did double duty. It claimed both to describe how people ought to choose *and* how they do in fact choose. The obvious possibility that these may differ was obscured by a circular use of the idea that people are rational: rational people do in fact choose in line with the theory – because the theory defines what counts as rational behaviour. This ruse was helpful in keeping the critics at bay (and many twenty-first-century economics textbooks remain evasive on the issue). Of course, insiders like Ellsberg and Savage were well aware that a theory of how people choose may not match their behaviour in reality; indeed, by 1961 Savage had already accepted that people often make choices which are inconsistent with the theory. The focus of the debate had moved on to whether the theory still provided a compelling account of how rational people *ought* to choose. So Ellsberg knew that if his experiment merely showed that ordinary people make choices inconsistent with the theory, the response from supporters of the Savage orthodoxy would be 'So what?'

Therefore, rather than asking ordinary people, Ellsberg asked supporters of the Savage orthodoxy – academics and graduate students working on decision theory – to participate in his experiment. And when, as most did, they chose in a way inconsistent with the use of probabilities, Ellsberg explained their 'error' to them and asked if they wanted to change their minds. Most did not: they stuck with their original choices, violating Savage's theory, even after the opportunity to reflect and reconsider. (According to Ellsberg, Savage himself was one such 'unrepentant violator' of his own theory, but no independent evidence has emerged to corroborate Ellsberg's story.)[15] The lesson was clear. It is absurd to insist that a rational decision-maker must invent probabilities in the face of uncertainty, if even supporters of that view do not follow it in practice when given full opportunity to reflect and reconsider.

Ellsberg's strategy – getting supporters of orthodox decision theory to make choices inconsistent with it – was clever. But perhaps too clever. It gave the defenders of orthodoxy no excuse, no place to hide, no way to save face. Which left them just one option: ignore the

Ellsberg Paradox altogether. Ellsberg himself made it easier for them to do so, because his mercurial mind had already moved on to other things. By the time 'Risk, Ambiguity and the Savage Axioms' was published, Ellsberg was a consultant to the US Defense Department and the White House. In 1961 he drafted the guidance to the Joint Chiefs of Staff on the operational plans for general nuclear war; the following year, unsurprisingly, saw him preoccupied with the Cuban Missile Crisis. As for promoting his ideas in academic circles, Ellsberg had effectively gone AWOL. He had, in one way or another, become obsessed with the Vietnam War. After working on plans to escalate US involvement in Vietnam, Ellsberg spent two years in Saigon, and then returned to RAND to work on a top-secret review of US decision-making regarding Vietnam. Then it happened.

Ellsberg switched from hawk to whistle-blower. His work at RAND had convinced him that the US Administration had expanded military operations in Vietnam without approval from Congress and had misled the public about its real intentions. Ellsberg spent many hours secretly making photocopies of the 7,000-page review (he took his thirteen-year-old son Robert along to help). In 1971, after failing to persuade senators on the Foreign Relations Committee to make the review public, Ellsberg sent it to nineteen newspapers and, after the publication of what became known as the 'Pentagon Papers', turned himself in. He faced a potential 115 years in jail on conspiracy charges. But, unintentionally, the Plumbers saved him.

The Plumbers were a motley crew of ex-CIA operatives who were friends of friends of Nixon and used criminal methods to try to get evidence against enemies of Nixon (such as breaking into the office of Ellsberg's former psychoanalyst). Once it was clear that the case against Ellsberg was based on government gross misconduct and illegal evidence-gathering, the judge dismissed all charges against him. Ellsberg avoided jail, but had attained international notoriety, a 1970s precursor to Julian Assange and Edward Snowden. His new reputation provided another excuse, if decision theorists needed one, not to think about the Ellsberg Paradox for a while longer.

FIVE BLACK SWANS AND NOBEL PRIZES

In the meantime, the emerging orthodoxy combined bell-curve thinking and the efficient-market hypothesis to suggest that uncertainty in financial markets could be tamed or neutered altogether. In academia, this culminated in the award of five Nobel prizes to financial economists: three in 1990 (Harry Markowitz and two others building on his work), and two more in 1997, for Robert Merton and Myron Scholes. In financial markets, the culmination of the idea that uncertainty can be neutered came with the emergence of hedge funds claiming to do just that. Merton and Scholes practised what they preached and were senior managers of the hedge fund Long-Term Capital Management. LTCM made huge profits, but its approach ignored the possibility of black swans. When one came along in the shape of a major default and devaluation by the Russian government, LTCM went bust. That was 1998 – just a year after Merton and Scholes had won the Nobel Prize.

Alas, regarding their blindness to the problems of orthodox thinking about uncertainty, most financial economists and bankers are serial offenders. In recent history the orthodoxy has been challenged by Black Monday in 1987, the collapse of LTCM, the dot.com bubble and the financial crisis beginning in 2007 (to name the most obvious challenges). In each case the main response has been silence, or the argument that, since such events are black swans, no one could be expected to see them coming. There has been little admission that we need new thinking about uncertainty which explicitly incorporates the possibility of black swans and – since there is inherently no hope of predicting them – the importance of taking precautions to help cope with their unexpected arrival.

The biggest obstacle to overthrowing the old orthodoxy is our deep-seated reluctance to admit the limits of our knowledge in the face of uncertainty and our dogged faith in the quantification of uncertainty following from that reluctance. We have already noted the preference for bell-curve thinking over the hard-won yet meagre rewards of Mandelbrotian maths. More generally, the idea that we can reduce uncertainty to a single number, a probability, appeals to our desire for simplicity, security and stability. Once captured in a single number, uncertainty can seemingly be controlled. We can choose the amount of risk we will tolerate.

In parallel with the desire to control our destiny comes a set of beliefs suggesting that we can do so. Many people have a deep-rooted, barely conscious belief that there are stable patterns in history which will continue into the future. This connects to the way we understand most things in terms of narratives and stories. Understanding the future as a narrative evolving from the present is not just a way of literally 'making sense' of uncertainty, replacing doubt with explanation. It is cognitively easier too. The novelist E. M. Forster famously contrasted a simple succession of facts – 'The king died and then the queen died' – with a plot: 'The king died, and then the queen died of grief.' There is more information in this plot, yet it is no harder to remember: it is cognitively more efficient.[16]

However, there is a catch. Daniel Kahneman and Amos Tversky provided the first clear evidence. The Linda Problem remains one of their most famous experiments:

> Linda is thirty-one years old, single, outspoken, and very bright. She majored in philosophy. As a student, she was deeply concerned with issues of discrimination and social justice, and also participated in anti-nuclear demonstrations.
> Which is more probable?
> 1. Linda is a bank teller.
> 2. Linda is a bank teller and active in the feminist movement.[17]

Most people choose option 2. But option 2 *must* be *less* probable than option 1, because option 1 is true both when Linda is active in the feminist movement *and* when she is not. Our tendency to impose narratives as a way of coping with lack of knowledge plays havoc with using basic laws of probability. Put another way, the combination of our reliance on narrative understandings and our desire to use probabilities to describe uncertainty is potentially disastrous. Still, we must be careful not to overstate the problem. Yes, ordinary folk reach for narratives to help cope with uncertainty, but experts reach for their tools, theories and computer models. Experts may fool themselves with optimistic bell-curve thinking, but at least they don't fall for an error as basic as the Linda Problem.

Except that they do, as Kahneman and Tversky discovered when they ran similar experiments with doctors and other trained experts. And there is clear evidence that expert decision-makers are reluctant to abandon another narrative – the optimistic orthodoxy about decision-making under uncertainty described in this chapter, the one beginning with von Neumann's jottings on the back of an envelope, then proceeding via Savage through a series of improvements and applications leading to Nobel prizes and other glory.

Here is celebrated former Chairman of the US Federal Reserve Alan Greenspan in testimony to the US Congress in October 2008 after the financial crisis had hit:

> In recent decades, a vast risk-management and pricing system has evolved ... A Nobel Prize was awarded ... This modern risk-management paradigm held sway for decades. The whole intellectual edifice, however, collapsed in the summer of last year ...

So far so good.

> ... because the data inputted into the risk-management models generally covered only the past two decades, a period of euphoria.[18]

So, for Greenspan, the validity of bell-curve thinking and the quantification of uncertainty remains unquestioned, and perhaps unquestionable. All that went wrong was that we used only twenty years of data. This fundamentally misunderstands the problem. Black swans never come along often enough to estimate their probability reliably from past data. Whether in the financial markets or elsewhere, the probability of rare events cannot be estimated from past frequencies precisely *because* they are rare. And, logically, unforeseen events must be unforeseen in advance, so their probability cannot be estimated. Surprises must be surprising.

The rarity of black swans provides another reason why we act as though they don't exist when attempting to measure uncertainty using probabilities. People who ignore black swans and use bell-curve thinking can seem to manage uncertainty successfully for a long period. And, in the meantime, they are likely to be well rewarded for this apparent success. In the long run, a black swan will appear, but then again, as Keynes put it, 'in the long run we are all dead.' Or retired with a healthy pension.

Yet this argument might seem too glib. Why do people – such as bankers who manage risks – get so well rewarded if their reasoning is flawed? We have already mentioned some reasons: the orthodoxy, from Nobel Prize-winners down, has become so dominant that alternative views have barely been heard, and these alternatives don't offer the comforting illusion of taming uncertainty but instead a blunt description of the limits of our knowledge. There is a less obvious reason too. People are usually paid according to their performance rather than the reasoning behind it. And, in many sectors, such as finance, performance is wholly relative. If your rivals, against whom your performance is judged, are all using the same orthodox methods for 'risk management', then you will cover your back by doing so too. As the saying in the tech sector once went: nobody ever got fired for buying an IBM. Making the orthodox choice is safe. If things go wrong, your rivals will have fared no better, and you can all say that you relied on standard scientific theories and models. You save face. Fund managers call it 'benchmarking against the market'; Keynes called it following the herd.

In contrast, abandoning the orthodoxy means making your own judgements – and being responsible if things go badly or your rivals do better. You are, as the UK's chief financial regulator put it, 'in a much more worrying space because you don't have an intellectual system to refer each of your decisions'.[19]

Economists and other defenders of the orthodoxy have given decision-makers a licence to avoid making judgements, a licence to abrogate responsibility to the decision theory. Yet this tantalizing power of decision theory to do away with making judgements about the future rests on a fundamental error. Perhaps because it is a philosophical rather than mathematical error, the defenders of the orthodoxy do not seem to have noticed. A theory of decision-making using personal probabilities cannot describe how you *ought* to choose, because when you remove the mathematical wrapper a personal probability is just an expression of how likely you believe something will be. And your beliefs cannot determine what you ought to choose, because they can be mistaken. I might choose to continue as a heavy smoker because I believe that smoking does not increase my risk of cancer. But we can't say that I ought to continue smoking, or that my decision to continue smoking is justified, based on my belief that smoking does not increase the risk of cancer – because that belief is false.[20] A theory which prescribes what we should choose, justifying particular choices in the face of uncertainty – which is exactly what the modern orthodoxy claims to do – needs objective standards, facts external to the decision-maker. It cannot be based just on their subjective beliefs.

Frank Ramsey, the pioneer of personal probabilities, knew this. Unlike Savage, Ramsey did not argue that personal probabilities can tell us what someone *ought* to choose. Ramsey saw personal probabilities as a conceptual device to explain the choices that people *do* make. (And Ellsberg's experiment subsequently cast doubt on even that.)

It was Savage and his followers who went further, giving beliefs and opinions, once represented as personal probabilities, the same status as objective facts. This brings us to the hidden arrogance of our modern orthodoxy in thinking about uncertainty. It leads us into an elaborate exercise in self-justification. The maths conceals the underlying arrogance: we justify our choices by reference to our own beliefs. But believing something does not make it true. We ignore the facts – and especially the facts about our lack of knowledge of the future. It is our contemporary Greek tragedy. We act with hubris, excessive self-confidence in defiance of the gods of chance. Hubris always leads to nemesis. And sometimes the stakes are much higher than they are in a global financial crisis.

THE MAKING OF A NUMBER

Although there is fierce debate over the details there is a strong scientific consensus that if we continue on our current path of carbon emissions into the atmosphere we are heading for a planet on average around 4°C warmer. (This average temperature rise conceals a complex picture of different dimensions of climate change – more extreme temperatures, floods, droughts, desertification, hurricanes, storm surges, and so on.) But how much does it matter?

On 30 October 2006, probably the most influential answer to this question to date was provided by a report for the UK government, the 'Stern Review on the Economics of Climate Change'. The Stern Review captured headlines worldwide with its claim that doing nothing about climate change would cost between 5 per cent and 20 per cent of global GDP, every year. Economist Nick Stern's conclusion was based on an elaborate economic model, and the review stimulated an explosion in similar modelling research by other economists, leading to the current consensus: the damage associated with 4°C warming will be around 5 per cent of global GDP per year. Five per cent of global GDP is still a big number, and a convenient figure which politicians, business leaders and others with the power to make a difference can retain in their minds. The difference between 5 per cent and 20 per cent arises from differences in the incredible array of assumptions, simplifications and omissions needed to get to these neat numbers.

It is hard to know where to begin. To get to a higher number like 20 per cent you need to consider risks posed by climate change that are less well understood by science, and so use more guesswork in putting a money value on the damage such risks might do – and a money value is of course what is needed to add up all damages and express them as a percentage of GDP. On the other hand, to get to a lower number like 5 per cent you need more naïve or optimistic assumptions about the extent of climate change, and you need to ignore some of its possible impacts. Here is a far from comprehensive list of potential damages that are ignored in reaching the 5 per cent figure: thawing of the Arctic permafrost, release of methane, air pollution from burning fossil fuels, variations in sea-level rise leading to inundation of small island states and coastal communities, and conflict resulting from large-scale migration to escape the worst-affected areas.

As for the impacts of climate change that *are* included in reaching a single magic number (whether 5 per cent or 20 per cent), few of them are absolutely certain. So to reach a total value for the damage caused by climate change, the money value of each uncertain impact must be multiplied by the probability of the impact occurring. Unfortunately, for many of the most important impacts there is pure uncertainty. We don't know their probability; we don't even know with any confidence the range of plausible probabilities. We simply do not know.

Reliable numbers are equally hard to find when we turn to determining the money value of every impact of climate change. Take perhaps the most important impact of all – the premature, probably grim deaths of millions of people. In 2002 the World Health Organization suggested that around 150,000 deaths annually might be caused by a temperature rise of less than 1°C (due to more heatwaves, malaria and dehydration, among other reasons). Since the harm to human health increases disproportionately as the temperature rises, a 4°C rise would probably cause more than half a million premature deaths per year.[21]

As we saw in Chapter 6, Tom Schelling introduced to economics a controversial method for putting a money value on (preventing) premature death. This value is derived from how much money people need to be paid to tolerate increased risk. The calculations are usually based on data comparing wages in more-or-less risky but otherwise identical jobs. But whatever the source of the data, we will find that how much money people accept to tolerate increased risk and how much they are willing to spend to avoid it depends on their income. Poor people tolerate risky jobs more readily than rich people, because they need the wage. They spend less on avoiding risk because they have less to spend. Thus Schelling's method gives a lower value to life saving (preventing premature death) in a poor society than in a rich one. That is, the value of a 'statistical life' is less in a poor country than in a rich one. This isn't just an intellectual game. It led directly to the influential Intergovernmental Panel on Climate Change, in its 1995 report, valuing lives lost in rich countries at $1,500,000 but those in poor countries at $100,000.[22]

Most economists recognize that valuing some lives more highly than others is widely seen as unacceptable. But another approach they adopt instead is no better: many economic models simply ignore potential loss of life from climate change altogether by assuming a fixed global population. Assuming away half a million premature deaths a year is a stunning move, yet there is an even more powerful assumption hidden in the economists' calculations, the one wielding the biggest influence on the final numbers such as '5 per cent of GDP'.

This assumption is the 'discount rate' used to convert *future* costs and benefits of climate change into numbers comparable with *current* costs and benefits. Discounting means that the future impacts are discounted – given a reduced value in the calculations – compared to identical impacts now. And the further into the future some impact will occur, the more it is discounted, with a compounding effect of great power over long periods: in standard economic models with standard discount rates total global GDP in 200 years is discounted to be equivalent to around $4 billion dollars in current terms (the GDP of Togo, or just 2.5 per cent of the fortune of Jeff Bezos, the Amazon founder and world's richest person in 2019). The upshot is that if we are trying to decide how much it is worth spending to prevent the destruction of the earth 200 years from now – on the basis of lost future GDP, which is just what economic models try to do – the answer would be no more than a minor dent in Jeff Bezos's fortune. At least when applied over long time horizons, discounting seems absurd because it trivializes catastrophe in this way.

The history of discounting takes us back to the prodigious Frank Ramsey. He was the first person to pin down two key arguments for discounting in mathematical terms, by means of an elegantly concise formula, the Ramsey Rule, which remains the inspiration for the way in which future impacts of climate change are discounted in economic models today. Ramsey's first argument is breathtakingly direct: so-called 'pure discounting', the basic assertion that lives in the future are less important than lives now. If you think this sounds like straightforward discrimination against future generations, most philosophers, religions and ethical codes agree with you. Ramsey may have described this justification for discounting mathematically, but he argued that it was ethically indefensible (and he would surely have also recognized the absurdity of discounting applied over 200-year periods). Alas, while most climate economists nowadays revere Ramsey's mathematical models, they ignore his warnings about the immorality of misusing them. It is no exaggeration to say that most economic models of the impact of climate change discriminate indefensibly against future generations through the use of 'pure discounting' of future impacts.

Ramsey's second argument for discounting is subtler. If, on average, people will be much wealthier in the future, then money will matter a bit less to them: an extra dollar is less valuable the richer you are. It follows that climate-change impacts in the future will matter less too, compared to current impacts of the same monetary value: the same monetary value will be worth less in the future. So we should reduce the weight attached to future impacts in our calculations. This is a better argument than justifying discounting through discrimination – but not much. It recklessly assumes that economic growth will continue much as it has done in the past, so that future generations will be meaningfully richer than us. It ignores the likelihood, taken seriously not just by environmentalists but also by the entire insurance industry, that climate change will disrupt economic activity enough to make business-as-usual economic growth rates no more than a distant memory. Ignoring the threat posed by climate change to economic growth in this way is an astonishing omission in an economic appraisal of the impact of climate change. At best it can be explained because it makes the maths more manageable and links the models more closely to Ramsey's original analysis, which economists have grown up with from textbooks. But yet again the ultimate effect of this omission is a misleading reduction in the cost of climate change expressed as a proportion of global GDP. If an economist wanted to rig the economic appraisal in a way hidden from democratic scrutiny by non-economists, technical shenanigans with the discount rate would be a good way to do it.

But even if there might be a few villains among mainstream economists here, there are many more who are painfully aware of the limitations of a model that boils down all the scientific, economic, political and social uncertainties and dimensions to a single percentage of GDP. After the publication of the Stern Review, Nick Stern realized that almost all the uncertainties in the models bias them in the same direction: 'Grafting Gross Underestimation of Risk onto Already Narrow Science Models' is how he labels the situation in a leading economics journal. And Stern is exasperated by the attention given to the percentage-of-GDP numbers. He points out that the models generating these numbers comprised just 30 out of 692 pages in the Stern Review: the rest was devoted to other ways of thinking about climate change. Nevertheless, Stern and most climate economists remain loyal to these models, arguing that global decisions about climate policy should be based on improved models spewing out bigger numbers for the cost to global GDP caused by climate change.

For anyone hoping for significant action to try to reduce climate change, the economists' strategy is a worrying one, given their continuing dominance over policy-making. The reaction to the Stern Review shows that once a percentage-of-GDP number is mentioned it will drown out all other ways of talking and thinking about the damage caused by climate change. If you don't want politicians and the media to focus solely on one easy-to-remember number, don't give them one. And using a new model to get a bigger number does not help.

Because in the end no one cares much.

That unchecked climate change might cost 5 per cent of global GDP is already a much bigger number than it might seem. Both the First World War and the Second World War made barely a dent in global GDP (overall, the Second World War probably *increased* global GDP compared to what would have happened otherwise).[23] In comparison, a 5 per cent fall is significant. But the real message of this comparison is that the death of tens of millions of people – the Holocaust and human suffering on an unprecedented scale – went largely undetected in measures of GDP. Clearly, we cannot assume that the impact of global catastrophe will be reflected in measures of GDP, whether these catastrophes are wars or climate change.

If the orthodoxy on the cost of 4°C warming changed from 5 per cent to 20 per cent of global GDP, it is far from clear that this would have much effect on the global debate over climate change: perhaps most people have a gut understanding of the limitations of GDP numbers when contemplating huge global changes. Despite the seeming dominance of economic language in politics, ultimately, the numbers don't matter much.

Still, if we abandon the orthodoxy, we face the same problem faced by the followers of Keynes insisting, when faced with pure uncertainty, that 'we simply do not know'. How to decide instead? If not an overarching economic reckoning of the costs of climate change set against the costs of trying to do something to mitigate it, all measured in terms of money, then what?

SOME NUMBER IS BETTER THAN NO NUMBER?

Some risks have two characteristics that make them much harder to deal with. First, pure uncertainty. Second, the possibility of catastrophe – not just a bad outcome but different-in-kind bad, often featuring irreversible damage or loss, or complete collapse of the underlying system, organization or framework within which decisions are taken. Arguably, both climate change and global financial crises share these two characteristics. With such risks, traditional thinking in economics – which advocates precisely maximizing benefits-minus-costs and the aggressively efficient use of means in pursuit of ends – is reckless. Instead, the overriding priority must be avoiding catastrophe: we need resilience and security rather than maximization and efficiency. In nature, this priority is often pursued through the opposite of efficiency, namely redundancy – for example, humans having two kidneys rather than one. In politics and law this way of thinking is associated with the 'precautionary principle'. In broad terms, the principle recommends approaches to practical decision-making which focus on resilience, security and taking precautions.[24] The emphasis is on being aware of what we don't know and the likelihood that the future will be surprising (who could have guessed that CFCs, chemicals discovered to be ideal for cooling machines like fridges, would turn out to cause global warming?). These alternative ways of thinking about risk reject the dominant orthodoxy of putting a price tag and a probability on every possible future impact of every choice. Instead they advocate focusing much more on a careful, detailed, multidimensional appraisal of the possible impacts, and much less on trying to guess their probabilities. We simply do not know these probabilities and, even if we did, that knowledge is of little use without a good understanding of what we have the probability *of*. Unlike the Governor of the Bank of England, many people in the summer of 1914 correctly forecast that a war was likely. But it hardly mattered, because no one realized that the war would be on a hitherto unimaginable scale.

Put another way, we cannot plan to reduce the risk of catastrophe without agreement on what counts as a catastrophe. We are forced to ask, 'What matters most to us?' And also in the case of climate change, 'What will matter most to future generations?' These questions are clearly beyond the scope of any science of society. We must move beyond money as a crude measure of goodness or badness. And technical economics is of no help in thinking through our obligations to future generations. Just the name of the theory of 'discounting the future' is enough to tell us what it does. Baroque discounting calculations are not needed; they serve only to conceal our disregard for the future.

Over the past fifty years or so economists and economic ideas have been central to the trend towards quantification of all risks and values. This trend formed part of the rebranding of economics as a neutral science akin to physics rather than a mode of analysis based on political and ethical assumptions. The Social Science Research Building at the University of Chicago has the following inscription (attributed to the physicist Lord Kelvin but not in fact an actual quotation) carved on its façade: 'When you cannot measure, your knowledge is meager and unsatisfactory.' Economists have taken this to mean: yes, the numbers have their flaws, but *some number is better than no number*. Frank Knight, the most un-Chicago of Chicago economists in his emphasis on pure, unmeasurable uncertainty, was less optimistic. He saw the inscription as licensing economists to conclude 'Oh well, if you cannot measure, measure anyhow.'[25]

One simple problem with the 'some number is better than no number' mantra is our inability to ignore irrelevant numbers. Kahneman and Tversky's 'anchoring effect' describes how people, including experienced decision-makers, are influenced by irrelevant starting points or anchors, including numbers they *know* to be irrelevant. For instance, German judges who rolled dice before sentencing issued longer sentences after rolling high numbers.[26]

And economic numbers – probabilities and money values – bring their own particular problems, so that, again, some number can be worse than no number. Some things which matter get ignored because they are difficult or impossible to quantify. As Einstein allegedly said: not everything that can be counted counts, and not everything that counts can be counted. We have seen examples through this chapter and others (such as RAND ignoring the loss of pilots' lives because its analysts couldn't agree how to put a dollar value on them). Worse still, once the number has been produced we often forget what was ignored in the process of producing it – and so we forget that the number may be systematically biased. One example is the GDP estimates of the cost of climate change. A less obvious kind of bias arises when we ignore the risk of bad things happening (avoiding such risks is worthwhile in advance, even if the risks don't materialize). Bad things which didn't happen get ignored because they are much harder to quantify than good things which did. This is one underlying reason why, in investment banks, risk-taking traders are paid much more than those in the bank responsible for risk control or compliance with regulations designed to limit risk-taking. The insistence on quantification supports a bias towards recklessness.

Another danger of obsessive quantification: the process of producing the number distorts or misrepresents the concept we are trying to measure. Ultimately, the original concept can disappear altogether, being redefined in terms of the number. Beginning with Harry Markowitz's work, economists and financial types have quietly redefined risk as volatility with almost no one noticing – even though this redefinition affects everyday life in countless ways, from pensions to insurance. This is just one example of the transformative power of economic numbers. Introducing them into a decision or debate is not a neutral step, let alone always an improvement yielding greater precision. Instead, economic numbers are all too often anti-democratic, because they obscure the ethical and political issues behind a technical fog. And as we have seen, regarding the future, economic numbers bias decisions towards recklessness and ignoring the interests of future generations.

If there is to be a shift away from trusting in such numbers, back towards trusting in our own judgements, it will be made piecemeal, from the bottom up, by individual decision-makers. There are some small reasons for optimism.

First, the orthodoxy in decision theory has always claimed the scientific high ground, pointing to its sophisticated mathematical underpinnings. But recent developments at the cutting edge of decision theory have begun to provide mathematical respectability for alternative principles (such as the precautionary principle), so very smart people may start to take them seriously. Second, while making judgements involves taking responsibility, at least it gives us something to do. Nowadays, a computer doesn't just perform calculations. With artificial intelligence it can tweak and refine the mathematical model it is using along the way. As artificial intelligence proliferates and humans increasingly contemplate their redundancy, confronting pure uncertainty and ethical dilemmas with cautious, tentative but uniquely human qualitative judgement begins to look appealing after all.

9

You Deserve What You Get

In most richer countries inequality is rising and has been rising for some time. Many people believe this is a problem, although there is disagreement about its importance. But in any case it seems there is not much we can do about it – and besides, the cure may be worse than the disease. Globalization and new technology have created an economy in which those with highly valued skills or talents can earn huge rewards. Inequality inevitably rises. Attempting to reduce inequality via redistributive taxation is likely to fail because the global elite can easily move to another tax jurisdiction or a tax haven. Insofar as increased taxation does hit the rich, it will deter wealth creation, so we all end up poorer.

One strange thing about these arguments, whatever their merits, is how they stand in stark contrast to the economic orthodoxy that existed from roughly 1945 to 1980, which held that rising inequality was not inevitable and that various government policies could reduce it. What's more, these policies appear to have been successful. Inequality fell in most countries from the 1940s to the 1970s. The inequality we see today is largely due to changes since 1980. In both the US and the UK, from 1980 to 2016 the share of total income going to the top 1 per cent has more than doubled.[1] The material living standards of this top 1 per cent have rapidly pulled away from the rest of the population: after allowing for inflation, the earnings of the bottom 90 per cent in the US and UK have barely risen at all over the past twenty-five years. We can see the same trend at an individual level. In 1950 the world's highest paid CEO was Charlie Wilson, the boss of General Motors. He was paid $586,000 – equivalent to more than $5 million today. But in 2007 GM paid their CEO $15.7

million, roughly three times as much (and GM made a $39 billion loss that year). More generally, fifty years ago a US CEO earned on average about twenty times as much as the typical worker. Today the CEO earns 354 times as much.[2] In short, while the period from 1945 to 1980 is not so long ago, within living memory, as far as inequality is concerned it is about as remote as Mars. So what has changed?

The arrival of an immense package of ideas – in the form of a fundamental shift in mainstream economic and political thinking in favour of free markets – undoubtedly played a large part. As Margaret Thatcher put it, 'It is our job to glory in inequality and see that talents and abilities are given vent and expression for the benefit of all.'[3] However, the Reagan/Thatcher turn in economic ideas, already dissected at length by some brilliant historians, is far from complete as an explanation of rising inequality.[4] To see why, we must look elsewhere, beginning with an economist whose impact on thinking about inequality remains enormous.

REASONS NOT TO TALK ABOUT INEQUALITY

Vilfredo Pareto is one of the most influential economists most people have never heard of. He is an enigmatic figure in the history of economics, an abrasive, volatile, argumentative, aristocratic cynic whose life and ideas are hard to categorize. His working life began quietly: after a degree in engineering, he worked as a railway engineer in Florence. But by his death in 1923, ten months after the fascist leader Benito Mussolini became Italian Prime Minister, his ideas were hailed by the fascists as their main intellectual inspiration. In those ten months they showered him with honours – although Pareto refused most of them. Along his journey from railway engineer to hero of the fascists, Pareto had been a staunch defender of free markets and small government before flirting with socialism and Marxism. He was a radical democrat, involved in street protests and polemical journalism. But then he publicly declared himself an *anti*-democrat. As an economist, he focused on abstract mathematical economic theory, before becoming bored of it once he decided its relevance to reality was limited.

A cynical explanation for some of these ideological flip-flops might be found in Pareto's personal circumstances. Pareto campaigned for radical social change. But then he inherited a fortune. Shortly afterwards Pareto's wife left him, running off with their young cook. Whether in response to his wife's actions or his inheritance, Pareto moved to a luxurious house overlooking Lake Geneva. Naming it Villa Angora, he lived alone there, except for his housekeeper and an entourage of twelve pedigree angora cats, whom he thought of as examples to humanity.[5] It was in this otherworldly setting that Pareto refined the two ideas that have come to dominate how most economists think about inequality today. It is the ghost of Pareto – not the much better-known Marx, Keynes, Friedman or Hayek – that has done most to shape the mainstream political consensus on inequality in the richer nations of the early twenty-first century, a consensus around the inevitability of substantial inequality and the difficulty of devising policies to reduce it.

In mainstream economics a fundamental idea – perhaps *the* fundamental idea – is efficiency. Mostly, when economists speak of efficiency it is a shorthand for *Pareto efficiency*. In engineering, there is an unambiguous increase in the efficiency of a system or process if output is maintained while reducing inputs, or output is increased using unchanged inputs. Either way, there is a costless improvement. Pareto the ex-engineer applied the idea to economic systems: a costless improvement occurs when at least one person gains and no one loses (economists now call this kind of improvement a *Pareto improvement*). And Pareto efficiency is achieved when no further Pareto improvements are possible: all costless gains have been taken, so any further gains for some will be unavoidably accompanied by losses for others.

For economists from the 1930s onwards the idea of Pareto efficiency was transformative. It transformed awkward, politically charged debates about the distribution of the fruits of capitalism, about winners and losers, into scientific-sounding arguments about efficiency. A Pareto improvement, when at least one person gains and no one loses, could be seen as an unambiguous improvement, as objective and unarguable as engineering efficiency improvements in some manufacturing process. And beyond Pareto improvements, nothing objective (and hence 'scientific') can be said. All other changes involve both winners and losers, so deciding whether the change is on balance a good thing involves 'unscientific' value judgements – appeals to morality to weigh up the gains and losses. In the self-image of economics-as-science which came to dominate after the Second World War, value judgements were seen as having no place in economics. Paretian ideas had given economists a convenient excuse to pay little attention to the winners and losers arising from changes in government policy or the wider economy. In other words, the effects on inequality were largely ignored. Economists simply identified the Pareto improvements and left it at that – 'economics has nothing more to say'. This view has been passed down to the present via generations of economics textbooks. In contemporary debate the ghost of Pareto lies behind the idea that the goodness or badness of increased inequality is merely 'a matter of opinion' and that serious, politically impartial policy analysis done by advisers in government and business must focus on efficiency considerations, not equity, fairness or inequality.

The bizarre, Pareto-inspired reluctance of orthodox economists to talk about inequality doesn't just sideline other perspectives on inequality from Smith to Keynes. It ignores Pareto's own work too. Textbooks refer to Pareto efficiency on every other page – but they make no mention of Pareto's other big idea about inequality.

And this idea was big. After a careful study of as much income and wealth data as he could find (going as far afield as Peru and as far back as tax records from Basel, Switzerland, in 1454), Pareto concluded that in *all* countries, at *all* times, the distribution of income and wealth follows the *same* pattern of high inequality. Pareto had begun by noting that 80 per cent of the land in Italy was owned by 20 per cent of the people: his research is the origin of the '80/20 rule' familiar today. Pareto discovered a deep and general pattern: if we put all members of society in order of income (or wealth), moving from the poorest to the richest, income (or wealth) does not rise smoothly or follow a line. Instead it barely rises at all initially, then by a relatively small amount over the majority of the population, then it shoots up hugely once we reach the top 1 per cent. As we have seen, people default to bell-curve thinking – in this context, the idea that the pattern of inequality is all about the disparity between the very rich (or very poor) and the great mass of people in the middle. But this misses a key fact about inequality: it does not stop at the top. In the mathematical language of the previous chapter (which was not known in Pareto's day), Pareto had discovered that income and wealth follow a scale-invariant distribution: the pattern of inequality stays the same, regardless of scale. In the late 2010s, the richest 1 per cent in the US received around 20 per cent of all the income. Pareto's scale-invariance idea implies that, *within* this top 1 per cent group, the same pattern of inequality holds. And Pareto was right: today in the US, the top 1 per cent *within* the top 1 per cent (the top 0.01 per cent) also earn around 20 per cent of the total earned by the top 1 per cent overall. In other words, millionaires differ. There is a high degree of inequality *among* millionaires – *and* the same degree of inequality amongst billionaires. It is like opening up successive nested Russian dolls.[6] The CEOs of the top 500 companies in the US may earn a fortune, but in some recent years the top 25 US hedge-fund managers have earned more than these 500 CEOs combined.[7]

While Pareto was right about the facts of inequality, his explanation for them is controversial, at best. Pareto argued that the stable pattern of inequality across time and place reflected innate differences in ability and talent across people. Significant inequalities in income and wealth are the inevitable and natural result of significant inequalities in ability and talent. Pareto insisted that democratic societies risked stagnation and decay if they attempted to ameliorate these inequalities, or to limit the natural tendency of superior people to rise to the top. He believed that we should 'compare the social body to the human body, which will promptly perish if prevented from eliminating toxins'.[8] This was just the kind of language which Mussolini, with his master-race fantasies, found so appealing. While it may seem to have nothing to do with mainstream opinion in the twenty-first century, elements of this Paretian worldview persist today in the idea that there are some exceptionally talented people in the world who deserve to keep the overwhelming majority of the wealth they create. Trying to resist this tendency towards the concentration of wealth in the hands of a few supreme wealth creators, so the argument goes, is likely to be futile, and attempts to do so will usually be harmful to wider society. Another reason why inequality becomes barely worth talking about.

In the modern version, the conclusion is essentially the same: rising inequality is natural and inevitable. But it is justified by an economic argument around globalization and new technology. Globalization means that most goods and services have a potentially global market. Supplying such a large market is much more profitable, so if your own skills are indispensable to that supply chain the rewards are potentially much greater. And new technology has boosted the earnings premium available to workers with the skills to make the most of it. One implication is that the earnings of university graduates will rise faster than average earnings.

However, familiar as it may be, this explanation does not fit the facts. Instead we see the pattern Pareto identified – rising inequality *within* the group. A small number of graduates have enjoyed enormous earnings growth, but most graduate earnings have *not* risen faster than average earnings, even though these graduates include most of the highly skilled workers in the economy.[9] The story of rising inequality is not one of increasing rewards to highly skilled workers because of globalization and new technology but a stunning rise in rewards to a very small group among them.

Any argument that rising inequality is largely inevitable in our globalized economy faces a further crucial objection. Since 1980 some countries have experienced a big increase in inequality (the US and the UK); some have seen a much smaller increase (Canada, Japan, Italy), while inequality has been stable or falling in France, Belgium and Hungary.[10] So rising inequality cannot be inevitable. And the extent of inequality within a country cannot be solely determined by long-run global economic forces, because, although most richer countries have been subject to broadly similar forces, their experiences of inequality have differed. Given their common economic experiences, the explanation of any differences is likely to be non-economic. This returns us to the familiar political explanation for rising inequality – the huge shift in mainstream economic and political thinking triggered by the election of Reagan and Thatcher. Its fit with the facts is undeniable. Across developed economies, the biggest rise in inequality since 1945 occurred in the US and UK from 1980 onwards.

The power of a grand political transformation seems persuasive. But it cannot be the whole explanation. It is too top-down: it is all about what politicians and other elites do to us. The idea that rising inequality is inevitable begins to look like a convenient myth, one that allows us to avoid thinking about another possibility: that through our electoral choices and decisions in daily life we have supported rising inequality, or at least acquiesced in it. Admittedly, that assumes we know about it. Surveys in the UK and US consistently suggest that we underestimate both the level of current inequality and how much it has recently increased.[11] But ignorance cannot be a complete excuse, because surveys also reveal a change in attitudes: rising inequality has become more acceptable – or at least, less unacceptable – especially if you are not on the wrong end of it.[12]

Inequality is unlikely to fall much in the future unless our attitudes turn unequivocally against it again. Among other things, we will need to accept that how much people earn in the market is often not what they deserve, and that the tax they pay is not taking from what is rightfully theirs. All of which is easy to accept when applied to hedge-fund managers, harder to accept when applied to entrepreneurs – and much, much harder to accept when applied to you and me.

We will come to you and me, but let's start with Bill Gates.

IT'S TOUGH AT THE TOP

As *The Economist* put it, 'Societies have always had elites . . . The big change over the past century is that elites are increasingly meritocratic and global. The richest people in advanced countries are not aristocrats but entrepreneurs such as Bill Gates.'[13] As well as often being dubbed 'world's richest person', Bill Gates seems to be a nice guy. A leading philanthropist, he seems the model of someone who used their substantial talent and worked extremely hard to achieve great success. Yet a closer look at his rise tells a less heroic story.[14] Thanks to family wealth, he went to Lakeside, a private school in Seattle that had something few schools in the world had in the late 1960s – a computer. Gates was hooked early on. After more lucky breaks, Gates dropped out of Harvard and set up Microsoft (with another former Lakeside computer enthusiast). By the late 1970s the leading operating system in the nascent field of desktop computers was called CP/M (Control Program for Microcomputers). Microsoft's main business involved selling software to run on CP/M.

Around this time IBM, whose giant presence in the industry was matched by the giant size of its mainframe computers, wanted to launch a desktop and needed an operating system. Not only was CP/M the market leader, its creator Gary Kildall was ahead of his rivals, having already developed multitasking. (If this sounds like another era, it was. Kildall's company was originally called Intergalactic Digital Research.) However, for reasons which remain obscure, IBM approached Gates rather than Kildall to buy the licence for CP/M. Gates told them it wasn't his and referred them to Kildall. Yet somehow Gates still ended up doing the crucial deal with IBM, selling them a hurriedly bought and adapted version of CP/M. The exact reasons for Gates's success remain unclear. However, Kildall's boy-racer image did not fit in well with IBM's corporate culture; whereas the IBM CEO made it clear that he was pleased to hear of a deal with Microsoft, because he knew Bill Gates's mother well. It still took years for IBM and Microsoft to introduce an operating system that could handle multitasking.

We like hero stories, and the accumulation of wealth is no different. We like to see important advances in knowledge as the product of dogged determination and geniuses struggling against adversity. Yet history is awash with 'geniuses' who were very lucky. While Alexander Graham Bell is credited with inventing the telephone, it seems that Antonio Meucci had successfully developed it years earlier. Meucci filed a statement of intent to patent in 1871, five years before Bell. Bell is in the history books only because, in 1874, Meucci let the statement lapse because he could not afford the $10 renewal fee.[15]

It's not just that Bill Gates was lucky. His success depended greatly on the work of others, starting with Charles Babbage. Similarly, while Apple were lauded and rewarded for introducing a computer mouse to accompany their Mac desktop in 1984, it was Douglas Engelbart and Bill English who, with funding from the US Air Force, had invented the computer mouse back in the early 1960s.* When, in popular mythology, a single individual is strongly associated with a new product, invention or breakthrough, it is exactly that – a myth. Trying to tease out one person's contributions is a hopeless task. Professions of intellectual modesty tend to be more accurate than hero myths, a point well understood by one genius who changed the world. As Isaac Newton wrote to his rival Robert Hooke: 'You have added much several ways ... If I have seen further it is by standing on the shoulders of Giants.'

Moving from the individual perspective to the whole economy, the point stands. Attempts to trace the source of economic growth find that most of it is due neither to increases in labour productivity nor to investment. Coming from different theoretical perspectives, Nobel laureate economists Robert Solow and Herbert Simon reached the same conclusion: most growth ultimately stems from the economic consequences of advances in knowledge. George Akerlof, another Nobel economist, emphasizes that 'our marginal products are not ours alone ... [they] are due almost entirely to the cumulative process of learning that has taken us from stone-age poverty to twenty-first century affluence'.[16]

Were it not for ingrained hero myths, this might seem too obvious to state. And yet the traditional economic theory of the determination of wages and salaries assumes that a person's 'marginal product' – their extra contribution to economic output – can be neatly isolated and identified. The theory then asserts that every individual's earnings are a direct consequence of their marginal product: your pay reflects your contribution. Or, you get what you deserve, and you deserve what you get. The political context that originally inspired this marginal productivity theory was the emergence of a huge impoverished underclass after the Industrial Revolution and the charge from Marx and Engels that workers were being exploited.[17] Marginal-productivity theory satisfied the urgent need to justify the poverty pay of workers, in contrast to the much higher income of their bosses.

---

* Engelbart held a crucial patent for the mouse but never received any royalties because he allowed the patent to lapse in 1987.

The surprise is that, some 150-odd years later, economics textbooks still defend the theory.

One reason is that the theory is so difficult to disprove. Even assuming that your contribution could be somehow independent of our common inheritance of knowledge from the past, few people today work in splendid isolation, so it is hard to identify the added value due to your work alone. The CEO of a big corporation may take the credit for a large rise in profits, but how much of that rise is due just to their efforts? The converse is true too: it is hard to prove that the credit for a particular output is best attributed to others. The theory becomes impossible to disprove when it descends into tautology. This is easiest to see in the rare cases when someone's individual contribution *can* be identified (think sports stars and other solo performers). Often the only way to measure the value of this individual contribution is in terms of how much consumers or clients are willing to pay for it. Then the marginal productivity argument boils down to: your pay is justified because it reflects how much others are willing to pay you. In other words: your pay is justified because it reflects how much you are paid.

If this seems like a harmless semantic game, it is not. If the only measure of the value created by someone's work is consumers' willingness to pay for it, then we should ignore the intrinsic, non-market, value of goods and services. And we can justify top bankers being paid more than top neurosurgeons, and dog-walkers for the top 0.1 per cent being paid more than primary-school teachers.

Clearly, there must be more than marginal-productivity theory behind the widespread popularity of 'you get what you deserve, and you deserve what you get'. And hero myths – even if we believe them – can only justify the pay of a few exceptional people, not the rest of us. So we must dig deeper.

BECAUSE YOU'RE WORTH IT

At its heart, every argument in favour of inequality appeals direct to your ego: *you* are special and unique. *Ergo* you are different, *ergo* we are all different, *ergo* inequality is a fact of nature. Or at least, your uniqueness is manifested in your talent and hard work, which justify you getting the job you did or being paid more than other apparently similarly qualified colleagues. Or at least, you deserve what you earn because you worked hard to get where you are. At last, we can glimpse one crucial reason why we have done so little to reduce inequality in recent years: we downplay the role of luck in achieving success. Success usually requires a high degree of sustained effort over a long period, which is especially hard to summon up if we focus on the possibility of bad luck intervening to stymie our best efforts. So we favour narratives that marginalize the role played by luck. Parents teach their children that almost all goals are attainable if you try hard enough. This is a lie, but there is a good excuse for it: unless you try your best, many goals will definitely remain unreachable. Entrepreneurs who have successfully built up a business from scratch often recall with bemusement the naïve optimism they had when they started. If they had begun with a more realistic awareness of the huge risks and obstacles, they would probably never have started their business. In general, in many competitive situations, success may require a degree of self-delusion, overstating the difference our own individual efforts can make and understating the role of luck.[18]

Ignoring the good luck behind my success helps me feel good about myself and makes it much easier to feel I deserve the rewards associated with success. These forces are at work even in the most unpromising circumstances. Lottery winners frequently describe the elaborate techniques they used to pick their winning numbers. Research among stock-market investors has shown that they often attribute most of their successful investments to good judgement and most of their failures to bad luck. And, of course, people with high earnings see them as the deserved result of talent and hard work.

Yet the stubborn persistence of you-deserve-what-you-get and related beliefs suggest that these beliefs may go beyond self-conscious exercises in providing a moral justification for your own high income or wealth. High earners may truly believe that they deserve their income because they are vividly aware of how hard they have worked and the obstacles they have had to overcome to be successful.

Unfortunately, our memories play tricks, systematically biasing the narrative of the path to success that we construct. The biggest culprit is probably the *availability heuristic* (another one of Kahneman and Tversky's major insights). When English speakers are asked whether English words beginning with the letter K are more frequent than words with K as the third letter, most choose the former. In fact, there are more words with K as the third letter, but words beginning with K are much more *available* to our minds because it is easier to think of examples. Availability is a mental shortcut which biases our judgements by leading us to give too much weight to readily available examples. Every high earner can easily remember several examples of their exceptional hard work (working all night, all weekend, and so on. Vivid examples of equally hard work by people we rarely know well (low earners) are more difficult to bring to mind. Similarly, it is easier to recall past obstacles and challenges I had to overcome than prevailing circumstances which worked in my favour. The latter are hard to capture with a single word (tailwind?) or image. Headwinds are easy to visualize, impossible to ignore, and hence easy to remember (imagine riding a bike into one). Tailwinds are easy to forget, even when on a bike.[19]

But there is a puzzle here. If the explanation for you-deserve-what-you-get and related beliefs is psychological and hence universal, why does support for these beliefs differ so much in different countries? More than that: why is support for these beliefs stronger in countries where there seems to be stronger evidence that contradicts them?

Support for you-deserve-what-you-get seems strongest in the country where there is perhaps the most conflicting evidence: the United States.[20] Attitude surveys have consistently shown that, compared to US residents, Europeans are roughly twice as likely to believe that luck is the main determinant of income and that the poor are trapped in poverty. Similarly, people in the US are about twice as likely as Europeans to believe that the poor are lazy and lack willpower and that hard work leads to higher quality of life in the long run. Yet in fact the poor (the bottom 20 per cent) work roughly the same total annual hours in the US and Europe. And crucially, economic opportunity and intergenerational mobility is more limited in the US than in Europe. A person's income is more likely to reflect their economic background (their parents' income) in the US: the correlation between parents' income and children's income is higher in the US than the

European average. In the US the correlation is around 0.5, about the same as between the heights of parents and their children.[21] US children born to poor parents are as likely to be poor as those born to tall parents are likely to be tall. And research has repeatedly shown that many people in the US don't know this: perceptions of social mobility are consistently over-optimistic.

European countries have, on average, more redistributive tax systems and more welfare benefits for the poor than the US, and therefore less inequality, after taxes and benefits. Many people see this outcome as reflecting the differing attitudes in US and Europe described above. But cause-and-effect may run the other way: you-deserve-what-you-get beliefs are strengthened by inequality. Psychologists have shown that people have motivated beliefs: beliefs that they have chosen to hold because the beliefs serve some function or meet a psychological need. Now, being poor in the US is no fun, given the meagre welfare benefits and high levels of post-tax inequality. So Americans have a greater need than Europeans to believe that you-deserve-what-you-get and you-get-what-you-deserve. These beliefs play a powerful role in motivating yourself and your children to work as hard as possible to avoid poverty. And these beliefs can help alleviate the guilt involved in ignoring a homeless person begging on your street.

This is not just a US issue. Britain is an outlier within Europe, with relatively high inequality and low economic and social mobility. Its recent history fits the cause-and-effect relationship here. Following the election of Margaret Thatcher in 1979, inequality rose significantly. *After* inequality rose, British attitudes changed. More people became convinced that generous welfare benefits make poor people lazy and that high salaries are essential to motivate talented people. However, intergenerational mobility fell: your income in Britain today is closely correlated with your parents' income. The pattern recurs worldwide: countries with higher inequality are those with lower intergenerational mobility, and vice versa. Economists have dubbed the graph showing this relationship the 'Great Gatsby Curve'.[22]

If the American Dream and other narratives about everyone having a chance to be rich were true, we would expect the opposite relationship: high inequality (is fair because of) high intergenerational mobility. Instead we see a very different narrative, more of a coping strategy: people cope with high inequality by convincing themselves it is fair after all. We adopt narratives to justify inequality because society is highly unequal, not the other way round. So inequality may be self-perpetuating in a surprising way. Rather than resist and revolt, we just cope with it. Less *Communist Manifesto*, more self-help manual. And inequality is self-perpetuating in other ways too.

YOU GET WHAT YOU CAN GET AWAY WITH

We have seen that much of the rise in inequality is driven by changes at the very top. The rewards going to the top 1 per cent have risen greatly, both in comparison with the bottom 99 per cent and as a proportion of GDP. Why? We have already ruled out some answers: it is not due to global economic forces or new technology, while explanations from marginal productivity theory are either false or tautological. The answer is both simple and astonishing. Simple because, in essence, the top 1 one cent just decided to pay themselves much more. And astonishing because, at least initially, we invited them to do so.

This kind of absurd invitation violates common sense so, unsurprisingly, its genesis lies in economic theory. In textbook economics, a prerequisite for successful capitalism is that firms seek to maximize profits. But profit-maximizing firms are unlikely in reality, because profits traditionally go to shareholders, whereas the CEO and senior managers who make the decisions are more likely to be interested in enlarging their own salary or status. Economists proposed 'optimal contracting' as the way to make firms more like the profit-maximizing textbook 'ideal': give senior managers a relatively modest basic salary, along with the opportunity to earn a substantial bonus contingent on good profits (or some other outcome serving the interests of investors, such as a rising share price). While CEOs and other managers with these new 'pay-for-performance' contracts could earn much more, the entire economy would benefit, economists argued, because firms would be run more efficiently. In 1990 two of the most prominent cheerleaders for pay-for-performance, Michael Jensen and Kevin Murphy, wrote in an article in the *Harvard Business Review*: 'Are current levels of CEO compensation high enough to attract the best and brightest individuals to careers in corporate management? The answer is, probably not.'[23]

Jensen and Murphy's piece proved massively influential: together with other leading economists, they provided a fig leaf for corporate greed. In the fifteen years following 1990 the average total 'compensation package' of CEOs in the top 500 US companies more than tripled (after allowing for inflation). By 2004 Jensen and Murphy had recanted, commenting on their earlier view that CEO pay should be higher: 'Jensen and Murphy would not give that answer today.'[24]

We have the benefit of hindsight, of course, but still, the flaws in the argument for massive pay rises for CEOs seem glaringly obvious. First, the argument assumes that any increase in profits must be due entirely to the actions of CEOs and other senior managers; second, the argument assumes that if profits rise, somehow in the long run everyone in the economy will be better off. Actually, we can ignore these heroic assumptions because something cruder went wrong with pay-for-performance contracts: they were – and still are – rigged in favour of CEOs and other top managers.

The key reason is not hard to find. Pay-for-performance contracts are determined by boards of directors. And, as Jensen and Murphy belatedly noticed: 'The CEO does most of the recruiting for the board ... board members serve at the pleasure of the CEO. The CEO generally sets the agenda for the board. Virtually all information board members receive from the company originates from or passes through the CEO.'[25] The result, from the perspective of perhaps the world's most successful investor, billionaire Warren Buffett, is that 'The deck is stacked against investors when it comes to the CEO's pay.' The practical realities of pay-for-performance have finally filtered back to its originators, the economic theorists who invented 'optimal contracting'. Bengt Holmström recently won a Nobel Prize for his work on optimal contracting – but used his acceptance speech to perform a pirouette similar to Jensen and Murphy's.

Holmström concluded that 'bringing the market inside the firm is such a misguided idea, something I failed to understand [earlier] and advocates of market-like incentives in firms seem to miss today'.[26]

Better late than never, although the more inventive self-enrichment efforts of the top 1 per cent have now moved elsewhere. Most of these efforts involve changing the rules underpinning economic activity in their favour. Economists call it *rent-seeking*: any action undertaken with the principal purpose of redistributing income, wealth or resources in your favour – in contrast to most economic activity, which in some sense creates wealth or adds value to economy or society. The only objective of rent-seekers is grabbing a bigger slice of the pie; they do nothing to enlarge the pie for everyone. The telltale sign of rent-seekers at work is the appearance of some obscure or little-discussed rule or regulation which has no conceivable justification but turns out to be worth a fortune to the rent-seekers. In many countries, for example, government-controlled and -funded healthcare systems have curiously forbidden themselves to negotiate lower prices with manufacturers. In the US, this little-noticed legal rule has effectively gifted the drug companies more than $50 billion a year.[27] But probably the favourite playground of rent-seekers is the financial sector. The former head of the Securities and Exchange Commission (Wall Street's chief regulator) described how Wall Street lobbyists 'would quickly set about to defeat even minor threats. Individual investors, with no organized [group] to represent their views in Washington, never knew what hit them.'[28] The general lesson is clear, and now supported by extensive research: as the very rich become even richer, they exert more influence throughout the political process, from election-campaign funding to lobbying over particular rules and regulations. The result is politicians and policies which help them but are inefficient and wasteful.[29] Left-wing critics have called it 'socialism for the rich'. Even Warren Buffett seems to agree: 'There's been class warfare going on for the last 20 years and my class has won.'

We saw earlier that once inequality increases, it can be self-perpetuating, as attitudes evolve to accommodate and justify it. And now we see a parallel dynamic at work: an initial impetus coming from economists (such as advocating pay-for-performance contracts) followed by a vicious circle in which inequality begets further in-equality. As the top 1 per cent grow richer they have both more incentive and more ability to enrich themselves further. Their success in doing so begins the cycle all over again.

But the biggest increase in inequality has come from this process playing out in another arena: tax. High earners have most to gain from income tax cuts and more spare cash to lobby politicians for these cuts. Once tax cuts are secured, high earners have an even stronger incentive to seek pay rises because they keep a greater pro-portion of after-tax pay. And so on.

Here is the evidence. Over the last fifty years developed economies with the smallest increase in the share of pre-tax income going to the top 1 per cent are also those with smallest cuts in the top rate of income tax (the rate applicable to the highest earners). Conversely, countries where the top 1 per cent have gained the most *before* tax are also those countries in which they have enjoyed the biggest tax cuts.[30] No surprises about the countries in this last group: although there have been cuts in the top rate of income tax across almost all developed economies since 1979, it was the UK and the US that were first and that went furthest.[31] In 1979 Thatcher cut the UK's top rate from 83 per cent to 60 per cent, with a further reduc-tion to 40 per cent in 1988. In 1981 Reagan cut the top US rate from 70 per cent to 28 per cent. Although top rates today are slightly higher (35 per cent in the US and 45 per cent in the UK), the numbers are worth mentioning because they are strikingly lower than in the postwar period, when top tax rates averaged 75 per cent in the US and even higher in the UK. That people saw things differently then is illustrated by President Eisenhower, war hero and Supreme Com-mander of the Allied Forces in the Second World War (so hardly a commie). Under Eisenhower, the top US income tax rate rose to 91 per cent. Eisenhower really seemed to believe in high tax on the rich: in a private letter to his brother he wrote about his acceptance of the New Deal, involving generous social-security and unemployment payments funded partly through income tax. Eisenhower described those opposed as a few 'Texas millionaires, and an occasional politi-cian or businessman from other areas. Their number is negligible and they are stupid.'[32]

Some elements of the Reagan/Thatcher revolution in economic policy, such as Milton Friedman's monetarist macroeconomics, have subsequently been abandoned. But the key policy idea to come out of *micro*economics has become so widely accepted today that it has acquired the status of common sense: that tax discourages economic activity and, in particular, income tax discourages work. This doctrine did not emerge from a new idea in economic theory. Instead it boiled down to a brilliant new presentation of old ideas, in the right place at the right time. The new doctrine seemingly transformed public debate about taxation from the dismal science of the turbulent 1970s, an endless argument over who gets what, to the promise of a bright and prosperous future for all. The *for all* bit was crucial: no more winners and losers. Just winners. And the basic ideas were simple enough to fit on the back of a napkin.

TAX IS THE NEW THEFT

One evening in December 1974 a group of ambitious young conservatives met for dinner at the Two Continents Restaurant in Washington DC. With Jude Wanniski, an editor at the *Wall Street Journal*, were the Chicago University economist Arthur Laffer, Donald Rumsfeld (then Chief of Staff to President Ford) and Dick Cheney, then Rumsfeld's deputy and a former Yale classmate of Laffer's.[33] While discussing President Ford's recent tax increases, Laffer pointed out that, like a 0 per cent income tax rate, a 100 per cent rate would raise no revenue because no one would bother working. Logically, there must be some tax rate between these two extremes which would maximize tax revenue. Although Laffer does not remember doing so, he apparently grabbed a napkin and drew a curve on it, representing the relationship between tax rates and revenues.* The 'Laffer curve' was born and, with it, the idea of 'trickle down economics'. The key

---

* A napkin fitting the description has appeared: see http://www.polyconomics.com/gallery/Napkin003.jpg. However, since Laffer does not remember the incident, this was presumably drawn more recently, as though by popular request. And it seems to be dated September, which does not match the December lunch described by Wanniski.

implication which impressed Rumsfeld and Cheney was that, just in the way that tax rates lower than 100 per cent must raise more revenue, cuts in income tax rates more generally could raise revenue. In other words, there could be winners, and no losers, from tax cuts.

But *could* does not mean *will*. No empirical evidence was produced in support of the mere logical possibility that tax cuts could raise revenue, and even the economists employed by the incoming Reagan administration some six years later struggled to find any evidence in support of the idea. Yet it proved irresistible to Reagan the perennial optimist, who essentially overruled his expert advisers, convinced that the 'entrepreneurial spirit unleashed by the new tax cuts would surely bring in more revenue than his experts imagined'.[34] (If this potent brew of populist optimism and impatience with economic experts seems familiar forty years later, Laffer was also a campaign adviser to Donald Trump.)[35]

For income tax cuts to *raise* tax revenue, the prospect of higher after-tax pay must motivate people to work more. The resulting increase in GDP and income may be enough to generate higher tax revenues, even though the tax rate itself has fallen. Although the effects of the big Reagan tax cuts are still disputed (mainly because of disagreement over how the US economy would have performed without the cuts), even those sympathetic to trickle-down economics conceded that the cuts had negligible impact on GDP – and certainly not enough to outweigh the negative effect of the cuts on tax revenues. But the Laffer curve did remind economists that a 'revenue-maximizing top tax rate' somewhere between 0 per cent and 100 per cent must exist. Finding the magic number is another matter: the search continues today. It is worth a brief dig into this research, not least because it is regularly used to veto attempts to reduce inequality by raising tax on the rich. In 2013, for example, UK Chancellor of the Exchequer George Osborne reduced the top rate of income tax from 50 per cent to 45 per cent, arguing Laffer-style that the tax cut would lead to little if any loss of revenue. Osborne's argument relied on economic analysis suggesting that the revenue-maximizing top tax rate for the UK is around 40 per cent.

Yet the assumptions behind this number are shaky, as most economists involved in producing such figures acknowledge.[36] Let's begin with the underlying idea: if lower tax rates raise your after-tax pay, you are motivated to work more. It seems plausible enough, but in practice the effects are likely to be minimal. If income tax falls, many of us cannot work more, even if we wanted to do so. There is little opportunity to get paid overtime, or otherwise increase our paid working hours, and working harder during current working hours does not lead to higher pay. Even for those who have these opportunities, it is far from clear that they will work more or harder. Instead they may decide to work *less*: since after-tax pay has risen, they can choose to work fewer hours and still maintain their previous income level, leaving their material standard of living unaffected. So the popular presumption that income tax cuts must lead to more work and productive economic activity turns out to have little basis in either common sense or economic theory.

There are deeper difficulties with Osborne's argument, difficulties not widely known even among economists. It is often assumed that if the top 1 per cent are incentivized by income tax cuts to earn more, those higher earnings reflect an increase in productive economic activity. In other words, the pie gets bigger. But some economists (including the influential Thomas Piketty) have shown this is not true for CEOs and other top corporate managers following the tax cuts in the 1980s. Instead, they essentially funded their own pay rises by paying shareholders less – which led in turn to lower dividend tax revenue for the government. Allowing for this and related effects – the rich redistributing the pie rather than making it bigger – Piketty and colleagues have argued that the revenue-maximizing top income tax rate may be as high as 83 per cent.[37]

The income tax cuts for the rich over the past forty years were originally justified by economic arguments: Laffer's rhetoric was seized upon by politicians. But to economists his ideas were both familiar and trivial. Modern economics provides neither theory nor evidence proving the merit of these tax cuts. Both are ambiguous. Although politicians can ignore this truth for a while, it suggests that widespread opposition to higher taxes on the rich is ultimately based on reasons beyond economics.

When the top UK income tax rate was raised to 50 per cent in 2009 (until Osborne cut it to 45 per cent four years later) the musicals composer Andrew Lloyd Webber, one of Britain's wealthiest people, responded bluntly: 'the last thing we need is a Somali pirate-style raid on the few wealth creators who still dare to navigate Britain's gale-force waters'.[38] In the US Stephen Schwarzman, CEO of private equity firm Blackstone, likened proposals to remove a specialized tax exemption (from which he greatly benefited) to the German invasion of Poland.[39]

While we may scoff at these whines from the super-rich, most people unthinkingly accept the fundamental idea behind them: that income tax is a kind of theft, taking income which is rightfully owned by the person who earned it. It follows that tax is at best a necessary evil, and so should be minimized as far as possible. On these grounds, the 83 per cent top tax rate discussed by Piketty is unacceptable. There is an entire cultural ecosystem which has evolved around tax-as-theft, recognizable today in politicians' talk about 'spending taxpayers' money', or campaigners celebrating 'tax freedom day'. It is not just populism. Tax economists, accountants and lawyers refer to the 'tax burden' – and if you think 'tax burden' is a neutral label, then for the sake of consistency you should be happy for the term 'public spending' to be replaced with 'public benefits'.

But the idea that you somehow own your pre-tax income, while obvious, is false. To begin with, you could never have ownership rights prior to, or independent from, taxation. Ownership is a legal right. Laws require various institutions, including police and a legal system, to function. These institutions are financed through taxation. The tax and the ownership rights are effectively created simultaneously. We cannot have one without the other. Perhaps we overlook this inherent interdependency between tax and property rights because *as individuals* we can fantasize about escaping from it: clearly, an individual could receive all their pre-tax income and have enforceable ownership rights over it – providing everyone else pays the tax to maintain the system to enforce these rights.

However, if the only function of the state is to support private ownership rights (maintaining a legal system, police, and so on), it seems that taxation could be very low – and any further taxation on top could still be seen as a form of theft.

Implicit in this view is the idea of incomes earned, and so ownership rights created, in an entirely private market economy, with the minimal state entering only later, to ensure these rights are maintained. Many economics textbooks picture the state in this way, as an add-on to the market. Yet this, too, is a fantasy. In the modern world all economic activity reflects the influence of government. Markets are *inevitably* defined and shaped by government. There is no such thing as income earned before government comes along. My earnings partly reflect my education. Earlier still, the circumstances of my birth and my subsequent health reflects the healthcare available. Even if that healthcare is entirely 'private', it depends on the education of doctors and nurses, and the drugs and other technologies available. Like all other goods and services, these in turn depend on the economic and social infrastructure, including transport networks, communications systems, energy supplies and extensive legal arrangements covering complex matters such as intellectual property, formal markets such as stock exchanges, and jurisdiction across national borders. Andrew Lloyd Webber's wealth depends on government decisions about the length of copyright on the music he wrote. In sum, it is impossible to isolate what is 'yours' from what is made possible, or influenced, by the role of government.[40]

Talk of taxation as theft turns out to be another variation on the egotistical tendency discussed earlier – to see my success in splendid isolation, ignoring the contribution of past generations, current colleagues and government. Undervaluing the role of government leads to the belief that if you are smart and hard-working, the high taxes you endure, paying for often wasteful government, are not a good deal. You would be better off in a minimal-state, low-tax society. One reply to this challenge points to the evidence on the rich leaving their home country to move to a lower tax jurisdiction: in fact, very few of them do.[41] Here is a more ambitious reply from Warren Buffett:

> Imagine there are two identical twins in the womb . . . And the genie says to them, 'One of you is going to be born in the United States, and one of you is going to be born in Bangladesh. And if you wind up in Bangladesh, you will pay no taxes. What percentage of your income would you bid to be born in the United States?' . . . The people who say, 'I did it all myself' . . . believe me, they'd bid more to be in the United States than in Bangladesh.[42]

REVENGE OF THE *LUMPENPROLETARIAT*

The *Lumpenproletariat* was Karl Marx's term for the underclass, the poorest, marginalized members of society, usually with little if any secure work or income, and vulnerable to being conned into supporting political leaders who claim to want to help them, but don't. (In the US after the election of Donald Trump, the word *Trumpenproletariat* went viral online.) Yet the *Lumpen/Trumpenproletariat* have more power than it seems. Around the world, employers large and small assume that an easy way to boost profits is to pay unskilled workers as little as possible – just enough to prevent them walking away. This strategy has the blessing of traditional economic theory, which treats labour as just another input to the production process, as if workers were just another kind of machine. And we saw how this mechanistic view of humanity spread beyond economics via Frederick Taylor and the early behavioural psychologists. But humans can take revenge.

If they know they are being paid as little as possible, people will work as little as possible in return. As one apocryphal worker described life in a Soviet factory, 'They pretend to pay us and we pretend to work.' To be clear, this is not a Marxist or Communist argument about the hidden power of downtrodden workers: Soviet production was hopelessly inefficient largely because it failed to recognize this power. Among modern economists the argument has been pioneered not by Marxists but by two Nobel laureate economists and a subsequent Chair of the US Federal Reserve: George Akerlof, Joseph Stiglitz and Janet Yellen have shown how profits can rise if a firm pays more than the bare minimum to prevent workers from seeking employment elsewhere. If instead the firm pays a substantially higher 'efficiency wage', this motivates workers to give their best, maximizing efficiency and productivity. They do so because they feel valued and respected by their employer – and also want to keep their job because they know they would probably earn less elsewhere.

Efficiency wages have profound implications for thinking about inequality. When increased inequality in pre-tax incomes arises from paying workers the bare minimum, the negative effect on productivity and profits is damaging for the wider economy. The pie shrinks. Inequality here doesn't just make the poor and the unskilled worse off; the rest of us lose too.

Reduced productivity caused by paying workers below their efficiency wage is not the only way that rising inequality can be costly, even to those on middle and higher incomes. Setting aside the wider social costs of inequality, there remain important – but little discussed – reasons why high inequality is costly even in narrow economic terms.

We have seen how the soaring rewards of the top 1 per cent are the result of their political and economic power and changing attitudes, rather than a reflection of their greater economic contribution. The growing mismatch between the rewards and contribution of the 1 per cent is very costly to the wider economy, much more so than the direct cost of lavish remuneration packages alone. The costs are clearest in the financial sector, since it employs such a large proportion of the 1 per cent (and an even larger proportion of the 0.1 per cent). These costs are recognized by insiders sympathetic to the sector, not just its critics. Leading central bankers have emphasized that rigged pay-for-performance contracts have increased the likelihood of bank bail-outs and other harms to the broader economy, by encouraging excessive speculation and risk-taking in financial markets.[43] The rigged contracts are less pay-for-performance, more heads-I-win-tales-you-lose: they let bankers keep a big part of the returns from successful bets without having to shoulder equivalent losses from failures.

Another problem with excessive remuneration packages in finance is that they lure too many talented people into the sector – people who would make a greater economic contribution elsewhere. On top of this waste of human resources, there are the resources wasted solely on getting excessive remuneration – merely redistributing the pie, rather than enlarging it. More rent-seeking, in other words. A rough estimate of the scale of the waste comes from the classic rent-seeking activity, lobbying. In the US in 2011 alone over $3 billion was spent on lobbying.[44]

Turning to the other end of the income distribution, poverty is not just a tragedy for the poor. It is an appalling waste of productive capacity in the rest of the economy. The poor have little access to affordable long-term credit, so they cannot afford the education and training available to the better off, and they struggle to borrow enough to develop a business idea. Starting a business, always a risky process, is especially dangerous for those with a minimal state-welfare safety net and no cushion of family wealth to protect them should the business fail. As well as the economic wastefulness of poverty, there is growing macroeconomic evidence that rising poverty and inequality are partly responsible for the lower levels of economic growth seen in many countries in recent years.[45] The explanation is straightforward: since real incomes at the bottom have stagnated, demand from the poor for goods and services has inevitably stagnated, too, adversely affecting economic growth. (Reduced consumption by the poor has not been offset by increased consumption by the rich, because the poor spend a much higher proportion of their income than the rich. So as money moves from poor to rich, overall consumption falls.)

This is not the place to go into the details of specific policies to reduce inequality. We looked briefly at one key aspect of one key policy: increasing top rates of income tax may well raise more revenue, as well as acting directly to reduce inequality in after-tax pay. To go deeper, you can turn to the many leading economists who have argued that more unequal societies are, if anything, associated with lower rather than higher economic growth; that tax rises for the rich do not harm economic growth or lead to a flight of talent abroad; and that redistributive measures involving greater welfare spending can be both affordable and feasible in an economy facing global competition.[46]

Yet perhaps these sophisticated economic arguments all miss the point. The crucial *economic* objection to any serious attempt to reduce inequality may be more basic and self-interested. There is a large and politically influential group – let's call them the affluent middle classes – who are much richer than average but poorer than the top 1 per cent. They have a vague sense of losing out from recent rises in inequality (and, as we've seen, they are right), and a much clearer, sharper sense that tax rises and other redistributive policies would definitely make them worse off. But here they are wrong.

Most of us with above-average incomes spend a large part of them on goods and services which are, to an economist, atypical. They have an unusual characteristic: their supply is effectively fixed or, if it can increase, it does so only rarely. The clearest examples of goods with a fixed supply (original art works and furniture, vintage cars and wine) are not our concern here because, even among the affluent middle classes, few people spend much of their income on them. But we do spend a large proportion of our incomes on housing – and usually the kind of housing that is in inherently short supply, either because the style or features are not possible to reproduce in new buildings, or because the location has inherently scarce features. There are inevitably only so many people who can live in comfort near the city centre, or with a view of the park, or with access to the best school for their children. This latter kind of scarcity is social rather than physical, and brings us to a range of other goods which are scarce because they need to be: their value or desirability is *due to* their scarcity. High-end labels – Gucci handbags, Ferrari sports cars – appeal in this way, enabling owners to signal their uncommon wealth or taste. The affluent middle classes spend a little on these. They spend much more on educational services (elite schools, elite postgraduate degrees) which confer advantage over others in the job market – because they are scarce. Economists call all these things *positional goods*, because buying them depends on outbidding other people for the limited supply: it depends not on your absolute income, but on your relative position in the income distribution.

The upshot is that middle-class dissatisfaction about those with higher incomes need not be due to envy, as some commentators suggest, but to legitimate positional concerns, such as falling behind in the competition to get your child into a better school. Yes, there is a kind of irrationality here, but it is collective rather than individual (it's the Prisoner's Dilemma of Chapter 2). When you are at a sports match, standing up to get a better view – to improve your relative position – is individually rational, but soon everyone else stands up, too, and we are all worse off. Similarly, most of us are trapped in the rat race, competing to buy the nice houses with access to the better schools. If everyone's income rises, the question of who gets which house remains unchanged. House prices rise, though: we all have to spend more to get the same house. We all stand up. If everyone then pays more tax, the opposite happens. Post-tax incomes fall, who gets which house remains unchanged, we all sit down.[47] Paying more tax, then, need *not* imply that your material living standards decline. If others face the same tax rise too, then your relative position will be unchanged, and so, too, your access to sought-after positional goods.[48]

Of course, there are caveats and exceptions to this argument. Clearly, it does not apply to tax rises on poorer members of society, who will be spending a large proportion of their income on necessities rather than positional goods. On the other hand, tax rises on the wealthy can do more than merely leave living standards unchanged, because my argument so far has ignored the benefits of increased government spending. Notably, many familiar economic arguments ignore these benefits too: when income taxes rise, textbook tax economics holds that the benefit from working falls, because post-tax income does. But what about the benefits you may now receive from increased government spending? Ignoring these benefits leads to absurdities. When someone chooses to save some of their earnings into a private pension, we don't say that their benefit from working has fallen. But if instead the same proportion of someone's earnings is paid into a state-organized pension, funded through higher income tax, economists often say the benefit from working has fallen, because tax has risen.

There are complex issues here. One thing, however, is clear: that in assessing how people think about and respond to tax increases, economists often take an unduly one-sided view, which dovetails with a presumption of wasteful government spending encouraged by the public choice economists in Chapter 4. And political debate often echoes the tax economics: enthusiasts for tax cuts are usually blind to the state-funded services which must necessarily be cut too – in turn necessitating higher spending by citizens to buy replacement services privately. One irony of this selective blindness is that it leads to a society in which we cannot enjoy the private luxuries made possible by low taxes because of crumbling public infrastructure. Or, as one US economist advocating higher taxes puts it, with an example designed to appeal to the rich: 'No matter how wealthy you were, you'd probably prefer driving a $150,000 Porsche 911 Turbo on a well-maintained highway to driving a $333,000 Ferrari Berlinetta on a pothole-ridden road.'[49] The point is clear: even if the rich are only interested in their own living standards, they should not welcome tax cuts. The resulting deterioration in public services is making *them* worse off too. And yet . . .

IT'S *NOT* THE ECONOMY, STUPID

Much of the inequality we see today in richer countries is more down to decisions made by governments than to irreversible market forces. These decisions can be changed. We have entered an era of automation and artificial intelligence, which, some argue, makes increased inequality unavoidable: in essence, the geeks who design the robots and the 0.01 per cent who own them will be fabulously wealthy, while the rest of us will be jobless. Yet, as we've seen, there is nothing preordained about such an unequal outcome. We *can* control the direction of technological change, specifically by encouraging innovation which supports human workers and recognizes their irreplaceable role in growing areas of employment including care, leisure and entertainment.

However, we have to *want* to control inequality: we must make inequality reduction a central aim of government policy and wider society. In economic policy, inequality reduction should not be an afterthought but an overarching goal on a par with efficiency and economic growth – and so a factor to be explicitly considered in decision-making across all branches of government. This would not be a step into the unknown: detailed, well-researched policy proposals to reduce inequality have already been developed.[50] Finally, inequality reduction is not just something to wait for governments to do: an awareness of the impact on inequality should help shape our own choices as consumers, employers and employees.

The most entrenched, self-deluding and self-perpetuating justifications for inequality explored in this chapter are about morality, not economy. The great economist John Kenneth Galbraith nicely summarized the problem: 'One of man's oldest exercises in moral philosophy . . . is the search for a superior moral justification for selfishness. It is an exercise which always involves a certain number of internal contradictions and even a few absurdities. The conspicuously wealthy turn up urging the character-building value of privation for the poor.'[51]

There is a final reason to fear that such attitudes may yet become more entrenched. High economic inequality works as social fission, fracturing diverse communities and driving people into ghettoes of wealth or poverty. Many new apartment blocks in London have two entrances: a front entrance for the rich accessing luxury apartments and a side or back entrance for those in more modest accommodation. Increasingly, we rarely mix with people with very different economic circumstances and living conditions. So inequality becomes less noticeable and more easily forgotten. And when rich and poor rarely mix, myths about intrinsic differences between them are more likely to survive and spread.

Against this, there is a glimmer of hope now that inequality has risen enough to have a big effect on future generations. Even those with the purest faith in you-get-what-you-deserve and related beliefs acknowledge that being born poor is not the fault of the child. And there is growing awareness of the overwhelming evidence (such as the Great Gatsby Curve mentioned above) that being born poor means you are much more likely to stay poor. Once the role of luck and our broad inheritance – including knowledge from previous generations and being born in a richer country rather than a poor one – is widely accepted, we can confront the implications for taxation. A historical perspective helps us see that taxation can be proudly defended across the political spectrum. In their different ways, thinkers from John Stuart Mill to Tom Paine emphasized that when an individual becomes richer, their increase in wealth is partly of social origin and tax should be used to return this wealth to society. Tax is not about taking your money, but about paying back society for the social wealth it has bestowed on you, from education to roads to the knowledge inherited from past generations.[52]

Still, the self-obsessed super-rich will always be with us. And as Galbraith suggests, they will always invoke some worn-out morality. Not that it helps them. At a party on a super-yacht owned by a billionaire, two authors reflected on their surroundings. Kurt Vonnegut turned to his friend Joseph Heller and told him that their hedge-fund-manager host made more money in one day than Heller made in total from *Catch*-22 (despite that book selling more than 10 million copies). 'Yes, but I have something he will never have,' Heller replied. 'Enough.'

10

A Troubled Relationship: Modern Economics and Us

Most of us have a troubled, confused relationship with economics. We find it easy to ridicule. News reports frequently refer to some economic forecast which turned out to be completely wrong, or economic policy which is not delivering on the promises made by the economists who recommended it. And yet, as I've shown in the course of this book, a large part of recent history is our increasing deference to the ideas of economists. Once-controversial 'economistic' ways of thinking have become embedded in everyday life. Our relationship with economics is love–hate.

And it is deeply unequal. Many economists appear to see themselves as outsiders, scientific observers of society, looking down on ordinary people with the superior, disinterested gaze of Charles Darwin looking at squashed beetles through a magnifying glass. Some economists openly admit that they regard ordinary people as stupid. MIT economist Jonathan Gruber claimed that a recent healthcare law was deliberately drafted 'in a tortured way' in order to make it unintelligible, 'given the stupidity of the American voter'.[1] One UK economist concluded her book aimed at the public with 'ten rules of economic thinking', one of which is 'Where common sense and economics conflict, common sense is wrong.'[2] The libertarian economist Bryan Caplan goes further. He devotes an entire book to *The Myth of the Rational Voter*, alleging that non-economists repeatedly suffer from 'antimarket bias, antiforeign bias, make-work bias, and pessimistic bias'.[3] Caplan even holds that undergraduates taking introductory economics courses should be kept in the dark about the assumptions and limitations behind textbook economics. He advises their teachers to tell students, 'I'm right, the people outside this classroom are wrong, and you don't want to be like them, do you?'[4]

Although Caplan's views are extreme, many mainstream economists are frustrated that, despite their best efforts over many decades to teach basic economic principles to the general public, the public never seem to learn. Top of the list is usually the principle that free trade is better than protectionism. A quick search in the blogosphere is enough to uncover many serious economists complaining about the public failing to appreciate the merits of free trade. Economists often blame 'the media', or the wilful misrepresentation of economic ideas for political ends, for the public's woeful ignorance. Only very recently have a few economists begun to consider another explanation: ordinary people may be well aware of the views of economists (regarding free trade, and so on), but have good reasons for disagreeing with them. It is simple: many people knowingly reject many of the assumptions and theories which mainstream economists take for granted.[5]

Of course, academics and experts in many fields are privately dismissive of the views of laypeople. But what is distinctive about economists is that they also have relatively little interest in the views of *other* experts and academics. In the preceding chapters we have seen many instances of economic imperialism: the colonization of non-economic areas of life and academic subjects by economic ideas. And the traffic is mostly one-way. Modern mainstream economics has learned little from relevant disciplines, including law, psychology, sociology and history. In a paper modestly titled 'Economic Imperialism', published in one of the most prestigious economics journals, Harvard economist Edward Lazear implies that this colonizing strategy has been successful because, unlike other social sciences, economics is 'a genuine science'.[6] Evidence of economists' distinctive belief in the superiority of their discipline to other subjects comes from a survey of US academic economists, historians, psychologists, sociologists, political scientists and business-school professors. Most of them sensibly believe that 'interdisciplinary knowledge' is better than knowledge 'obtained by a single discipline'. Uniquely, the economists disagree.[7] Accordingly, economists are more insular: they cite research from outside their subject less than academics do in other subjects.[8]

Clearly, we need a new relationship with economics, one that is more equal, more open, more questioning, less deferential. We should be able to challenge economic orthodoxies – especially those discussed in previous chapters, which function to reshape our notions of value and morality. But before we explore this new relationship further, we must confront economists' standard reply when faced with criticism: 'We're not like that any more; economics has moved on.' Economists point to two reasons why past problems with economics have now been fixed. First, there has been a data revolution: economics research is now much less theoretical, and more grounded in quantitative data. Second, economic theories are now more realistic, notably the models of human behaviour emerging from behavioural economics.

This defence of economics is so ubiquitous that it demands discussion. Forging a new relationship with economics would be much easier if economists accepted that they haven't already fixed the problems.

On the 'data revolution': it is true that pure economic theorizing, far removed from the real world, carries less weight than it once did among academic economists. Moreover, 'big data' and improvements in information technology have allowed theories to be tested in a way that was previously impossible. So yes, economics research focused on empirical evidence has recently become more common.

Yet economists are still reluctant to 'get their hands dirty' with the messiness of real life. Most contemporary economists mainly use just one type of empirical evidence – large statistical datasets – which can be accessed without leaving your office. Nobel laureate Robert Shiller describes the problem as 'an attitude in the profession that collecting data is for lesser people'.[9] Before 'physics envy' led mainstream economics from the 1960s onwards to become dominated by mathematical modelling, economists had drawn on a broader mix of evidence including case studies and interviews – often involving going out and talking to people in the real economy.

Even if we ignore this problem of the narrow evidence base of modern economics, historians have shown that empirical research in economics today is still rarer than it was in the 1950s.[10] So the 'data revolution' claims made by recent economists are misleading. In fact, the history of empirical research since the 1940s has been one of permanent revolution – or, at least, a constant increase in the scale and range of economic data available, with economists perpetually complaining that research in economics was failing to make use of all the new data. As for the genuine revolution in information technology in recent years, the contrast between its impact on the self-styled 'science' of economics and on sciences like physics and biology is revealing. The IT revolution did not simply enable more empirical research in physics and biology. It transformed the theories being tested and stimulated the development of different kinds of theories. In economics there has been no analogous transformation. The core theoretical framework used by most economists most of the time remains unchanged.[11]

This point needs to be emphasized. Just because economic theories are now subject to more comprehensive testing against data, it does not follow that theory which fails to match up to the data is thrown out. The image of *homo economicus* (or, at least, a calculating individual who acts *as if* they are 'optimizing' something) still casts a long shadow. The theory being tested almost always takes this kind of optimizing behaviour as the norm, the starting point, even if exceptions are later admitted. It shapes the questions asked of the data, and how the answers derived from the data are interpreted. Throughout this book we have seen how economic theories and their transformation into formal mathematics shape what we see – and what we don't. At least two Nobel laureate economists have noted the problem. In Paul Krugman's words, 'we just don't see what we can't formalize'.[12] Similarly, George Akerlof argues that economic analysis is ignored unless it is written up in a research paper, and that can only happen if the analysis is mathematical: 'What I am worried about most of all, is what we don't see . . . the analysis that is never seen, that never becomes a paper . . . And it can't become a paper, because that's not what a paper in economics is all about . . . we know such vacuums exist.'[13]

To be fair, some economists have been more radical. They haven't merely tried to test theory against data. They have abandoned theory altogether. This is the hottest trend in economics research today, and it shows no sign of abating. These economists are the data geeks. The data geeks' main method is to identify a 'natural experiment' – two parallel sets of real-world circumstances which are in all relevant respects identical except for one crucial difference. By comparing outcomes in these two parallel worlds, the effect of that difference can be observed.

For example, we might be interested in whether doing military service reduces earnings in later life. We cannot simply compare the earnings of those who served with those who didn't because the two groups are not otherwise identical. People with a low level of educational attainment may be disproportionally attracted to military service: for them, lower earnings later in life may be due to their education (and hence the jobs they can get) rather than their military service. But one of the pioneering data geeks, Joshua Angrist, found the perfect 'natural experiment' to avoid this problem. Angrist relied on the random process used to draft US men for service in the Vietnam War. Those who served earned less in later life.[14] Natural experiments have exploded across economics research, claiming to prove beyond doubt that, among other things, changes in abortion law influence crime levels a few decades later, and watching Fox News makes US citizens more likely to vote Republican.[15]

Given the apparent power of the method, it's easy to see why natural experiments have become so popular. The conclusions seemingly come for free, out of thin air; that is, no theory is needed to support the conclusions, and in particular there are none of the usual assumptions that economists make about people optimizing or being rational. Alas, knowledge rarely comes for free in this way. Often, the randomization crucial to the validity of the natural experiment turns out to be not so random after all. Yes, a random number was assigned to each man to determine whether he would be drafted to serve in Vietnam (the lower a man's number, the more likely he would be drafted). But employers at the time knew this, so they were less likely to invest in training workers with low numbers – which in turn would help explain why these men were likely to earn less in later life.[16]

It is not just doubts about the 'proofs' supplied by natural experiments. In the last few years the statistical-significance tests of leading economics journals have been heavily criticized by, among others, statisticians.[17] A key scientific criterion, replicability, is often not met: published empirical research cannot be reproduced by other researchers. The so-called data revolution has not led to new, indisputable data-driven economic knowledge but to deepening controversy over what the data can demonstrate.

Beyond the statistical controversies, there is a more fundamental problem with using the data geeks' work to show how economics has changed for the better – because their work leaves out the economics. Once the data geeks have excluded economic theory, there is no distinctively 'economic' content left: their work is neither more nor less than statistical analysis. This exclusion of economics also helps explain the data geeks' interests. Studying the impact of abortion law on subsequent crime levels – however interesting and important – does not seem like appropriate subject matter for economics. Privately, many economists agree. But there is an irony here because, as we have seen, over the last fifty years mainstream economists have progressively rebranded themselves as scientists of society, claiming wider expertise than simply knowledge of the workings of the economy. So it is difficult for contemporary economists publicly to criticize the data geeks' work as not being economics – even though much of it clearly isn't.

The view of economics from outside is disturbing. We learn that economic theories populated by *homo economicus* are frequently the basis of economists' predictions about the real world. But how could anyone believe that *homo economicus* tells us anything about the behaviour of real people?

Economists nowadays present behavioural economics as the answer to these concerns. We are told it represents a major step forward in terms of realism. In truth, it is a minor tweak. The 'people' described by behavioural economics still bear no resemblance to real humans. They behave just as robotically as *homo economicus* but they also make mistakes. In essence, behavioural economics is just *homo economicus* with bugs. Notably, the error-prone robots of behavioural economics are, like *homo economicus*, predictable – they are 'predictably irrational'.[18] But real humans are not easily predictable because they are capable of genuine choices – choices which are not predetermined by their environment.

Behavioural economics provides no response to the ethical problems with mainstream economics. To begin with, behavioural economists are often blind to the dubious ethical assumptions and consequences of their policy advice, as we saw with Nudge. And the underlying message of behavioural economics is the same as that of Nudge – 'ordinary people are stupid'. This is hardly a promising basis for a more respectful relationship between economists and the public. Not least because, in important respects, the reverse is true. People are *much wiser* than mainstream economics assumes. Our calculating abilities may be far inferior to those of *homo economicus*, but we have other talents. Computers – and *homo economicus* – need data to work with. In settings where data is scarce, they fall silent. As discussed in Chapter 8, humans in the real world must make many of their decisions in a setting of pure, unmeasurable uncertainty, so a calculating approach reliant on probability information is impossible. Instead, we tell stories. People whose job involves making high-stakes decisions in conditions of pure uncertainty – whether in the world of medicine, finance or natural-disaster planning – all agree that scenario planning is crucial. Different possible future scenarios are effectively different stories we construct, and we need *imagination* to attempt to envisage new or unfamiliar futures, so scenario planning needs humans rather than *homo economicus*.

Clearly, a more equal relationship between economics and the rest of us requires that economics adopts a more complete and realistic picture of humans, one which recognizes that we have more capabilities than legacy desktop computers. But that is just the beginning. We need to reset our relationship with economics and economists. Here are some guiding principles for seeing economics and economists in a new way.

a. Economists are not separate from the economy.

A more equal relationship is impossible while economists cling to their self-image as scientists outside society, gazing down on us from above, like Charles Darwin observing some beetles. The analogy is wrong because the beetles don't change their behaviour in response to scientific theorizing about them. In contrast, as we have seen, economic ideas and theorizing alone can change our behaviour. And again, the weather forecast does not influence the weather – whereas economic forecasts move the economy. In promoting their subject as a science akin to physics or chemistry, economists imply an objective, arm's-length understanding of the economy, which they cannot deliver. It is a risky strategy which can easily backfire. For example, when economics is presented as a science, people are more likely to take economic forecasts seriously. If (when) those forecasts prove inaccurate, the credibility of economics more widely is questioned. In this way, promoting the 'scientific' image of economics can damage, rather than elevate, its standing among the wider public.

That economists and their ideas operate within, rather than outside or 'on', the economy, is not a new insight. The classic introduction to the history of economic ideas remains Robert Heilbroner's *The Worldly Philosophers*, a multimillion best-seller which remains in print nearly seventy years after its first publication. Heilbroner's core argument – convincingly illustrated in his discussion of Smith, Marx, Keynes and other great economists of the past – is that the evolution of capitalism is inseparable from the evolution of economic ideas. Causation runs in *both* directions. Capitalism is shaped by the ideas of great economists, as well as informing their thinking. It is time to abandon the fantasy of 'outsider' economists, above and beyond the economies and societies they study.

b. There are few 'facts' in economics.

Another consequence of economists' obsession with seeing themselves – and being seen – as scientists is their denial of the political and ethical ideas woven through economics. Many economists are fond of quoting from a letter Keynes wrote to a close colleague in which he asserted, 'Economics is a science of thinking in terms of models joined to the art of choosing models which are relevant to the contemporary world.'[19] But what they leave out is how Keynes concludes the letter: 'economics is essentially a moral science and not a natural science. That is to say, it employs introspection and judgements of value.'

As I've shown, ethical presumptions and value judgements are comprehensively embedded in economics, in many varied and often subtle ways. At the risk of losing some of these subtleties, we can boil down the ethical stance of contemporary economic orthodoxy to two core ideas. First, market transactions work as a kind of moral bleach, leaving outcomes ethically whiter than white and blemish-free. The argument that both parties to a voluntary transaction must be better off, otherwise it wouldn't take place, is used to wash away all considerations of justice, fairness, responsibility, exploitation, and so on. Second, if a judgement of value is required, a market transaction – hypothetical or actual – provides the answer: a thing is worth just what someone is willing to pay for it.

While many economists concede the influence of political and ethical judgements in large parts of their discipline, they also assert the objective and 'value free' nature of some core principles such as the 'law of demand', which states that when the price of something rises, demand for it will fall. But unlike the laws of physics, there are few objective economic facts on which to base economic laws. Even if we specify a unique time and place, most goods and services do not have a single price. The seemingly objective measurement process dissolves into a series of subjective judgements about which goods are truly the 'same' as other goods, for the purposes of determining their (average) price. Moreover, much raw economic data is simply conjured into existence by diktat, often on the advice of economists, such as when an interest rate change is announced. And for many complex financial products such as derivatives, the usual 'scientific' relationship between theory and observational data is reversed: if the observed market price and the price in economic theory differ, the former moves to align with the latter.[20]

Ultimately, most economic numbers are in some way constructed by economists, rather than simply being observed in the world like the variables of Newtonian mechanics. Again we see that economics is not a neutral set of ideas and tools for observing and analysing the economy from the outside. Instead, it operates *within* the economy, shaping and influencing it.

c. The economy is not separate from us.

We should reject those, economists and others, who present economic ideas and the economy as beyond our influence. The economy is not like a natural system, with laws and forces over which humans have no control. The economy is not a monolithic other thing.

It is true that pernicious economic ideas have become deeply embedded into our everyday thinking but, as we have seen, this transformation is relatively recent. Escape from the influence of subtle, taken-for-granted ideas may seem impossible at times, yet another way of seeing the world lies within living memory. And we have more power than we often imagine. The economy is the sum of the choices and activities of billions of people. Its future is in our hands. We can decide the kind of economy we want. Nevertheless, of course, we need expert advice.

This brings us to a key question. What should we ask of economics and economists?

1. *Economists must communicate better, taking care to explain the reasons behind their conclusions.* Mention of 'economists communicating with the wider public' might summon up a caricature of hesitant academics struggling to explain convoluted theories using abstruse jargon and qualifying every statement with several caveats. Yet nowadays the opposite is all too common. Economists entering public debate make clear, confident claims and back them up with a sketch of the argument behind their conclusions. What could be wrong with that?

A big problem is that economists fail to explain crucial bits of their argument. Often, a black box is produced – 'economic theory has shown that', or 'a statistical relationship has been proven', and so on. Such shorthand is not an attempt to deceive us but usually reflects economists' belief that the relevant theory or statistics are too complex for non-economists to understand. In a few cases there is some truth in this, but it is also true that, within academic economics, technical wizardry is too often prized for its own sake. So economists have usually had little incentive or practice in attempting to explain complex ideas in simple terms. Sometimes they simply have a warped perspective of what is complex. As we've seen, many economists see behavioural economics as a set of 'deviations' from the textbook mathematical model of *homo economicus*. From this perspective, behavioural economics can be understood only if you already know that mathematical model – along with some harder maths on top to incorporate the deviations into the model. The effect is to make the simple ideas underpinning behavioural economics seem too complex to explain to the public.

Whatever the reasons, economists must try harder. If they want us to heed their analysis, we must trust it – and that requires it to be broadly intelligible. Being told at a crucial step in an economic argument that 'X has been proven' makes us feel patronized and inclined to ignore the argument altogether.

Another difficulty is that economists' public recommendations or conclusions are sometimes over-simplified, leaving out the nuance and the caveats.

Take free trade versus protectionism. Harvard economist Dani Rodrik acknowledges that many economists have been guilty in public of over-simplistic advocacy of free trade. Yet in private, Rodrik reports, most economists are well aware that the answer to 'Free trade or protectionism?' is 'It depends.' The reason for economists' dogmatic public pronouncements, Rodrik argues, is their 'zeal to display the profession's crown jewels . . . market efficiency, the invisible hand . . . in untarnished form, and to shield them from attack by self-interested barbarians, namely the protectionists . . . The economists who let their enthusiasm for free markets run wild are in fact not being true to their own discipline.'[21] Rodrik is right that economic theory does not justify free-market zealotry: it must therefore come from the political ideology of some economists. But that is still a big problem. It is no use to be told that economists hold nuanced views in private, if their public statements default to simplistic endorsement of free markets out of a misguided desire to avoid confusing us. This simplification strategy is even less helpful when it is biased: economists' simplistic endorsement of free markets is much more common than their simplistic rejection of them.

Besides, the strategy usually backfires. For economists to have any hope of regaining our trust, they must be completely open about the limits of their knowledge. Most people realize that economic policy choices are rarely clear-cut because they depend on the relative priority we attach to conflicting objectives. (Which is more important: the increase in GDP from the removal of tariff barriers, or the rise in unemployment in industries suffering from greater foreign competition?) If we get economists' simplistic dogma, we just stop listening.

2. *Economists should state their political and ethical judgements openly and explicitly* – allowing us to argue with them on equal terms when we disagree. In previous chapters we have seen that economists are often silent on the political and ethical assumptions implicit in their arguments. One recurring reason has been economists' desire to appear scientific. A more prosaic explanation is their unease in discussing such matters, which is understandable enough: mathematically trained economists prize precision, but when it comes to verbalizing their core ethical judgements – such as basic principles of welfare economics – they are often inexperienced and can become vague and imprecise.*

Unfortunately, there is a less innocent explanation too. Some economists try to conceal their political loyalties – or the vested interests who might be funding their research.

This is not just the cynicism of outsiders. Mainstream economists, in their blogs and other candid moments, admit that one reason financial economists failed to criticize the deregulation of the financial sector in the years before the crisis was an unwillingness to 'bite the hand that feeds you'.[22] Eighty-two economists testified before Congress in hearings concerning the 2010 Dodd–Frank Act which increased regulation of the financial sector. A third of them failed, under oath, to declare their consulting income from firms that would be hit by the regulations.[23] Similarly, there is clear evidence that some

---

* For example, most economists confidently recite the definition of Pareto efficiency they learned from the textbooks: 'It's impossible to make anyone better off without making someone else worse off.' But this statement is inaccurate. Pareto efficiency focuses on giving people what they want (satisfying preferences) – which is not the same as making them better off. As psychologists have long known, people often make mistakes in pursuing their goals, or simply lack the information to know how best to achieve them. The textbook statement of Pareto efficiency implicitly assumes these problems don't exist.

economists publishing in prestigious academic journals are overly relaxed about conflicts of interest: financial economists' shyness in disclosing their consultancy work for the financial sector;[24] empirical research on ride-hailing platforms, which is overwhelmingly dominated by economists sponsored by Uber, or using data selected and provided by Uber, or both.[25]

What about the relevant professional code of conduct covering these activities – the ethics code of the American Economic Association (the world's largest association of professional economists)?

Until very recently, there wasn't one.

Doctors, engineers, sociologists, anthropologists and statisticians have long had formal ethical codes. Yet the impact of economists' activities is potentially even greater. In the early 1990s economist Jeffrey Sachs was advising Poland and other former Soviet Bloc countries on the painful transition to a market economy. Sachs wanted the transition to happen very quickly, before political opposition could mobilize: 'figure out how much society can take, and then move three times quicker than that'.[26] The complete absence of historical precedent for this 'shock therapy' did not prevent a strong consensus emerging among mainstream economists that it was the best strategy. Subsequent research – published in the leading UK medical journal the *Lancet* after rejection by several economics journals – revealed a 41 per cent rise in male death rates between 1991 and 1994, immediately following the shock privatization programmes in Russia, Kazakhstan and the Baltic states.[27]

In 1994 the Executive Committee of the American Economic Association was asked to consider introducing a code of conduct. One Committee member joked, 'Sure, we'll have a code – its first rule will be "Don't predict interest rates!"' Everyone laughed, and there was no further discussion of the matter.[28] In 1998 the hedge fund Long-Term Capital Management collapsed, threatening to destabilize the global banking system as it went down. Until the end, LTCM economists blamed their downfall on sabotage by rivals, and refused to accept that their bell-curve thinking was fundamentally flawed. Again, after the financial crisis Nobel laureate macroeconomist Tom Sargent, who had not once warned about imminent problems in the financial sector, asserted, 'it is just wrong to say that this financial crisis caught modern macroeconomists by surprise'.[29] David Miles, a macroeconomist who served on the Bank of England panel setting UK interest rates, took the opposite view, insisting that the crisis was inevitably a surprise, with no more clues in advance than the number on a winning lottery ticket: 'Any criticism of economics that rests on its failure to predict the crisis is no more plausible than the idea that statistical theory needs to be rewritten because mathematicians have a poor record at predicting winning lottery ticket numbers.'[30] And so it goes on. Recent austerity policies pursued in several countries were *explicitly* based on the research of Harvard economists Carmen Reinhart and Ken Rogoff, showing that economic growth falls sharply once the government debt-to-GDP ratio exceeds 90 per cent.[31] Except it didn't: in April 2013 a graduate student discovered a crucial error in their spreadsheet. It turned out that slow growth causes high debt, not the other way around, as Reinhart and Rogoff had implied. Reinhart and Rogoff did not apologize, trying instead to blame politicians for exaggerating their research. But Reinhart and Rogoff had not complained publicly before, at the time the politicians had been doing the exaggerating; rather, Reinhart and Rogoff had aggressively promoted debt reduction in Washington and elsewhere.[32]

3. *If economists want to regain the trust of the public, then they must be less arrogant, take responsibility for their advice and admit their mistakes.* If they don't, then a professional association or similar body should publicly censure them. In April 2018 the American Economic Association at last introduced a code of professional conduct. But it stands in sharp contrast to the codes of other professions: the AEA code is under 250 words long, with just eight words referring to conflicts of interest. It is a small first step. Economists should encourage and welcome dialogue with the public, not just about conflicts of interests (where the problems in many cases are too obvious to merit discussion), but also a wider conversation about their place in society and the responsibilities which follow from that.

As a starting point, we could begin with John Maynard Keynes's remark: 'If economists could manage to get themselves thought of as humble, competent people, on a level with dentists, that would be splendid!'[33]

What would an economics inspired by dentistry look like?[34] Dentistry is entirely focused on solving the problems of real people in the real world. So the research agenda of economists would be determined by such problems, not by theoretical developments within economics. And the methods and tools used to address these problems would not be restricted by the prevailing culture of economics: there would be no requirement to express all analysis mathematically in an attempt to be more 'rigorous' or 'scientific'. We have seen this culture at work in the development of postwar microeconomics. It has had an equally powerful impact on macroeconomics. Here is Roger Farmer, a leading mainstream macroeconomist: 'The macroeconomics of the last thirty years has consisted of rediscovering truths that were known [to economists] in the 1920s ... Whereas 1920s theory was verbal, the macroeconomics of 2011 is formalized with a rigour that was not possible in 1928 because the mathematical tools did not exist.'[35] Translated, without the hyperbole: recent 'progress' in macroeconomics has been limited to devising mathematical proofs of what we already knew almost a century ago. Some behavioural economics suffers from the same limitation: with framing effects (Chapter 7) economists showed in experiments that people make different decisions depending on how the alternatives are described.[36] Who knew?

Economics as dentistry would have no interest in proving what we already know because that is of no use to its clients, real people with real problems. Instead, economists would use whichever methods and tools are most helpful in addressing these problems. Some mainstream economists have recently argued that modern economics does just that: it consists of a smorgasbord of tools (models), and good economists are adept at picking the right one for the task in hand. But this is a misleading description: yes, economists are open to using different tools in different contexts, as long as the tools are those of mainstream economics. A genuine 'what works' approach would not restrict the smorgasbord to current orthodoxy. It would also draw on the rich diversity of ideas from outside the mainstream, in schools of thought ranging from Marx to Hayek. This brings us to education.

4. *Educating economists.* [37] This is not the place for detailed discussion of economics curriculum reform – but it is important because,

compared to many subjects, a relatively high proportion of those with a first degree in economics draw on it in their subsequent careers. So undergraduates should learn 'what works'. Since economics is not an experimental science like physics or chemistry, it should not be taught like one, with textbooks presented as describing the economic laws of nature. The history of economic ideas is one of cul-de-sacs and false starts: economics does not make smooth and steady progress towards the truth. Therefore, current orthodoxy does not automatically incorporate all the best ideas from the past. At present, almost all undergraduate economics courses and textbooks focus exclusively on the orthodoxy. Instead, courses should introduce students to the breadth of useful ideas and theories in different schools of thought, probably via the history of economic ideas – which shows how different schools emerged to address particular problems in particular times and places, rather than one theoretical approach being best placed to solve them all. And if we step outside the orthodoxy there is the pleasant surprise of finally discovering economists with a healthy scepticism about economics and economists. The tone of Joan Robinson, a friend and friendly critic of Keynes, is refreshing: 'The purpose of studying economics is not to acquire a set of ready-made answers to economic questions, but to learn how to avoid being deceived by economists.'[38]

Another implication of the vocational role of economics is that undergraduate economists should learn about economies. Remarkably, in most existing courses, they don't. With the focus in most courses overwhelmingly on economic theory and learning mathematical and statistical skills, there is little time to study real-world economies and their constituent parts, let alone the relevant history and politics of these economies.

The effect of this gaping hole in the training of most economists was seen in the financial crisis of 2007–10, which exposed how little some financial economists, whether working in academia or regulatory agencies, knew about the actual operation of financial institutions and financial markets. It was left to financial historians, journalists and other commentators to explain how these institutions and markets really work. (Allegedly open-minded mainstream economists are still reluctant to acknowledge this point. Dani Rodrik should drop one of his 'Ten Commandments for Non-economists': 'economists don't (all) worship markets, but they know better how they work than you do').[39]

A closing message. Many critics of economics have invoked Keynes's comment about economists as dentists as part of a plea to economists to show more humility. But the critics seem not to have noticed that the rest of us have an active role here too. If economics needs deflating to a more humble and modest position in our culture, then we need not wait for economists to let the air out. Ultimately, we have the power to put economics back in its proper place. We should not delay.

Further Reading

At the end of his superb account of the collaboration between Daniel Kahneman and Amos Tversky, *The Undoing Project*, Michael Lewis provides a note on sources. But he warns the reader that when researchers write papers for publication in academic journals, they 'aren't trying to engage their readers, much less give them pleasure. They're trying to survive them.'

In other words, most academic journal papers in fields such as economics don't try to enter into dialogue with their readers. Instead they attempt to provide a bulletproof argument to bully even the most hostile reader into submission. Here, I offer some suggestions for friendlier entry points into the academic literature. But these books don't shy away from technical economics or philosophical analysis, where necessary.

1. THE SHAPE OF THINGS TO COME

Two very different discussions of the rise and influence of the Mont Pèlerin Society may be found in:

Cockett, R. (1995). *Thinking the Unthinkable*. London, Fontana.

Mirowski, P. (2013). *Never Let a Serious Crisis Go to Waste*. London, Verso.

More scholarly:

Mirowski, P. and D. Plehwe, eds. (2015). *The Road from Mont Pèlerin*. Harvard, Harvard University Press.

A good introduction to the impact of economic ideas:

Hirschman, D. and E. Berman (2014). 'Do Economists Make Policies? On the Political Effects of Economics'. *Socio-Economic Review*, 12, 779–811.

2. TRUST NO ONE

History of game theory:
Nasar, S. (1998). *A Beautiful Mind*. London, Faber.
Poundstone, W. (1992). *Prisoner's Dilemma*. New York, Anchor Books.
Critical discussion of game theory is hard reading. Two papers I like:
Risse, M. (2000). 'What is Rational about Nash Equilibria?' *Synthese*, 124 (3), 361–84.
Guala, F. (2006). 'Has Game Theory been Refuted?' *Journal of Philosophy*, 103, 239–63.

3. WEALTH BEATS JUSTICE: THE CURIOUS COASE THEOREM

Authoritative, accessible history of ideas:
Medema, S. (2009). *The Hesitant Hand*. Princeton, Princeton University Press.
A witty take on misunderstandings of Coase, from a Chicago insider:
McCloskey, D. (1998). 'The So-called Coase Theorem'. *Eastern Economic Journal*, 24 (3), 367–71.
Posner and the law and economics movement:
Teles, S. (2008). *The Rise of the Conservative Legal Movement*. Princeton, Princeton University Press.

4. THE GOVERNMENT ENEMY

Two superb books. On the shaping of social-choice theory and public choice theory by the politics and culture of the Cold War, and the influence of the Cold War on economics more generally:
Amadae, S. (2003). *Rationalizing Capitalist Democracy*. Chicago, University Chicago Press.
On the influence of public choice theory on contemporary politics:
Hay, C. (2007). *Why We Hate Politics*. Cambridge, Polity Press.

5. FREE-RIDING, OR NOT DOING YOUR BIT

Outstanding historical scholarship and philosophical analysis:
Tuck, R. (2008). *Free Riding*. Cambridge, Harvard University Press.

6. THE ECONOMICS OF EVERYTHING

Debating the appropriate scope of markets:
Sandel, M. (2012). *What Money Can't Buy: The Moral Limits of Markets*.
  London, Allen Lane.
Satz, D. (2010). *Why Some Things Should Not be for Sale*. Oxford, Oxford
  University Press.
How market thinking has become embedded in everyday life:
Roscoe, P. (2014). *I Spend Therefore I Am*. London, Penguin.

7. EVERYONE HAS A PRICE

An economist pushing against the boundaries of the mainstream economics
  of incentives:
Bowles, S. (2016). *The Moral Economy*. New Haven, Yale University Press.
A broader, deeper analysis from a philosopher:
Grant, R. (2012). *Strings Attached*. Princeton, Princeton University Press.

8. TRUST IN NUMBERS

Entertaining and insightful on the ideas behind the global financial crisis:
Lanchester, J. (2010). *Whoops!* London, Penguin.
Sprawling but unmissable, and influential, on the flaws in bell-curve
  thinking:
Taleb, N. (2010). *The Black Swan*. London, Penguin.

9. YOU DESERVE WHAT YOU GET

On the rise of the Laffer curve and, more generally, the political/cultural
  shift towards markets in the US:
Rodgers, D. (2011). *Age of Fracture*. Harvard, Harvard University Press.
There are several excellent books on inequality, but few combine accessibil-
  ity, insight and encyclopaedic knowledge as well as:
Atkinson, A. (2015). *Inequality*. Cambridge, Harvard University Press.
On why we accept inequality:
Frank, R. (2016). *Success and Luck*. Princeton, Princeton University Press.

10. A TROUBLED RELATIONSHIP:
MODERN ECONOMICS AND US

Contrasting perspectives on what is wrong with modern economics, and
what to do about it:

De Martino, G. (2011), *The Economist's Oath*. New York, Oxford University Press.

Earle, J., et al. (2017). *The Econocracy*. London, Penguin.

Fourcade, M., et al. (2015). 'The Superiority of Economists'. *Journal of Economic Perspectives*, 29 (1), 89–114.

Rodrik, D. (2016). *Economics Rules*. New York, Norton.

Acknowledgements

In one way or another, I've been worrying about the effect of recent economic ideas on our common-sense morality for twenty years or more. Many discussions have influenced my thinking, within academia and often beyond, and alas I cannot name all the participants here. I have had the privilege to teach many talented students who have often brought fresh insights to old debates. Their passion and enthusiasm have spurred me along as well.

Another privilege has been the supportive working environment of Emmanuel College, Cambridge, a place of countless informal conversations across disciplinary boundaries. These have repeatedly prompted me to search for a wider perspective than the view from within economics.

Two superb books which provided early inspiration were Daniel Rodgers's *Age of Fracture* and Richard Tuck's *Free Riding*.

I owe a special debt of gratitude to friends and colleagues who have commented in detail on drafts of one or more chapters: Geoff Browne, Ha-Joon Chang, John O'Neill, Derrick Robinson, Antoine Tinnion and Lucy Yang. I have also been assisted on specific points by Jeremy Caddick, Lawrence Klein and Nick White.

I have been lucky to have a superb editor in Tom Penn at Penguin, whose commitment and enthusiasm have been a great support. His close reading of my drafts has been invaluable, keeping my arguments focused when they threaten to veer off course. I have also benefited from the meticulous copy-editing of Sarah Day and the work of the wider Penguin team.

This book would not have been written without the advice and guidance of two people. Ha-Joon Chang has influenced my work in many ways, but two stand out. First, his insistence that almost all economic theory can be expressed in straightforward, ordinary language, so there is no reason why economists and non-economists should not be able to discuss economics on equal terms. Second, Ha-Joon's preference for the specific over the general. Most economists love generalities and abstraction, but we lead specific, not abstract, lives in economy and society – and it is the contextual specifics of time and place which make all the difference.

My agent, Ivan Mulcahy, has had an equally transformational influence on my writing. Ivan convinced me that writing about serious topics can be fun to read – and even fun to write. And we live our lives through stories.

Finally, this book would not have been possible without Hilary's support on the occasions when I began to doubt the whole project. Hilary was always there to remind me of something, or rather someone, so much more important than my work – our son, Julian. His enthusiasm for life is a ceaseless delight. I dedicate this book to them both.

Notes

1. THE SHAPE OF THINGS TO COME

1 'Aaron Director, Economist, Dies at 102', *New York Times*, 16 September 2004.

2 Keynes, J. (1978), *The Collected Writings of John Maynard Keynes*, eds. E. Johnson and D. Moggridge (London: Royal Economic Society), vol. 27, 374.

3 Hayek in a letter to Karl Popper, 13 February 1947. Quoted in Stedman-Jones, D. (2012), *Masters of the Universe* (Princeton: Princeton University Press), 78.

4 Cockett, R. (1995), *Thinking the Unthinkable* (London: Fontana), 174.

5 Ibid., 175–6.

6 Hayek, F. (1944), *The Road to Serfdom* (London: Routledge), 93. Unlike some contemporary economists, Hayek realized that economic motives are nevertheless bounded by 'customs and tradition'. I thank Ha-Joon Chang for pressing this point.

7 Speech to a World Bank/IMF meeting in Bangkok, 1991.

8 Smith, A. (1976), *The Theory of Moral Sentiments*, eds. D. Raphael and A. Macfie (Oxford: Oxford University Press), 61.

9 In a recent experiment by the *Reader's Digest*, around half of 192 dropped wallets were returned.

10 Arrow, K. (1972), 'Gifts and Exchanges', *Philosophy and Public Affairs*, 1 (4), 354–5.

11 Quoted in Sandel, M. (2012), *What Money Can't Buy: The Moral Limits of Markets* (London: Allen Lane), 130.

12 Hirschman, A. (1984), 'Against Parsimony', *Bulletin of the American Academy of Arts and Sciences*, 37 (8), 24.

13 Aristotle, *Nicomachean Ethics*, book II, chapter 1.

14 Damasio, A. (1994), *Descartes' Error* (New York: Putnam), 193–4.

15 Stiglitz, J. (2012), *The Price of Inequality* (London: Allen Lane), 192.

16 Keynes, J. M. (1936), *The General Theory of Employment, Interest and Money* (London: Macmillan), 383–4.

2. TRUST NO ONE

1   The RAND Hymn, 1961, quoted in Nasar, S. (1998), *A Beautiful Mind* (London: Faber), 104.
2   Nasar, 71.
3   *Fortune*, March 1951.
4   *Life*, 25 February 1957.
5   Keynes, J. (1978), *The Collected Writings of John Maynard Keynes*, eds. E. Johnson and D. Moggridge (Royal Economic Society), vol. 10, 173–4.
6   Letter to Morgenstern, 8 October 1947, explaining von Neumann's refusal to review Paul Samuelson's *Foundations of Economic Analysis*. Quoted in Morgenstern (1976), 'The Collaboration between Oskar Morgenstern and John von Neumann on the Theory of Games', *Journal of Economic Literature*, 14 (3), 810.
7   Morgenstern's diary, April–May 1942. Quoted in Leonard, Robert J. (1995), 'From Parlor Games to Social Science: Von Neumann, Morgenstern, and the Creation of Game Theory 1928–1944', *Journal of Economic Literature*, 33 (2), 730.
8   Nasar, 94.
9   Ibid.
10 Quoted in Heims, S. (1980). *John Von Neumann and Norbert Wiener: From Mathematics to the Technologies of Life and Death* (Cambridge: MIT Press), 327.
11 Quoted in Poundstone, W. (1992), *Prisoner's Dilemma* (New York: Anchor Books), 168.
12 Quoted in Ferguson, N. (2017), *The Square and the Tower: Networks and Power, from the Freemasons to Facebook* (London: Allen Lane), 260.
13 Hertzberg, H. (2001), 'Comment: Tuesday, and After', *New Yorker*, 24 September 2001, 27. Quoted in Amadae, S. (2003), *Rationalizing Capitalist Democracy* (Chicago: University of Chicago Press), 6.
14 Russell, B. (1959), *Common Sense and Nuclear Warfare* (London: Allen and Unwin), 30.
15 Nasar, 242, 244.
16 Ibid., 379.
17 Goeree, J., and Holt, C. (1999), 'Stochastic Game Theory', *Proceedings of the National Academy of Science*, 96, 10564–7.

18 Mirowski and Nik-Khah in D. Mackenzie, F. Muniesa and L. Siu (eds.) (2007), *Do Economists Make Markets? On the Performativity of Economics* (Princeton: Princeton University Press).

19 Sadrieh, A. (2010), 'Reinhard Selten a Wanderer', in A. Ockenfels and A. Sadrieh (eds.), *The Selten School of Behavioral Economics* (Berlin, Springer-Verlag), 5.

20 Gintis, H. (2009), *The Bounds of Reason* (Princeton: Princeton University Press).

21 For a rigorous development of the argument sketched below see F. Guala (2006), 'Has Game Theory been Refuted?', *Journal of Philosophy*, 103, 239–63.

22 https://www.aip.org/history-programs/niels-bohr-library/oral-histories/30665.

3. WEALTH BEATS JUSTICE: THE CURIOUS COASE THEOREM

1 Woodbury, S. A., and Spiegelman, R. G. (1987), 'Bonuses to Workers and Employers to Reduce Unemployment: Randomized Trials in Illinois', *American Economic Review*, 77 (4), 513–30.

2 Shapiro, Fred R., and Pearse, Michelle (2012), 'The Most-cited Law Review Articles of All Time', *Michigan Law Review*, 110 (8).

3 Ronald Coase, autobiographical essay upon winning the Nobel Prize for economics. See https://www.nobelprize.org/nobel_prizes/economic-sciences/laureates/1991/coase-bio.html.

4 Ibid.

5 Coase, R. H. (1959), 'The Federal Communications Commission', *Journal of Law and Economics*, 2, 7.

6 Kitch, E. W. (1983), 'The Fire of Truth: A Remembrance of Law and Economics at Chicago, 1932–1970', *Journal of Law and Economics*, 26 (1), 221.

7 Coase, R. (1988), *The Firm, the Market, and the Law* (Chicago, University of Chicago Press), 1.

8 Coase, R. (1960), 'The Problem of Social Cost', *Journal of Law and Economics*, 3, 2.

9 Posner, R. (1995), *Overcoming Law* (Harvard, Harvard University Press), 418.

10 Quoted in S. Medema (2009), *The Hesitant Hand* (Princeton: Princeton University Press), 106.

11 Quoted in Kitch, 192.

12 Greenspan, A. (2013), *The Map and the Territory* (Penguin: 2013).

13 Teles, S. (2008), *The Rise of the Conservative Legal Movement* (Princeton: Princeton University Press), 99–100.

14 Posner, R. (1992), *Sex and Reason* (Cambridge: Harvard University Press), 437.

15 Landes, W., and Posner, R. (1987), *The Economic Structure of Tort Law* (Cambridge: Harvard University Press), 312.

16 Friedman, M. (1953), *Essays in Positive Economics* (Chicago: University of Chicago Press), 5.

17 Landes, E., and Posner, R. (1978), 'The Economics of the Baby Shortage', *Journal of Legal Studies*, 7 (2), 323.

18 http://edition.cnn.com/2014/09/02/travel/airline-seat-recline-diversion/.

19 'Coase in Flight', *National Review*, 29 July 2011.

20 Quoted in Kill, J. et al. (2010), 'Trading Carbon' (Moreton-in-March, UK: FERN).

21 Woolf, V. (1966), 'Mr. Bennett and Mrs. Brown', *Collected Essays*, I (London: The Hogarth Press), 320.

22 Larkin, P. (1985), *All What Jazz* (London: Faber), 17. This fascinating juxtaposition of modernism in art and economics, and the link to Coase, is drawn from D. McCloskey (1998), 'The So-called Coase Theorem', *Eastern Economic Journal*, 24 (3), 367–71.

23 Coase (1988), 174.

4. THE GOVERNMENT ENEMY

1 Starr, R. (2008), 'Kenneth Joseph Arrow', in S. Durlauf and L. Blume (eds.), *The New Palgrave Dictionary of Economics* (London: Palgrave Macmillan).

2 Nasar, S. (1998). *A Beautiful Mind* (London: Faber), 108.

3 Arrow in Breit, W., and Hirsch, B. T. (2009), *Lives of the Laureates: Twenty-three Nobel Economists* (Cambridge: MIT Press), 36. On Russell and Tarski: see Feferman in *Alfred Tarski and the Vienna Circle* (1999), Jan Wolenski and Eckehart Köhler (eds.) (New York: Springer), 48.

4 Black, D. (1991), 'Arrow's Work and the Normative Theory of Committees', *Journal of Theoretical Politics*, 3, 262.

5 Interview with Alec Cairncross, quoted in McLean, I., McMillan, A., and Munroe, B. (1996), *A Mathematical Approach to Proportional Representation* (Dordrecht: Kluwer), xvi.

6 Arrow, K. (1951), *Social Choice and Individual Values* (New York: Wiley), 59.

7 Arrow, Kenneth J. (1978), 'A Cautious Case for Socialism', *Dissent*, September, 472–82.

8 Reisman, D. (2015), *James Buchanan* (Basingstoke: Palgrave Macmillan), 3.

9 Ibid.

10 Ibid.

11 Downs, A. (1957), *An Economic Theory of Democracy* (New York: Harper), 27.

12 See for example C. Pissarides (1980), 'British Government Popularity and Economic Performance', *Economic Journal*, 90, 569–81.

13 Buchanan, J., and Wagner R. (1977), *Democracy in Deficit* (San Diego: Academic Press), 65.

14 Friedman, Milton (1993), 'George Stigler: A Personal Remembrance', *Journal of Political Economy*, 101 (5), 772.

15 For a good discussion see Robert H. Wade (2014), 'Economists' Ethics in the Build-up to the Great Recession', in George DeMartino and Deirdre McCloskey (eds.), *The Oxford Handbook of Professional Economic Ethics* (Oxford: Oxford University Press).

16 The IBM Simon is regarded as the first mobile phone, released in 1994 at about $1,000 when a ticket at Lincoln Center in New York was around $30. In 2017 a mid-range smartphone is around $200 while the same ticket is $100.

17 For detailed but approachable discussion, and the statistics quoted here, see W. Baumol (ed.) (2012), *The Cost Disease* (New Haven: Yale University Press).

18 Ibid., 50.

19 Baumol, W. (2001), 'Paradox of the Services', in T. ten Raa and R. Schettkat (eds.), *The Growth of Service Industries* (Cheltenham: Edward Elgar), 24.

20 Florio, M. (2006), *The Great Divestiture* (Cambridge: MIT Press).

21 Much of this section has been influenced by the superb analysis in Hay, C. (2007), *Why We Hate Politics* (Cambridge: Polity Press), chapters 3 and 5.

22 Lord Falconer, Secretary of State for Constitutional Affairs, quoted in Hay, 93.

5. FREE-RIDING, OR NOT DOING YOUR BIT

1 Quoted in Strain, C. (2016), *The Long Sixties* (New York: Wiley), 188.

2 Smith, A. (1776), *The Wealth of Nations*, book 1, chapter X, part II.

3 Weintraub, Stanley, 'GBS and the Despots', *Times Literary Supplement*, 22 August 2011.

4 For the development of economics, a crucial feature of the new understanding of 'perfect competition' was the assumption that the contribution of each producer to the market is effectively zero, not just negligible. Much of orthodox producer theory is based on this mathematical error.

5 See Tuck, R. (2008), *Free Riding* (Cambridge: Harvard University Press). Tuck's superb philosophical and historical analysis inspired much of my discussion in this chapter.

6 Oppenheimer, Joe A. (2008, 2nd edn), *The New Palgrave Dictionary of Economics*, Steven N. Durlauf and Lawrence E. Blume (eds.). http://www.dictionaryofeconomics.com/article?id=pde2008_O000094&edition=current&q=mancur%20olson&topicid=&result_number=1.

7 Mancur Olson obituary, *Economist*, 5 March 1998.

8 Olson, M. (1971, rev. edn), *The Logic of Collective Action* (Cambridge: Harvard University Press), 64.

9 Ibid.

10 *The New York Times*, 12 July 1989.

11 *Wall Street Journal*, 22 January 2009.

12 *Independent*, 13 December 2012.

13 It is hard to estimate the precise shortfall because the tax-avoidance efforts of corporations such as Google centre on concealing what proportion of their taxable activity arises in a particular country. One estimate suggests that Google ought to be paying around an extra £700 million in tax in the UK alone ('Ending the Free Ride', *Civitas*, November 2014; http://www.civitas.org.uk/pdf/EndingtheFreeRide). Another methodology suggests the largest 243 listed companies globally should together be paying at least $82 billion more tax a year ('The $82bn Listed-company Tax Gap', *Financial Times*, 12 April 2015).

14 In *An Introduction to the Principles of Morals and Legislation*, Jeremy Bentham made exactly this point in arguing that it is in each individual's self-interest to pay tax.

15 De Viti de Marco, A. (1936), *First Principles of Public Finance* (London: Jonathan Cape), 114.

16 Tuck, 60.

17 See Hart, H. L. A., and Honoré, T. (1985), *Causation in the Law* (Oxford: Oxford University Press), which explains causation in the legal system as a manifestation of Mill's view of causation.

18 A widespread view of causation holds that for something to count as a 'cause', then if it had not occurred, the 'effect' would not have occurred. This counterfactual view of causation is rejected here, in favour of the sufficiency theory of causation first developed by John Stuart Mill in *A System of Logic*. For a balanced discussion of causation see J. Collins et al. (2004), *Causation and Counterfactuals* (Cambridge, MIT Press).

19 International Energy Agency data; see https://www.iea.org/coal2017/.

20 See for example S. Barr (2008), *Environment and Society* (Aldershot: Ashgate).

21 My arguments in this section draw heavily on M. Lane (2011), *Eco-Republic* (Princeton: Princeton University Press), chapter 3.

22 This point is inspired by Kahneman's representativeness principle. See D. Kahneman (2011), *Thinking Fast and Slow* (London: Penguin).

23 Inaugural address to the Fisheries Exhibition, London, 1883. Quoted in Lane. See http://alepho.clarku.edu/huxley/SM5/fish.html.

24 Unger, P. (1996), *Living High and Letting Die* (Oxford: Oxford University Press).

25 The current consensus is that any so-called 'solution' involves deeply counter-intuitive modifications to our beliefs about basic logical principles. Effectively, we 'solve' the Sorites paradox by generating other equally challenging paradoxes. R. Keefe and P. Smith (1996), *Vagueness: A Reader* (Cambridge: MIT Press), includes some leading candidate 'solutions', with an excellent introduction.

26 Based on D. Parfit (1984), *Reasons and Persons* (Oxford: Clarendon), 80, with minor modifications.

27 At least if we ignore the complications raised earlier, such as uncertainty about what others will do, or my contribution making a small difference, because the project is literally the sum of individual contributions, and more contributions imply a more successful project.

28 Assuming that I prefer the outcome where the project happens and I contribute to it to the outcome where the project does not happen and I don't contribute. (Without this assumption, free-riding is irrelevant: I definitely won't contribute, even without free-rider thinking.)

29 Hilton, B., *A Mad, Bad and Dangerous People*, quoted in D. Runciman, 'Why Not Eat an Éclair?', *London Review of Books*, 9 October 2008.

30 See Runciman.

6. THE ECONOMICS OF EVERYTHING

1 *New York Post*, 14 May 2013.

2 See Sandel, M. (2012), *What Money Can't Buy: The Moral Limits of Markets* (London: Allen Lane) for most of these examples, as well as many other thought 1-provoking case studies of the expanding scope of markets.

3 Becker interview in K. Horn (2009), *Roads to Wisdom* (Cheltenham: Edward Elgar).

4 Tim Harford has written several columns praising Becker's work (e.g. 'Gary Becker – The Man Who Put a Price on Everything', *Financial Times*, 6 May 2014), while John Kay (2003) notes drily that 'no parody is required' (*The Truth about Markets* (London: Penguin), 186).

5 Becker, G. (1991, enlarged edn), *A Treatise on the Family* (Cambridge: Harvard University Press), 124.

6 Ibid., 98.

7 Herfeld, Catherine (2012), 'The Potentials and Limitations of Rational Choice Theory: An Interview with Gary Becker', *Erasmus Journal for Philosophy and Economics*, 1, 73–86.

8 Becker, G. (1976), *The Economic Approach to Human Behavior* (Chicago: University of Chicago Press), 5.

9 Ibid., 8.

10 Becker (1991), 339.

11 Interview with Gary Becker in *Region*, June 2002, Federal Reserve Bank of Minneapolis: https://www.minneapolisfed.org/publications/the-region/interview-with-gary-becker.

12 Friedman, M. (1953), *Essays in Positive Economics* (Chicago: University of Chicago Press), 21.

13 Becker (1976), 5.

14 Robert Solow in R. Swedberg (ed.) (1990), *Economics and Sociology* (Princeton: Princeton University Press), 276.

15 Davies, W. (2014), *The Limits of Neoliberalism* (London: Sage), 86.

16 Becker, G. (1976), *The Economic Approach to Human Behavior* (Chicago: University of Chicago Press), 10.

17 Blinder, A. (1974), 'The Economics of Brushing Teeth', *Journal of Political Economy*, 82 (4), 887–91. Becker told James Heckman about his support for the paper: see 'Private notes on Gary Becker' at https://bfi.uchicago.edu/sites/default/files/file_uploads/Heckman-tribute-text.1.20.14.pdf.

18 Becker, G. (1993), 'The Economic Way of Looking at Behavior', *Journal of Political Economy*, 101 (3), 391.

19 Becker, (1976), 7–8.

20 Breit, W., and Hirsch, B. (eds.) (2009), *Lives of the Laureates* (Cambridge: MIT Press), 402.

21 Clark, K., 'In Praise of Original Thought', *US News and World Report*, 24 October 2005, 52.

22 Breit and Hirsch, 408.

23 Schelling, T. (1984), *Choice and Consequence: Perspectives of an Errant Economist* (Cambridge: Harvard University Press), 59.

24 Banzhaf, H. Spencer (2014), 'The Cold-war Origins of the Value of Statistical Life', *Journal of Economic Perspectives*, 28 (4), 216.

25 Schelling, T. (1968), 'The Life You Save May be Your Own', in S. Chase (ed.), *Problems in Public Expenditure Analysis* (Washington: Brookings Institution), 128–9.

26 Becker, G., and Posner, R. (2009), *Uncommon Sense* (Chicago: University of Chicago Press), 38.

27 Becker, Gary S., and Elias, J. (2007), 'Introducing Incentives in the Market for Live and Cadaveric Organ Donations', *Journal of Economic Perspectives*, 21 (3), 9.

28 For an excellent discussion of kidney markets see P. Roscoe (2014), *I Spend Therefore I Am* (London: Penguin).

29 Nancy Scheper-Hughes, founder of Organs Watch, quoted in D. Satz (2010), *Why Some Things Should Not be for Sale* (Oxford: Oxford University Press), 198.

30 Levitt, S., and Dubner, S. (2005), *Freakonomics* (London: Allen Lane), 10.

31 Schelling, 116.

32 The argument in this paragraph is heavily influenced by Debra Satz's discussion of Schelling's *Titanic* example. See Satz, 84–9.

7. EVERYONE HAS A PRICE

1 Aitken, Hugh G. J. (1985; first published 1960), *Scientific Management in Action: Taylorism at Watertown Arsenal, 1908–1915* (Princeton: Princeton University Press).

2 Quoted in David Montgomery (1989), *The Fall of the House of Labor: The Workplace, the State, and American Labor Activism, 1865–1925* (Cambridge: Cambridge University Press), 251.

3 Taylor, F. (1911), *Principles of Scientific Management* (New York: Harper), 7.

4 O'Connor, S. 'Amazon Unpacked', *Financial Times*, 8 February 2013.

5 Levitt, S., and Dubner, S. (2005), *Freakonomics* (London: Allen Lane), 20.

6 Hayek (1956), *Collectivist Economic Planning* (London: Routledge), 4.

See R. Grant (2012), *Strings Attached* (Princeton: Princeton University Press), 33, for these striking examples. Grant's penetrating analysis of incentives has inspired several of the arguments in this chapter.

Frey, B., Oberholzer-Gee, F., and Eichenberger, R. (1996), 'The Old Lady Visits Your Backyard: A Tale of Morals and Markets', *Journal of Political Economy*, 104, 1297–313. Similar reactions have been observed in other communities offered money in return for accepting nuclear dumps: see H. Kunreuther and D. Easterling (1996), 'The Role of Compensation in Siting Hazardous Facilities', *Journal of Policy Analysis and Management*, 15, 601–22.

9 Gneezy, U., and Rustichini, A. (2000), 'A Fine is a Price', *Journal of Legal Studies*, 29, 1–18.

10 A comprehensive survey is Deci, E., Koestner, R., and Ryan, R. (1999), 'A Meta-analytic Review of Experiments Examining the Effect of Extrinsic Rewards on Intrinsic Motivation', *Psychological Bulletin*, 125, 627–68.

11 Bowles, S. (2016), *The Moral Economy* (New Haven: Yale University Press), 9.

12 Quoted in ibid., 79.

13 Kinnaman, T. (2006), 'Examining the Justification for Residential Recycling', *Journal of Economic Perspectives*, 20 (4), 219–32.

14 Gneezy and Rustichini, 29, 1–18.

15 Gasioroska, A., Zaleskiewicz, T., and Wygrab, S. (2012), 'Would You Do Something for Me?' *Journal of Economic Psychology*, 33 (3), 603–8.

16 A comprehensive recent review of the evidence is Niza, C., Tung, B., and Marteau, T. M. (2013), 'Incentivizing Blood Donation: Systematic Review and Meta-analysis to Test Titmuss' Hypotheses', *Health Psychology*, 32, 941–9. In response, in a letter to the editors of *Health Psychology*, economists Lacetera, Macis and Slonim criticize Niza et al.'s research on the basis that 'basic economics principles predict that increasing the value of incentives will increase effectiveness'. But, on their own, these principles are mere assertions; they are irrelevant to the empirical testing of whether financial incentives to give blood are effective. See: http://www.apa.org/pubs/journals/features/hea-letter-to-editor-a0032740.pdf and http://www.apa.org/pubs/journals/features/hea-letter-to-editor-response-a0032740.pdf.

17 Dutton, J. E., Debebe, G., and Wrzesniewski, A. (2016), 'Being Valued and Devalued at Work', in B. Bechky and K. Elsbach, *Qualitative Organizational Research: Best Papers from the Davis Conference on*

278

Qualitative Research, Volume 3 (Information Age Publishing). See also A. Wrzesniewski and J. E. Dutton (2001), 'Crafting a Job', *Academy of Management Review*, 26 (2), 179–201.

18 Berlin, I. (1969), *Four Essays on Liberty* (Oxford: Oxford University Press), 30 n. 9.

19 Ibid., 131.

20 Grant, R. (2012), *Strings Attached* (Princeton: Princeton University Press), 117.

21 The empirical evidence on the effects of financial incentives on school students is ambiguous, for several reasons: there are many variations in incentive schemes across schools, so direct comparisons are difficult; few studies trace the effects of incentives over the long term; and few studies can distinguish between genuine improvements in educational performance and spurious performance increases due to more cheating. See Grant, 111–32, for a balanced discussion.

22 A minor rewording of the original in Amos Tversky and Daniel Kahneman (1981), 'The Framing of Decisions and the Psychology of Choice', *Science*, 211, 453.

23 Whitehead, M. et al., 'Nudging All over the World: Assessing the Global Impact of the Behavioural Sciences on Public Policy', Economic and Social Research Council, September 2014.

24 Sunstein, C. (2014), *Why Nudge?* (New Haven: Yale University Press).

25 For the evidence, and much more on how Nudge thinking remains unhelpfully shackled to economic orthodoxy, see R. Bubb and R. Pildes (2014), 'How Behavioral Economics Trims Its Sails and Why', *Harvard Law Review*, 127, 1593–678.

26 Thaler, R., and Sunstein, C. (2008), *Nudge* (New Haven: Yale University Press), 249.

27 For example, see http://www.bbc.co.uk/news/business-22772431 and http://www.bbc.co.uk/news/world-south-asia-15059592.

28 In a major review of forty-one research studies examining the response to incentives, only three studied incentives in the real world. Bowles, S. (2008), 'Policies Designed for Self-interested Citizens may Undermine "The Moral Sentiments"', *Science*, 320, 1605–9. See http://www.sciencemag.org/content/suppl/2008/06/19/320.5883.1605.DC1/Bowles_SOM.pdf

29 See the interesting discussion in J. Wolff (2015), 'Paying People to Act in Their Own Interests: Incentives versus Rationalization in Public Health', *Public Health Ethics*, 8 (1), 27–30.

30 Teachout, Z. (2014), *Corruption in America* (Cambridge, Harvard University Press).

31 Schumpeter's *History of Economic Analysis* (1954), a massive and influential history of economic thought, does not mention the word 'incentive' once.

32 Kahneman's Nobel Prize autobiographical statement.

33 Interview with Michael Lewis, *Vanity Fair*, 11 September 2012.

8. TRUST IN NUMBERS

1 Mackenzie, D. (2001), *Mechanizing Proof* (Cambridge, MIT Press), 23.

2 Dowd, Kevin et al. (2008), 'How Unlucky is 25-Sigma?', Centre for Risk and Insurance Studies, Nottingham University Business School; https://www.nottingham.ac.uk/business/businesscentres/crbfs/documents/cris-reports/cris-paper-2008-3.pdf.

3 King, M. (2016), *The End of Alchemy* (London: Little, Brown), 193.

4 See the superb intellectual portrait in D. Mellor (1995), 'Cambridge Philosophers I: F. P. Ramsey', *Philosophy*, 70, 242–62. Mellor adds that Ramsey's version of Wittgenstein here is an improvement on the original, because it sums up a major objection to the *Tractatus*, one which Wittgenstein (probably) came to endorse.

5 Keynes, J. M. (1937), 'The General Theory', *Quarterly Journal of Economics*, 51, 213–14.

6 Friedman, M., and Friedman, R. (1998), *Two Lucky People* (Chicago: University of Chicago Press), 146.

7 For this example and much more detail on the difference between bell-curve and scale-invariant phenomena see N. Taleb (2010), *The Black Swan* (London: Penguin), chapter 15.

8 BBC News, 15 September 2008: http://news.bbc.co.uk/1/hi/7616996.stm. Quoted in D. Orrell (2012), *Economyths* (London: Icon), 90.

9 Freedman D., and Stark, P. (2003), 'What is the Chance of an Earthquake?', Technical report 611, Department of Statistics, University of California, Berkeley. For an accessible introduction which has influenced my discussion here see D. Orrell, chapter 4.

10 I owe this example to J. Lancaster (2010), *Whoops!* (London: Penguin), 137.

11 Bernstein, P. (1998), *Against the Gods* (New York: Wiley), 250.

12 Wells, T. (2001), *Wild Man: The Life and Times of Daniel Ellsberg* (New York: Palgrave Macmillan), chapter 2.

13 Ibid., 128.

14 Ellsberg, D. (1961), 'Risk, Ambiguity and the Savage Axioms', *Quarterly Journal of Economics*, 75, 643–69.

15 See C. Zappia (2015), *Daniel Ellsberg on the Ellsberg Paradox* (University of Siena, Department of Economics), notes 13 and 15.

16 Taleb, 70.

17 Tversky, A., and Kahneman, D. (1983), 'Extensional versus Intuitive Reasoning: The Conjunction Fallacy in Probability Judgment', *Psychological Review*, 90 (4), 293–315.

18 Greenspan, A., Statement to the House, Hearing of the Committee on Oversight and Government Reform, 23 October 2008.

19 Turner, A., 'How to Tame Global Finance', *Prospect*, 27 August 2009.

20 Mellor, D. H. (2007), 'Acting under Risk' in T. Lewens, *Risk: Philosophical Perspectives*, (London: Routledge).

21 Stern, N., 'Ethics, Equity and the Economics of Climate Change Paper 1: Science and Philosophy', *Economics and Philosophy*, 30 (3): 397–44, 423.

22 Aldred, J. (2009), 'Ethics and Climate Change Cost-benefit Analysis', *New Political Economy*, 14 (4), 469–88.

23 Jaeger, C., Schellnhuber, H., and Brovkin, V. (2008), 'Stern's Review and Adam's Fallacy', *Climatic Change*, 89, 207–18.

24 For further details on the ideas in this paragraph, see the postscript to Taleb.

25 Bernstein, P. (1998), *Against the Gods* (New York: Wiley), 219.

26 Englich, B., Mussweiler, T., and Strack, F. (2006), 'Playing Dice with Criminal Sentences', *Personality and Social Psychology Bulletin*, 32, 188–200.

9. YOU DESERVE WHAT YOU GET

1 Atkinson, A. (2015), *Inequality* (Cambridge: Harvard University Press), 18. The late Tony Atkinson was a world authority on inequality and this is the best recent book for a careful and thorough discussion of the facts of inequality.

2 Mishel, L., and Sabadish, N., *CEO Pay in 2012 was Extraordinarily High Relative to Typical Workers and Other High Earners* (Economic Policy Institute, 2013).

3 Speech at the Royal Geographical Society Presidential Dinner, London, 1991.

4 On histories of the effect of Reagan's and Thatcher's ideas, one inspiration for this book was Daniel Rodgers's superb *Age of Fracture* (Harvard: Harvard University Press, 2011). See especially chapter 2.

5 Strathern, P. (2001), *Dr Strangelove's Game* (London: Hamish Hamilton), 227.

6 Atkinson, 19–20.

7 See *Economist*, 13 October 2012, 'The Rich and the Rest', and research cited there.

8 Quoted in Benoit Mandelbrot; Hudson, Richard L. (2004), *The (Mis) behavior of Markets: A Fractal View of Risk, Ruin, and Reward* (New York: Basic Books), 155.

9 Hacker, J., and Pierson, P. (2010), 'Winner-Take-All Politics', *Politics and Society*, 38 (2010), 152–204.

10 See for instance Atkinson, 80–81 and J. Stiglitz (2012), *The Price of Inequality* (London: Allen Lane), 27–8.

11 Norton, M., and Ariely, Dan, 'Building a Better America – One Wealth Quintile at a Time', *Perspectives in Psychological Science*, 6 (2011), 9–12; Davidai, S., and Gilovich, T. (2015), 'Building a More Mobile America – One Income Quintile at a Time', in ibid., 10, 60–71; survey conducted by Fondation-Jean-Jaurès at https://jean-jaures.org/nos-productions/la-perception-des-inegalites-dans-le-monde.

12 See for instance M. Luttig (2013), 'The Structure of Inequality and Americans' Attitudes toward Redistribution', *Public Opinion Quarterly*, 77 (3), 811–21. However, there is little consensus among researchers on recent changes in attitudes to inequality. See M. Orton and M. Rowlingson (2007), *Public Attitudes to Economic Inequality* (York: Joseph Rowntree Foundation).
There is some empirical support for the idea that people in the middle and upper-middle part of the income distribution do not object to recent rises in inequality, because their share of total income has not declined. See J. G. Palma (2011), 'Homogeneous Middles vs. Heterogeneous Tails, and the End of the "Inverted-U"', *Development and Change*, 42, 1 January, 87–153.

13 'The Few', *Economist*, 20 January 2011.

14 Evans, H. (2004), *They Made America* (New York: Little, Brown).

15 Alperovitz, G., and Daly, L. (2008), *Unjust Deserts* (New York: The New Press), 60.

16 Akerlof, G. (2000), 'Comment' in G. Perry and J. Tobin, *Economic Events, Ideas, and Policies* (Yale: Brookings Institution Press), 35.

17 See the classic K. Polanyi, *The Great Transformation* (Boston: Beacon Press, 1965).

18 This paragraph draws heavily on R. Frank (2016), *Success and Luck* (Princeton: Princeton University Press, 2016).

19 See the work of Tom Gilovich, as described in R. Frank, 80.

20 Bénabou, Roland, and Tirole, Roland (2006), 'Belief in a Just World and Redistributive Politics', *Quarterly Journal of Economics*, 121/2, 699–746.

21 Corak, M. (2016), 'Inequality from Generation to Generation' (Institute of Labour Economics, Bonn: IZA Discussion Paper No. 9929). The memorable analogy between family incomes and family heights comes from Alan Kreuger, Chair of Obama's Council of Economic Advisers.

22 The Great Gatsby Curve gained wide attention from a speech on 12 January 2012 by Alan Kreuger, Chair of Obama's Council of Economic Advisers. See https://www.americanprogress.org/events/2012/01/12/17181/the-rise-and-consequences-of-inequality/.

23 Jensen, M., and Murphy, K. (2012), 'CEO Incentives', *Harvard Business Review*, 68 (1990), 138–53, quoted in N. Häring and N. Douglas, *Economists and the Powerful* (London: Anthem Press), 109.

24 Jensen, M., Murphy, K., and Wruck, E. (2004), 'Remuneration', European Corporate Governance Institute Working Paper.

25 Ibid.

26 Holmström, Bengt (2017), 'Pay for Performance and Beyond', *American Economic Review*, 107/7, 1753–77, 1774.

27 Baker, Dean, *The Savings from an Efficient Medicare Prescription Drug Plan*, Washington DC, Centre for Economic and Policy Research, January 2006.

28 Hacker and Pierson, 192.

29 Solt, F. (2008), 'Economic Inequality and Democratic Political Engagement', *American Journal of Political Science*, 52/1 (2008), 48–60.

30 Atkinson, 180–83, shows the correlations, although stresses that causation is hard to infer from cross-country comparisons over long time periods.

31 Frank provides a convenient table of top income tax rates in thirty mostly rich countries in 1979, 1990 and 2002. Compared to 1979, the rates are lower in every country in 2002.

32 Quoted in L. Mcquaig and N. Brooks (2013), *The Trouble with Billionaires* (London: Oneworld), 204.

33   Laffer, A., *The Laffer Curve: Past, Present, and Future*, Heritage Foundation Report, 1 June 2004.

34   Quoted in Rodgers, 73.

35   http://www.politico.com/story/2017/05/15/donald-trump-fake-news-238379.

36   An excellent overview is provided by Atkinson, 183–7.

37   Piketty, T., Saez, E., and Stantcheva, S. (2014), 'Optimal Taxation of Top Incomes', *American Economic Journal: Economic Policy*, 6, 230–71.

38   Quoted in Mcquaig and Brooks, 40.

39   Surowiecki, James, 'Moaning Moguls', *New Yorker*, 7 July 2014.

40   For related development of these ideas, see L. Murphy and T. Nagel (2002), *The Myth of Ownership* (Oxford: Oxford University Press) and Ha-Joon Chang (2002), 'Breaking the Mould: An Institutionalist Political Economy Alternative to the Neo-Liberal Theory of the Market and the State', *Cambridge Journal of Economics*, 26/5, 539–59.

41   See Young, C. (2017), *The Myth of Millionaire Tax Flight: How Place Still Matters for the Rich* (Stanford: Stanford University Press). And there was very little evidence of flight by the rich, or difficulty in attracting talented people to the UK, even during the period of historically high top rates of income tax in the UK in the 1970s: Fiegehen, C., and Reddaway, W. (1981), *Companies, Incentives and Senior Managers* (Oxford, Oxford University Press), 92.

42   Quoted in Mcquaig and Brooks, 249–50.

43   King, M. (2016), *The End of Alchemy* (London: Little, Brown).

44   Stiglitz, 119.

45   Cynamon, Barry Z., and Fazzari, Steven M. (2016), 'Inequality, the Great Recession and Slow Recovery', *Cambridge Journal of Economics*, 40/2, 373–99; Stockhammer, Engelbert (2015), 'Rising Inequality as a Cause of the Present Crisis', *Cambridge Journal of Economics*, 39/3, 935–58; Wisman, Jon D. (2013), 'Wage Stagnation, Rising Inequality and the Financial Crisis of 2008', *Cambridge Journal of Economics*, 37/4, 921–45.

46   Atkinson; Piketty, T. (2014), *Capital in the Twenty-first Century* (Cambridge: Harvard University Press); Stiglitz.

47   This is a simplified summary. People enter the market with different housing assets (some inherit a house) and some prices rise much faster than others, so there can be relative winners and losers from rising average house prices. But these complications do not undermine the main argument.

48 The price of some positional goods (such as desirable houses) will fall; in other cases, where prices reflect international demand (sports cars), the price may not fall but living standards are unlikely to be much affected from having to scale back from, say, a Ferrari Berlinetta to a Porsche 911 Turbo at half the price. See below.

49 Frank, 91.

50 For the UK, see Atkinson, *Inequality*, 237–9. For the US, see Stiglitz, 336–55.

51 Interview with Rupert Cornwell, *Toronto Globe and Mail*, 6 July 2002.

52 For more discussion and references see Mcquaig and Brooks, 121–3.

10. A TROUBLED RELATIONSHIP: MODERN ECONOMICS AND US

1 Avik, Roy, 'ACA Architect: "The Stupidity of the American Voter" Led Us to Hide Obamacare's True Costs from the Public', *Forbes*, 10 November 2014.

2 Coyle, D. (2002), *Sex, Drugs and Economics* (New York: Texere), 226.

3 Caplan, B. (2007), *The Myth of the Rational Voter* (Princeton: Princeton University Press), 30.

4 Caplan, 201.

5 Sapienza, Paola, and Zingales, Luigi (2013), 'Economic Experts versus Average Americans', *American Economic Review*, 103 (3), 636–42.

6 Lazear, E. (2000), 'Economic Imperialism', *Quarterly Journal of Economics*, 115 (1), 99–144. For an alternative account, see Edward Nik-Khah and R. Van Horn (2012), 'Inland Empire: Economics' Imperialism as an Imperative of Chicago Neoliberalism', *Journal of Economic Methodology*, 19 (3), 259–82.

7 Fourcade, M., Ollion, E., and Algan, Y. (2015), 'The Superiority of Economists', *Journal of Economic Perspectives*, 29 (1), table 2.

8 Van Noorden, R. (2015), 'Interdisciplinary Research by the Numbers', *Nature*, 525 (7569): 306–30.

9 Sommer, Jeff, 'Robert Shiller: A Skeptic and a Nobel Winner', *New York Times*, 19 October 2013.

10 Backhouse, R., and Cherrier, B. (2017), 'The Age of the Applied Economist', *History of Political Economy*, 49 (supplement), 1–33.

11 Backhouse, R., and Cherrier, B. (2017), ' "It's Computers, Stupid!" The Spread of Computers and the Changing Roles of Theoretical and Applied Economics', *History of Political Economy*, 49 (supplement), 103–26.

12 http://web.mit.edu/krugman/www/howiwork.html.

13 At the ASSA meetings, Chicago, January 2017. See https://www.aeaweb.org/webcasts/2017/curse.

14 Angrist, J. (1990), 'Lifetime Earnings and the Vietnam Era Draft Lottery', *American Economic Review*, 80 (3), 313–36.

15 Donohue, John J., and Levitt, Steven D. (2001), 'The Impact of Legalized Abortion on Crime', *Quarterly Journal of Economics*, 116 (2), 379–420; Martin, Gregory J., and Yurukoglu, Ali (2017), 'Bias in Cable News: Persuasion and Polarization', *American Economic Review*, 107 (9), 2565–99. The key point about this latter research is that it claims to prove that channels such as Fox News influence the voting behaviour of viewers – not just that such channels attract viewers already more likely to vote Republican.

16 Heckman, J. (1996), 'Comment', *Journal of the American Statistical Association*, 91 (434), 459–62.

17 Ioannidis, J. P. A. et al. (2017), 'The Power of Bias in Economics Research', *Economic Journal* 127: F236–F265.

18 Ariely, D. (2009), *Predictably Irrational* (New York: HarperCollins).

19 For example, Dani Rodrik (see below) uses this exact quote in 'The Fatal Flaw of Neoliberalism', *Guardian*, 14 November 2017. Keynes's letter to Roy Harrod is in his *Collected Writings*, vol. XIV, 295–7. See also: http://economia.unipv.it/harrod/edition/editionstuff/rfh.346.htm.

20 Mackenzie, D., Muniesa, F., and Siu, L. (eds.) (2007), *Do Economists Make Markets? On the Performativity of Economics* (Princeton: Princeton University Press); for a wide-ranging, approachable discussion of these issues see P. Roscoe (2014), *I Spend Therefore I Am* (London: Penguin).

21 Rodrik, Dani, 'The Fatal Flaw of Neoliberalism: It's Bad Economics', *Guardian* 14 November 2017.

22 Wren-Lewis, Simon, *mainly macro* blog, 9 October 2017: https://mainlymacro.blogspot.co.uk/2017/10/economics-too-much-ideology-too-little.html. Paul Krugman has voiced similar worries.

23 Flitter, Emily, Cook, Christina, and Da Costa, Pedro, 'Special Report: For Some Professors, Disclosure is Academic', Reuters, 20 December 2010. See: http://www.reuters.com/article/2010/12/20/us-academics-conflicts-idUSTRE6BJ3LF20101220.

24 Carrick-Hagenbarth, Jessica, and Epstein, Gerald A. (2012), 'Dangerous Interconnectedness: Economists' Conflicts of Interest, Ideology and Financial Crisis', *Cambridge Journal of Economics*, 36 (1), 43–63.

25 Häring, N., 'How UBER Money Dominates and Distorts Economic Research on Ride-hailing Platforms', *WEA Commentaries*, 7 (6), December 2017. See https://www.worldeconomicsassociation.org/files/2018/01/Issue7-6.pdf.

26 Quoted in G. DeMartino (2011), *The Economist's Oath* (New York: Oxford University Press), 8.

27 Stuckler, D. et al. (2009), 'Mass Privatisation and the Post-communist Mortality Crisis: A Cross-national Analysis', *Lancet*, 373 (9661), 399–407.

28 DeMartino, 65.

29 Interview with Federal Reserve Bank of Minneapolis, 26 August 2010. Seehttps://www.minneapolisfed.org/publications/the-region/interview-with-thomas-sargent.

30 Miles, David, 'Andy Haldane is Wrong: There is No Crisis in Economics', *Financial Times*, 11 January 2017.

31 For example, UK Chancellor George Osborne repeatedly referred to Reinhart and Rogoff's work in a key speech in the UK Parliament justifying spending cuts. See John Cassidy, 'The Reinhart and Rogoff Controversy', *New Yorker*, 26 April 2013.

32 Moore, Heidi, 'Rogoff and Reinhart Should Show Some Remorse and Reconsider Austerity', *Guardian*, 26 April 2013.

33 Keynes, J. M. (1963), *Essays in Persuasion* (New York: W. W. Norton & Co.), 373.

34 David Colander takes a similar approach (although I disagree with his views elsewhere about curriculum reform): see D. Colander (2016), 'Creating Humble Economists', in G. DeMartino and D. McCloskey (eds.), *The Oxford Handbook of Professional Economic Ethics* (New York: Oxford University Press).

35 Coyle, D. (2012), 'What's the Use of Economics?' (London: London Publishing Partnership), 121.

36 For a perceptive critique of behavioural economics, see G. Morson and M. Schapiro (2017), *Cents and Sensibility* (Princeton: Princeton University Press), 272–87.

37 For an excellent discussion from a student perspective see J. Earle, C. Moran, and Z. Ward-Perkins (2017), *The Econocracy* (London: Penguin).

38 Robinson, Joan (1955), *Marx, Marshall and Keynes* (Delhi: University of Delhi), 75.

39 Rodrik, D. (2016), *Economics Rules* (New York: Norton), 214–15.

Index